Additional Praise for *iProperty*

"Whether or not you think you have a well-oiled IP development machine, *iProperty* will double its speed and will boost your company's IP output, quality and value. the seeming simplicity of the process presented here belies the powerful results it can produce. Read it, or watch your competitors' IP machines pass you."

> Andy Gibbs, President & Choef Executive Officer
> PatentCafe®

"Companies starting, growing or financing a global technology business must have a cogent and comprehensive IP strategy. *iProperty* provides a nuanced and practical road map to develop and execute a master IP plan. Seasoned industry veterans and new entrepreneurs alike will find many valuable lessons embedded in this thoughtful book."

> B. Jefferson Clark, Managing Partner
> The Aurora Funds, Inc.

"*iProperty* provides a unique pathway for developing winning intellectual property strategies in the current global innovation economy. The book is a good read and will be widely consulted by researchers, industrialists, lawyers, knowledge economists, and others interested in the area of wealth creation through knowledge and intellectual property."

> Dr. Anindya Sircar, Chief IP Counsel
> Biocon Group of Companies, India

"*iProperty* is a must read for corporate executives and IP professionals. It shows how to build and integrate an IP arsenal into corporate strategies and how to manage and use this portfolio to win in the global marketplace."

> Richard Baker, Director of Intellectual Property Licensing
> 3Com Corporation

"The authors have developed a practitioner's handbook that shares important frameworks for planning and communicating the value of intellectual property to management, investors and other key global stakeholders. Essential tools for integrating profitable innovation with business strategy are presented side-by-side with examples of management success and shame. *iProperty* should be required reading for any manager with strategy as part of his or her professional mandate."

> Barry Brager, Managing Partner
> Preception Partners, Inc.

"*iProperty* presents strategy and techniques in a manner that is as useful for start-ups as it is for large companies. The approaches presented will make any technically innovative company think long and hard about how it protects its ideas."

> Ed Sawyer, CEO
> SBE Inc.

iProperty

*i*PROPERTY

Profiting from Ideas in an Age of Global Innovation

WILLIAM A. BARRETT, CHRISTOPHER H. PRICE,
AND THOMAS E. HUNT

BICENTENNIAL
BICENTENNIAL
1807
WILEY
2007
BICENTENNIAL
BICENTENNIAL

John Wiley & Sons, Inc.

Published by John Wiley & Sons, Inc., Hoboken, New Jersey.

Wiley Bicentennial Logo: Richard J. Pacifico

Published simultaneously in Canada.

For general information on our other products and services, or technical support, please contact our Customer Care Department within the United States at 800-762-2974, outside the United States at 317-572-3993 or fax 317-572-4002.

Wiley also publishes its books in a variety of electronic formats. Some content that appears in print may not be available in electronic books.

For more information about Wiley products, visit our web site at http://www.wiley.com.

Library of Congress Cataloging-in-Publication Data

978-0470-17179-0

Printed in the United States of America

10 9 8 7 6 5 4 3 2 1

He that will not apply new remedies must expect new evils; for time is the greatest innovator.

—*Francis Bacon*

Contents

Acknowledgments

BILL BARRETT

I would like to express my appreciation to these people:

Rich West, Michael Pollack, and Vamsee Pamula of Advanced Liquid Logic, Inc., for their support during the completion of this book, for creating a corporate environment that understands the value of iProperty, and for giving me an opportunity to put the theories into practice.

The outstanding intellectual property attorneys at Moore & Van Allen, PLLC in Research Triangle Park, North Carolina, for their support and encouragement, especially Mike Johnston and Marianne Fuierer; Eric Mills of Ward & Smith in Raleigh, North Carolina; Tony Chalk of the European intellectual property firm Harrison Goddard Foote; Dr. Anindya Sircar, chief patent counsel for Biocon, Ltd., Bangalore, India.

Professor Karl Jorda of Franklin Pierce Law Center for his insightful comments on Chapter 12.

Michael Francisco, associate editor of *Nature Biotechnology*; and Larry Plonsker, editor of *les Nouvelles*, the journal of the Licensing Executives Society International; and Joff Wild, editor of *Intellectual Asset Management Magazine*, for their help in obtaining permission to use works that first appeared in their respective publications and Joff's invaluable assistance with my research.

Anthony de Andrade of Global IP Net for permission to use data from Global IP Estimator.

Last, but not least, my wife, Cindy, for enduring the many hours I invested in this project and for not complaining about all of those lapses in conversation when my mind was wandering to some aspect of the book.

CHRIS PRICE

To my parents, Bob and Alice, who provided me with a sense of curiosity and the tools to explore questions, and to my wife, Susan, who is the core of our family and enables success for us all.

TOM HUNT

To my parents, Bill and Aileen, who taught me, through their example, the meaning of personal integrity.

To my children, Ian and Owen, who taught me, through their exuberantly competitive spirits, the meaning of the term "ownage."

To my wife, Karen, who, with her limitless capacity to find the good in every situation, has taught me that no obstacle is too great if I have her by my side.

All three co-authors also wish to thank Susan McDermott, our editor at Wiley, and Natasha Andrews–Noel, our production editor, for their professional and enthusiastic support.

FURTHER ACKNOWLEDGMENTS

Portions of Chapter 3 were adapted from William Barrett, "Building a Strategy for Maximizing Intellectual Property Value," *Nature Biotechnology* (January 2005).

Chapter 4 was adapted from Tom Hunt, "A Value Chain Approach to IP Management," *IAM* (November 2003).

Portions of Chapter 6 were adapted from William Barrett, "The Patent Gamble: Strategic Insights for Playing the Worldwide Patent Game," *Nature Biotechnology* (December 2003).

Chapter 7 was adapted from William Barrett and Christopher Price, "The Global Patent Value Matrix: Making Global Patent Strategy Decisions," *les Nouvelles* (December 2006), with permission from the Licensing Executives Society International.

Chapter 8 was adapted from Tom Hunt, "The Effect of Corporate Culture on IAM Initiatives," *Intellectual Asset Management* (April 2005).

Portions of Chapters 10 and 11 were adapted from William Barrett and Dave Crawford, "Integrating the Intellectual Property Value Chain," *Nature Biotechnology BioEntrepreneuer Supplement* (June 2002).

Portions of Chapter 12 were adapted from William Barrett, "Defensive Use of Publications in an Intellectual Property Strategy," *Nature Biotechnology* (February 2002).

About the Authors

William Barrett (Research Triangle Park, NC) is Vice President, Intellectual Property at Advanced Liquid Logic, Inc., in Research Triangle Park, North Carolina. Prior to that, Bill practiced patent law with Moore & Van Allen, PLLC, and was formerly senior director and legal counsel for Nobex Corporation. Bill has extensive experience in helping companies to develop and execute global intellectual property strategies; visualize, understand, and navigate their competitive intellectual property landscapes; and assemble, train, and facilitate effective intellectual property teams. He is a frequent author in the area of intellectual property management issues. Bill can be contacted at barrett@gpatents.com.

Christopher Price (Chapel Hill, NC) is a serial entrepreneur and has served as the CEO of several companies based on a variety of different classes of technology and has a passion for the conversion of science into products. He is an inventor on more than 34 patents and patent applications in the United States.

Thomas Hunt (Peterborough, NH) is Director of Intellectual Property at Markem Corporation of Keene, NH. Prior to that Tom was cofounder of ipCapital Group, Inc., an Intellectual Asset Management (IAM) Strategy Consulting firm in Burlington, VT and also served as program director of corporate intellectual property and licensing at IBM Corp. Tom has developed and refined IAM methodologies and processes that have been used in over 350 client companies since 1999. A patented inventor and business strategist, Tom is an accomplished author, industry expert, and speaker on the subject of strategic IAM.

Introduction
Rethinking Intellectual Property

In the old days, we referred to legal protections for ideas as "intellectual property," or "IP" for short. The common metaphor was a sedentary piece of real estate with a picket fence. But patent picket fences are insufficient for protecting ideas in the intense global competition of today *and tomorrow*, where the companies that thrive are only those that can deliver innovative products and services to consumers again, and again, and again. Of course, since "intellectual property" is a legal term, we cannot do away with it altogether. But we believe that it is time—past time—to re-envision the black-and-white world in which intellectual property is used to protect innovation. We call our new vision the world of *iProperty*.

iProperty is intellectual property plus a global strategy and global execution with a healthy dose of business-driven common sense. It is relevant to all innovating companies, big and small. The *i* represents not just "intellectual," which, according to Princeton's WordNet, is defined as "of or associated with or requiring the use of the mind." The *i* also reflects

- *i*magination—not just routine but the power to re-envision the future
- *i*deation—not just random ideas but proactive invention
- *i*nsight—not just raw intelligence but street sense
- *i*nnovation—not just ideas but commercialization
- *i*nternational—not just your own backyard but anywhere and everywhere
- *i*ntangible—not just land, factories, labor, and capital, but creative people and novel ideas

- *in*tegration—not just patent silos, but integration of science, technology, business vision and objectives, economics of intellectual assets and their protection

iProperty has a potent combination of speed, power, and strategic precision. If intellectual property is like real estate and picket fences, iProperty is like a fully loaded Mack® truck running on biofuel and with a driver on a Red Bull® caffeine drink, barreling down the road at 100 miles per hour with a specific destination in mind. A well-designed iProperty portfolio is like deploying a whole fleet of these Mack trucks targeting many specific destinations around the world. iProperty is not to be toyed with, and it is certainly not to be ignored. Innovators who ignore their own iProperty sacrifice the power to sustain competitive advantage in an age when competitive advantage is hard to attain and even harder to retain. Those who ignore the iProperty of others end up as road kill.

The world of iProperty does not accept the business-as-usual, leave-the-patents-to-the-patent-attorneys mindset. Effective iProperty companies realize that if ideas are the most valuable resource in the global economy, then companies that own their ideas have a competitive advantage over those who do not. When we say "own," we do not just mean own. When one of co-author Thomas Hunt's kids beats a friend in a game, the winner taunts the loser by saying "ownage!" *Ownage* is characterized not by putting up a good fight but by soundly defeating the opponent. Ownage implies ownership of the whole spacc in which the game is played, so that would-be competitors will think twice before entering your space and risking a sound thrashing. Ownage provides leverage that can be used for the benefit of a company's stakeholders, by stopping competitors, generating licensing revenues, enhancing company prestige, ensuring freedom of action, establishing standards, and building effective relationships.[1]

So, iProperty is about ownage. Companies that create and/or acquire access to the best and most economically valuable ideas and "own" them around the world, in the sense that they are protected in a manner that provides an effective barrier to competitors, have ownage. Ownage requires not only mastery of innovative product and service ideas from their conception until they are embodied in a strategically assembled portfolio of iProperty, but also the freedom to take those ideas to the market in every country of economic relevance without interference from the iProperty of competitors. Ironically, the need for ownage comes at a time when the global spread of innovation makes ownage more difficult to attain and defend than ever.

COMPETING FOR THE FUTURE

It is old news hardly worth mentioning that in today's global economy, company values and even economies are increasingly built on intellectual property. As stated in a 2006 report commissioned by the United Kingdom's House of Commons:

> In 1984 the top ten firms listed on the London Stock Exchange had a combined market value of $40 billion and net assets of the same value. Advance twenty years and the asset stock of the largest firms has doubled while their market value has increased nearly ten times.[2]

The report attributes this difference in value to intellectual assets, such as goodwill, reputation, and knowledge capital. According to one estimate, almost half of the gross domestic product of the United States is based on intellectual property![3] The factors of production were, for 200 years, thought of as land, labor, and capital; they are now people, ideas, and things.[4] As observed by Keith Cordoza, managing director of Ocean Tomo, a company that has created a stock index ranking companies based on the strength of their patent portfolios: "Today when I buy 100 shares of General Electric, it's not so I can own their vast inventory of factories. I buy that stock for the innovation and technology at GE, and that's embodied in their patent portfolio,"[5] and we would add the value of their trade secrets, know-how, and other forms of iProperty.

Why is it that most senior executives can tell you so little about the iProperty processes and portfolios of their companies? Executives who can quickly compare their companies with competitors in everything from the numbers of people to the square footage of manufacturing plants have hardly a word to say about iProperty. Moreover, due to their lack of attention, many of their beliefs and the statements they do make about their companies' iProperty are simply inaccurate.

In their bestselling book, *Competing for the Future*, Gary Hamel and C. K. Prahalad describe how they examine corporate managers to determine how they build a corporate perspective on the future.[6] First, they ask how much time they spend looking *outward* at external issues affecting their company. Of this outward-looking time, they ask how much time is spent looking *forward* 5 or 10 years at the future of their industry. Finally, of the time spent looking outward and forward, they ask how much is *spent with colleagues* developing "a deeply shared, well-tested view of the future." Hamel and Prahalad observe that senior management typically spends less than 3 percent of its time in such outward-looking, forward-looking activities building a shared corporate perspective on the future.

The issue is even more dismal when it comes to iProperty. Few corporations invest any significant business attention in their own internal processes for developing and managing intellectual property the old-fashioned way, much less the resources needed to develop a forward-looking iProperty perspective. Most simply follow the path of least resistance. Hamel and Prahalad diagnose the failure of foresight in this way:

> These questions go unanswered because to address them senior managers must first admit, to themselves and to their employees, that they are less than fully in control of their company's future. They must admit that what they know today—the knowledge and experience that justify their position in the corporate pecking order—may be irrelevant or wrong-headed for the future.[7]

There is perhaps no mustier and more difficult to access and change corner of the corporate world than the intellectual property silo. Whether the silo is in-house or at some distant intellectual property–crunching law firm, those invested with the task of protecting the company's intellectual property are frequently the least integrated members of the corporate community. We have collectively had the opportunity to see inside many corporations from the perspectives of attorney, consultant, and corporate executive, and we have seen efforts to break out of the old intellectual property mold to implement improved iProperty processes fully supported by senior management but stopped dead in their tracks by the patent counsel who report to them.

The problem can be even worse for companies that use outside patent counsel. Many patent firms in the United States and their counterparts in countries around the world seem to put more energy (and billable hours!) into expensive processes designed to defend the firm from liability than into understanding the clients' business and creatively solving clients' problems. If the problem does not fit the existing system, then there is no solution.

In the end, as Hamel and Prahalad say, "The urgent drives out the important; the future goes largely unexplored; and the capacity to act, rather than the capacity to think and imagine, becomes the sole measure of leadership."[8] Companies cannot expect to win consistently in the global innovation competition without paying attention to the way in which they manage iProperty assets.

WHAT IS iPROPERTY?

Unlike its tidy "intellectual property" counterpart, iProperty defies precise definition. It is a spirit of outside-the-box thinking that includes intellectual property concepts and a host of other ideas as well. iProperty is best thought of as a set of visionary concepts, strategies, and tactics used by companies for establishing ownage of their ideas in a manner that undergirds and prolongs their competitive success in the global economy. Its foundation is a realistic understanding of the current state of the global economic, legal, and cultural environments for protecting ideas. iProperty consists of three basic ingredients: technological ideas, novelty, and ownage.

By *technological ideas,* we mean ideas about technology, that is, how-to knowledge. Simply stated, technological ideas include any application of knowledge to tools, processes, organizations, and systems. Ideas are not confined to classic research and development activity but can, and should, emerge from every activity across the value chain, including regulatory, manufacturing, marketing, sales, and distribution. In addition to ideas relating to traditional technologies, such as semiconductor design and biotechnology, the term also includes some things not ordinarily thought of as technology, such as business processes. For simplicity, we refer to technological ideas simply as "ideas."

The second ingredient of iProperty is *novelty*. Novelty implies discontinuity with the past, advances in the state of the art, improved capabilities, and similar concepts. Novel ideas are new to the world. Old, unimproved ideas can be important intangible assets, but they do not create an opportunity for iProperty. If ideas include things like how to make a drug, how to assemble a computer, how to build a Web site, and how to sell a customer a DVD, then *novel* ideas include things like how to make a better drug, how to assemble a computer more reliably or economically, how to build a more viewer-interactive Web site, and how to help a customer use software to select a DVD that he or she is likely to find entertaining. We occasionally use the related term *invention* to refer to novel ideas or potentially novel ideas in the context of patent protection.

We distinguish novel ideas from innovation, in that innovation implies meaningful implementation or introduction to the market.[9] Every commercially implemented innovation starts in the mind of a person as an idea, and companies that wish to protect innovations effectively must begin by carefully identifying and protecting ideas.

The third component of iProperty is *ownage,* which we have already discussed. Intellectual property is about legal ownership, but iProperty goes way beyond legal ownership to the strategies and tactics that companies use to establish ownage. There are many ways to establish ownage, including traditional legal protections, such as patents and trade secrets, as well as concepts as diverse as processes for creating, capturing, and evaluating ideas; establishing open-source communities; giving away ideas to the world to prevent others from patenting them; creative contracting; assembling patent pools; and even paying attractive wages to workers in developing countries to reduce loss of trade secrets and know-how caused by employee turnover. The effectiveness of these and other approaches varies from country to country and from time to time. True ownage is not established by blindly following the strategies of the past; it is established by an insistence on understanding the present, insightfully anticipating the future, and creating and executing business and legal strategies for winning in current and future competitive contexts.

Most iProperty also has a fourth component: *enablement.* Enablement is a concept borrowed from patent law. It means that the idea must be workable. Companies often confuse enablement with another patent-related term, *reduction to practice,* which means that the idea has been physically implemented and made to work. However, enablement is a broader concept, and some ideas can be enabled without any reduction to practice simply by sketching them out on a piece of paper and/or describing their operation with words. We leave enablement out of the three core requirements for iProperty to emphasize that even ideas that lack enablement can be valuable if they are in the class of ideas that can be enabled. The development process is about enabling ideas, and every company that develops innovative products and services should be nurturing some unenabled ideas in its iProperty pipeline. However, we do not want to suggest that iProperty is about science fiction concepts like beaming people off the surface of planets or warp speed travel. . . at least not yet.

We understand that our focus on technological ideas excludes many economically important kinds of ideas, such as artistic works, business logos, and advertising script. This focus also excludes from our immediate discussion important and valuable forms of intellectual property, such as trademarks to protect brands and copyrights to protect music. These topics raise an entirely different set of challenges that are addressed adequately elsewhere.

Not every novel idea is worth the same investment in establishing ownage. Our discussions of iProperty assume existing processes for evaluating ideas in light of market opportunities and competitive pressures. If there is no potential for market interest, there is no need for iProperty. If there are seemingly insurmountable competitive threats to existing iProperty, companies can ideate anew or pursue other market opportunities.

Our concept of iProperty falls within the broader topic of "intangible assets," of which much has been written lately. However, in our experience, most writing about intangible assets scarcely mentions strategies and tactics for protecting those assets. We believe that there is a need for a more practical guide that not only introduces readers to real-world aspects of managing intellectual property, but that also seeks to pull the whole field of intellectual property management into the present and then gives it a not-so-gentle shove into the future: iProperty. It has been said that the best way to predict the future is to create it. We do not have all the answers, but we hope that by introducing our readers to some of the people, companies, and ideas that are creating the new world of iProperty, we can begin a dialogue that will help companies to develop and deploy their own unique iProperty strategies to produce tangible, bottom-line results.

Finally, encouraged by IBM's remarkable creation of a $1.7 billion technology outlicensing business, many companies are looking for approaches to monetizing their intellectual property assets. Companies can receive royalties and other payments from others, even competitors, in exchange for granting permission to use their patents, trade secrets, know-how, and other intellectual property assets.

The outlicensing trend has evolved significantly since the landmark book *Rembrandts in the Attic* encouraged companies to develop and monetize their intellectual property.[10] Current wisdom, as expressed by Microsoft's corporate vice president and deputy general counsel of intellectual property, Marshal Phelps, is that that "the default position is that all technology or know-how should be available for license, at the right time and under the right terms."[11] Our book does not delve into the intricacies of setting up an intellectual property outlicensing program, but we emphasize that it is a crucial strategy for monetizing iProperty assets.

As stated by Hewlett Packard's vice president of intellectual property, Joe Beyers, "It is a strategic imperative to properly protect the company's [intellectual property] and to maximize its overall return on its investment in innovation."[12] Our focus in this book is on the development of an iProperty portfolio that protects the company's investment in innovation and creates the best possible position from which the company can achieve this strategic imperative by implementing outlicensing and other intellectual property strategies. For readers interested in learning more about the development of an outlicensing program, we recommend *Making Innovation Pay*, edited by Bruce Berman.

iPROPERTY IS NOT EVIL

We want to make this clear right up front: iProperty is not evil. Patents, in particular, have been the frequent subject of public criticism in the United States, Europe, and around the globe. In a noteworthy and highly publicized case, BlackBerry users rode the litigation rollercoaster with BlackBerry maker Research in Motion as the company battled a patent infringement lawsuit by a company whose only significant assets were patents. In the pharmaceutical industry, patents have been increasingly viewed as the bully stick of big pharmaceutical companies who want to impose unreasonable prices on the consumers of their products, even to the point of maliciously denying drugs to dying people in poor countries. Patent laws are even blamed for the emergence of a new mythical beast called the patent troll, who uses patents only to impose expensive taxes on all unwary companies that want to use the troll's patent-protected ideas. As this book is being written, all of India is in an uproar over the recent granting of U.S. patents relating to methods of yoga.

Popular novelist Michael Crichton has even written a novel, titled *Next*, in which scientists patenting genes (and presumably their patent lawyers) are the villains. According to the book's cover, "We live in a time when one fifth of all our genes are owned by someone else, and an unsuspecting person and his family can be pursued cross-country because they happen to have certain valuable genes within their chromosomes...."[13] Rather misleading to say the least, but it apparently makes for good book sales.

Disaffection with the U.S. patent system has led many to declare that the system is broken.[14] A common complaint is that recent relaxation in the standards for patentability has resulted in large numbers of questionable patents, which one commentator argues has "increased the likelihood that a given invention will infringe one or more existing patents."[15] In their book, *Innovation and Its Discontents*, Brandeis University economist Adam Jaffe and Harvard business professor Josh Lerner contend that:

> in the space of less than a decade, we converted the weapon that a patent represents from something like a handgun or a pocket knife into a bazooka, and then started handing out the bazookas to pretty much anyone who asked for one.[16]

According to Jaffe and Lerner, this practice has resulted in "a dangerous and expensive arms' race," undermining rather than fostering the progress of technological innovation.[17] And while the United States has been busy strengthening patent rights, some have argued that the European Commission has been busy trying to weaken them. One commentator has accused the European Commission of fostering such a negative attitude about intellectual property rights that it is leading to "an innovation crash that is likely to hasten Europe's technological irrelevance."[18]

Some executives and company founders who hear these criticisms assume that iProperty is a tactic for socially unconscious corporate giants who think only about their bottom line and indiscriminately use intellectual property as a weapon of mass destruction. However, we contend that it is up to companies to compete within the law and with moral vision and that a company's iProperty strategy can support that moral vision.

iProperty is powerful, but its power can be used in a morally appropriate manner. For example, a company may want to use its powerful iProperty to stop an industry giant from taking its ideas while providing free use of the same iProperty to the academic community or to a particular open source community. Even Microsoft, identified in some circles as an alleged intellectual property villain, recently inked deals with Linux software distributors Novel Inc. and Xandros Inc. in which it agreed not to target users of the open-source software, even though Microsoft believes that 235 of its patents are being violated.[19] In the changing global landscape of innovation and competition, there are many creative and morally appropriate approaches to the use of iProperty for the success of business and society.

SHIFTING GLOBAL SANDS

Even if we assume that, as has been suggested, the system is broken or at least damaged, today's executives and managers must nevertheless use the system that exists to protect the ideas of their companies. The legal systems for protecting intellectual property "are what they are," but on many levels—technological, geographical, political, legal, and cultural—they are changing fast.

Virtually every country of economic importance is experiencing intellectual property changes; for example:

- **In the United States.** A variety of forces for change are impacting U.S. intellectual property laws, including bipartisan patent reform legislation, the Patent Reform Act of 2007, five recent U.S. Supreme Court cases relating to patent law, a 2007 Department of Justice and Federal Trade Commission joint report titled *Antitrust Enforcement and Intellectual Property Rights: Promoting Innovation and Competition*, and even new accounting standards for appraising intellectual property value by the American Society of Appraisers.[20] Further, as this book is going to press, the U.S. Patent & Trademark Office has just published in the Federal Register, 129 pages of painfully detailed regulations representing the most fundamental administrative change in U.S. patent policy in recent history, possibly ever. Within days of the regulations' publication, a lawsuit was filed in federal court requesting a judge to stop the implementation of the regulations, which are widely viewed by patent attorneys and others as dealing a devastating blow to the ability of companies, particularly small businesses and life sciences companies, to protect their inventions.

- **In Europe.** The European Union is considering changes to the European system that would, among other things, create a true European community patent and would change the way patents are obtained and litigated in Europe. As observed by Tony Chalk, a partner in the European intellectual property firm Harrison Goddard Foote, "If the countries of the European Union would ratify the Community Patent Convention, then patentees would have a single patent, enforceable across the whole of the EU, instead of the present messy bundle of National Patents, separately enforceable in all the different states."[21]

- **In India.** India passed a new patent law in 2005 to bring its system into compliance with its international obligations, and the Indian government's appetite for an effective patent system is currently being tested by litigation with international drug maker Novartis over a patent application covering its cancer drug Glivec®. The global public outcry has been so great, with many commentators fearing that an outcome in favor of Novartis would deprive poor people of drugs, that Novartis has added an "Information Center" to its Web site to try to provide clarity around the complex issues involved.[22]

- **In China.** The world's biggest intellectual property pirate, China, has a patent system that was created in 1984 and is just now reaching adolescence, but it is nevertheless scheduled for a third round of amendments that should be completed by the time this book publishes. In 2007, the U.S. formally filed a complaint with the World Trade Organization over Chinese failure to adequately live up to its international obligations for protecting intellectual property, a move that could open the door to retaliatory trade sanctions.

In general, these changes represent progress toward the global harmonization of intellectual property systems. But this progress remains incomplete, and decision makers must be ever aware of today's status and make reasoned predictions about the future status of intellectual property laws, systems, and cultures to build iProperty portfolios that will withstand the test of time. Like many other business decisions, such as those made on future market sizes, consumer preferences, the availability of capital, and political scenarios, decisions about iProperty are made in the face of a great deal of uncertainty and with a healthy dose of informed speculation. Yet it is in the shifting sands of a churning global economic reality that corporate leaders must make myriad iProperty decisions, such as what ideas to protect, and when, where, and how to do so, all while avoiding stepping on the land mines of others' iProperty.

INNOVATION HAPPENS. . . EVERYWHERE

When we started writing in 2005 on the subject of what we now term iProperty, outsourcing was principally confined to the use of unskilled labor in underdeveloped countries. Discussions and news reports were about manufacturing plants in China or call centers in India. Outsourcing of knowledge-heavy innovation was only just beginning. The question of the day was "Do you really think they'll outsource . . . engineering, code writing, chemistry, design, and so on?" By the time this book is published, outsourcing of knowledge-heavy innovation will be routine in almost every aspect of commerce. Innovation will no longer be confined to a few early hot spots such as Bangalore, India, and Shanghai, China. Highly skilled innovators will be creating new technologies and products in thousands of locations around the globe.

Many companies are exploiting this distributed talent by turning to a global product development paradigm in which engineering teams collaborate on product development from locations around the globe.[23] This mastery of sophisticated, global innovation capabilities will be particularly effective at producing new and valuable ideas and the economic benefits that flow from such ideas because these changes bring under the innovation umbrella an incredible diversity of innovators with different backgrounds, cultural frameworks, educational experiences, and ways of competing.[24] Success requires companies to harness this chaotic, global innovation engine and to protect important ideas that flow from it, while using those ideas to generate economic value in the form of exciting new products and services for customers.

But achieving this goal will not be easy. Many of today's myriad innovation hot spots are emerging in regions where legal and cultural protections for iProperty remain inadequate. We expect that continued improvements in many countries will, in the long run, yield huge innovation and investment dividends for innovator companies that have the vision, courage, and strategic thinking to enter these unsettled waters. For now, companies must evaluate investment decisions based on their best prediction of the *future* quality of protection for iProperty. The worst mistake that companies can make in the rapidly evolving iProperty arena is to fight the competitive battles of tomorrow using the strategies of yesterday. Success requires forward-thinking companies to confront today's reality and predict tomorrow's reality. Among other things, companies must make sense of the shifting global landscape of laws, regulations, political and legal climates, and business practices; integrate this information into their business planning activities; and build into their corporate cultures the ability to make sound iProperty judgments and effectively execute iProperty strategies and tactics.

WE ARE ALL GLOBAL NOW

At this point some of our readers may be thinking: "We're only a regional company; these global issues don't affect us." To this we say: "Look again," more closely this time. Size does not matter. No innovator company is too large or too small to invest in and benefit from rethinking its vision of iProperty. A company making and selling products in the two-county region surrounding Alabaster, Alabama, can be sued for infringement of a U.S. patent owned by a Chinese company just as easily as a large company selling the same product in every country in North America and South America.

And a small company in Research Triangle Park, North Carolina, can patent its own ideas in Singapore and cut a licensing deal with a Singaporean company paying royalties for products sold by the Singaporean company all over the Pacific rim. Yes, in the global economy, the North Carolina company can generate a revenue stream from Singapore and surrounding regions by developing and licensing its iProperty. Even better, that revenue stream does not require the company to invest in setting up factories, supply chains, warehouses, and the like in Singapore.

While it is true that all companies can benefit from investing (time, effort, and money) in the development and protection of their iProperty, the corollary is that no company that competes based on its ability to innovate is immune to the growing dangers posed by a world in which companies increasingly use iProperty strategies to protect their ideas. The changes in the global economy that we discuss in this book enhance the opportunities and intensify the risks. The global iProperty strategist must understand opportunities and risks associated with global innovation; determine when, where, and how to protect the company's ideas in light of these opportunities and risks; and identify and deal with threats posed by the iProperty of others. In today's increasingly integrated and globally competitive business world, these are challenging tasks.

THINK FOR A MOMENT

Before digging into the world of iProperty, we invite the reader to take a moment to consider a few questions. Think about how your company manages its intellectual property. Think about the future of your company, the rapid changes in the global economy, and how these changes are already impacting your ability to create and sustain the competitive advantages of your products or services. What role does innovation play now and in your future? What role does iProperty play in protecting your competitive advantages and supporting your business strategy?

Is your company setting the standard for the development and use of iProperty in its business, or are you following others and reacting as new strategies and tactics trickle down to you? Is your iProperty strategy characterized by an understanding of changes in the global economic and legal landscape, or is it characterized by the unsupported biases of one or more senior executives? What role does iProperty play in protecting your company's competitive advantages and in supporting your business strategy? Are your iProperty decisions guided by a documented and tested iProperty strategy? Do your managers understand how your iProperty assets affect the decisions and options of your competitors? Do you have a clear and well-thought-out vision about how the structure of your company's portfolio should grow and change on a global basis to achieve your long-term goals?

Can your executives articulate how your iProperty supports your business goals? Do their eyes glaze over when you talk about iProperty, or do they become more animated? Do your managers have a clear and consistent understanding of the current strengths and weaknesses of your iProperty assets and processes? Who in your company is attentively looking outward at competitor strategies and iProperty best practices? Whether your company is large or small, is there a person or, better yet, a team of people with a diversity of backgrounds in your organization tasked with the development of an iProperty strategy for your organization, or is iProperty strategy relegated to a patent attorney silo in some remote corner of the corporate castle? Are those who manage your iProperty assets using their energy to keep a docket and prevent missed deadlines, or are they iProperty architects envisioning the future and building a portfolio that will withstand anticipated pressures and take advantage of emerging opportunities? Is someone in your company paying attention to your corporate culture to make sure that employees at all levels are sensitive to iProperty values and issues?

These are the kinds of questions that companies that stake their livelihood on their ability to create novel ideas and deliver them in products and services to markets must ask if they want to use that ability not just to one-up their competitors but to establish iProperty ownage and use the resulting leverage to create novel futures for their companies, their industries, and the world. We explore the issues raised by these questions, and many others, as we venture into the world of iProperty.

NOTES

1. See Marshal Phelps, "Turning a Patent Portfolio into a Profit Center," in *Making Innovation Pay: People Who Turn IP into Shareholder Value,* ed. Bruce Berman (Hoboken, NJ: John Wiley & Sons, Inc., 2006), 30.

2. British Department of the Treasury, *Gowers Review of Intellectual Property*, (Norwich, United Kingdom: The Stationery Office, 2006).

3. "New Ideas about Ideas," *The Economist* (December 9, 2006), 66.

4. David Warsh, *Knowledge and the Wealth of Nations: A Story of Economic Discovery* (New York: W. W. Norton, 2007), introduction.

5. Keith Cordoza in discussion with the author, May 2007.

6. Gary Hamel and C. K Prahalad, *Competing for the Future* (Boston: Harvard Business School Press, 1994), 3–4.

7. Ibid., 5.

8. Ibid.

9. See Keith Smith, "Measuring Innovation," *The Oxford Handbook of Innovation*, ed. J. Fagerberg, D. Mowery, and R. R. Nelson (Oxford: Oxford University Press, 2004), 164.

10. Kevin Rivette, *Rembrandts in the Attic: Unlocking the Hidden Value of Patents* (Boston: Harvard Business School Press, 1999).

11. Phelps, "Turning a Patent Portfolio into a Profit Center." in *Making Innovation Pay: People Who Turn IP into Shareholder Value,* ed. Bruce Berman (Hoboken, NJ: John Wiley & Sons, Inc., 2006), 30.

12. Joe Beyers, "Managing Innovation Assets as Business Assets," in *Making Innovation Pay: People Who Turn IP into Shareholder Value,* ed. Bruce Berman (Hoboken, NJ: John Wiley & Sons, Inc., 2006), 162.

13. Michael Crichton, *Next* (New York: Harper Collins, 2006), front cover flap.

14. See "Patently Absurd," *Wall Street Journal* (March 1, 2006).

15. Nancy Gallini, "The Economics of Patents: Lessons from Recent U.S. Patent Reform," *Journal of Economic Perspectives* 16, no. 2 (2002); 131.

16. Adam Jaffe and Josh Lerner, *Innovation and Its Discontents* (Princeton, NJ: Princeton University Press, 2004), 35.

17. Ibid.

18. Ian Harvey, chairman of the Intellectual Property Institute and the former CEO of BTG plc, "Creativity Destruction," *Wall Street Journal Online*, May 31, 2007, http://online.wsj.com/article_print/SB118056787304019281.html.

19. "Microsoft, Xandros Ink Patent Pact," *Wall Street Journal Online*, June 4, 2007, http://online.wsj.com/article_print/SB118096792068623771.html.

20. Cameron Gray of Ocean Tomo observed the congruence of these various factors in "Clearing the Underbrush," *IAM* (June–July 2007), 23–26.

21. Tony Chalk, e-mail communication with the author, June 18, 2007.

22. Novartis, Inc., corporate Web site, www.novartis.com/newsroom/india-glivec-patent-case/index.shtml, accessed June 14, 2007.

23. Steven Eppinger and Anil Chitkara, "The New Practice of Global Product Development," *MIT Sloan Management Review* (Summer 2006), 22–30.

24. See Michael Porter, *The Competitive Advantage of Nations* (New York: The Free Press, 1990), 48.

*iP*ROPERTY

Part One

Global iProperty Context

1

Innovating World

Welcome to the Global Innovation Factory

Innovation is now a global phenomenon. It is both a *driver* of globalization, in that it creates the technologies that make globalization possible, and a *consequence* of globalization, which is causing an unprecedented redistribution and expansion of sophisticated innovative capabilities around the world. As a result of globalization, innovative ideas are now more important than ever for developing competitive advantage. One corollary is that protecting these ideas to sustain competitive advantage is also more important than ever. In fact, being better than competitors at protecting valuable ideas is in itself a competitive advantage. And yet, as more and more companies use the world's legal systems to protect their ideas, the landscape becomes more populated with hazards, so companies must also focus their attentions on avoiding the risks created by the iProperty of others.

The protections afforded by various countries are rapidly changing, generally in a positive direction but with frequent setbacks, and the cultural contexts in which these laws are framed and enforced are sometimes difficult for outsiders to understand. Companies must stay alert to and informed regarding the entire global context of protection and enforcement of iProperty in order to thrive. In this chapter, we discuss these and other topics as we set the stage for our discussion of iProperty strategies and tactics by viewing the evolving global economic stage from an iProperty perspective.

WHY THE WORLD IS INNOVATING

Today's innovator companies, whether large or small, local or international, are in a global competition. As such, they must focus on innovation and think about protecting the fruits of their innovation in global terms. Companies that consistently win in the global economic competition will be those consistent innovators with insight into current trends and foresight into how to protect and extend the competitive advantages conferred by their innovative capabilities. Exhibit 1.1 shows six key factors that characterize and shape the way the world does innovation:

1. **Innovation as a driver of globalization.** In today's economy, innovation is probably the key driver of unprecedented economic globalization.

2. **Urgency of innovation.** Economic globalization (global competition) makes innovation more important than ever for developing competitive advantage.

3. **Globalization of innovation.** Economic globalization stimulates the global distribution of sophisticated innovation capabilities.

4. **iProperty risks and opportunities.** Globalization of innovation stimulates the development and use of iProperty that creates new risks and affords new opportunities for every innovator company.

5. **Standardization of intellectual property laws.** Intellectual property laws are becoming more standardized in countries around

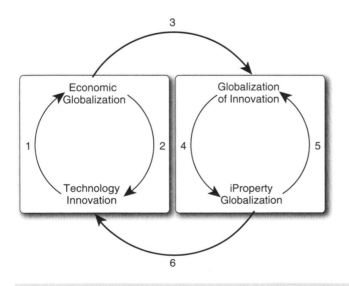

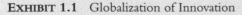

EXHIBIT 1.1 Globalization of Innovation

the globe, but significant differences remain, so innovators must grapple with global iProperty complexities.

6. **Increasing world economic output.** Globalization of innovation together with globally consistent iProperty standards will stimulate more innovation, advance economic globalization, and increase global economic output.

Innovation Drives Economic Globalization

Innovation is driving unprecedented economic globalization, which creates a variety of opportunities and risks in the iProperty world. How is this happening? To begin with, innovation is driving the global expansion of communication, collaboration, and competition. In *The World Is Flat*, an assessment of the global forces shaping our economic reality, Thomas Friedman writes:

> Clearly, it is now possible for more people than ever to collaborate and compete in real time with more other people on more different kinds of work from more different corners of the planet and on more equal footing than at any previous time in the history of the world.[1]

Underlying Friedman's list of superlatives is a series of innovations that includes more, faster, and more reliable technologies for communication, more optical cables crossing and satellites orbiting the planet, along with more and cheaper devices such as cell phones and computers for connecting into the global explosion of bandwidth. Better infrastructure and technologies now move people and goods around the world faster and more reliably than ever. Further, many developing countries are playing a game of technology leapfrog, in which they bypass traditional technologies, such as landline telecom systems, and jump to newer technologies, such as wireless communications. In India, for example, it is not uncommon to see farmers riding ox carts and talking on cell phones. These innovations are rapidly eliminating the old national barriers to business and supporting unprecedented, business-driven economic globalization. Yet, as we discuss further in Chapter 2, these innovations also create new threats to companies that want to protect their ideas.

Urgency of Innovation

One important effect of economic globalization is the transition to what Kenichi Ohmae, acclaimed Japanese management strategist, calls a "borderless business environment."[2] "Borderless business" enables companies to access larger markets, but also means that more competitors can access the same customers, thus intensifying competition. The Internet in particular levels the playing field for buyers, removes barriers for sellers to share product and service information, and enables companies previously isolated from one another to compete and collaborate directly, dramatically increasing the efficiency of markets.

Fierce global competition forces firms to source products from countries with lower capital and labor costs, even for products with comparatively high margins, such as pharmaceuticals. Companies in the United States outsource to India; companies in India outsource to Sri Lanka. The resulting difficulty of competing based on price motivates corporate leaders to look to novel ideas as their primary source of competitive advantage to avoid the otherwise inevitable commoditization. A recent Kauffman Foundation report concluded:

> Today's economy is driven by innovation—the development and adoption of new products, processes, and business models. Nations, states, regions, firms, and even individuals compete on their ability to accumulate, aggregate, and apply their assets to create value in new ways for increasingly diverse customers all over the world.[3]

Baruch Lev, a leading thinker in the area of intangible assets, refers to this phenomenon as "the urgency to innovate." According to Lev, "given the decreasing economies of scale (efficiency gains) from production . . . coupled with ever increasing competitive pressures, innovation has become a matter of corporate survival."[4] And while innovation may confer a competitive advantage, in the rapidly adapting global economy the competitive advantage will be short-lived without some form of protection from those who would simply copy the innovation.

How is the global redistribution of innovation impacting the way your company competes?

Bruce Greenwald, Columbia Business School professor of finance and asset management, and Judd Kahn, chief operating officer of Humingbird Management, LLC, recently emphasized the importance of "barriers to entry" as a force affecting the competitive environment: "It is so dominant that leaders seeking to develop and pursue winning strategies should begin by ignoring [other forces] and focus only on it.... No other feature of the competitive landscape has as much influence on a company's success as where it stands in regard to these barriers."[5] Lester Thurrow, former dean of the MIT Sloan School of Management, maintains that in addition to copyrights and brands, the "only remaining source of true competitive advantage [is] technologies that others do not have."[6] Walter Willigan of Pricewaterhouse Coopers echoes this sentiment:

> Successful corporations of the next century will not be able to rely solely on the age-old levers of competition viz., labor, capital and land. Rather they will have to supplement the management of these tangible assets with the effective management and exploitation of their intellectual property—patents, trademarks and technology.[7]

While strategic reliance on innovation is most apparent in companies that traditionally have made their living from technological advances in fields such as engineering and chemistry, the urgency to innovate and the corresponding need to use iProperty to protect that innovation impacts all innovating firms whose technologies are as diverse as biotechnology, banking, computer chips, and consumer goods. In a recent article, Michael Scharge, a research associate with MIT's Media Lab, chronicled the technological evolution of toasters. According to Scharge, when it comes to "countertop toasting technology," those who do not differentiate, segment, and innovate are doomed to fail.[8] He concludes that rather than signaling the commoditization of a product, intense price competition may signal the need for innovation: "innovate in order to differentiate ... identify hidden or untapped potential for new value creation." In today's economy, it appears that even toasters must be innovative.

Globalization of Innovation

The quest for innovation has gone global. Innovation hot spots are growing in virtually all corners of the globe. These hot spots provide critical concentrations of geographically localized innovation capabilities—including engineers, scientists, artists, entrepreneurs, and product manufacturing capabilities—and provide their host cities with international competitive advantage.[9] Businesses can find inexpensive services, from mechanical engineering to pharmaceutical scale-up and manufacturing. A recent article in *The Economist* concluded that China and India, hosts of many of the new innovation hot spots, are "changing the

very process of development." The article predicts that "the rise of India
and China as centres of innovation will radically shake up the technology
industry that is today based mainly in rich countries."[10] The Organization
for Economic Co-operation and Development estimates that by the end
of 2006, China will be the second-highest investor in research and development (R&D), with investments by government and business surpassing
$136 billion.[11] Further, we expect that the emergence of microfinancing,
very small amounts of money supplied to individual entrepreneurs, will
have massive impact at the grassroots level. These large and small investments are sure to fuel the growth of existing innovation hot spots as well
as the development of new ones.

Consider Albany Molecular, Inc. (AMRI), a leading chemistry-based
drug discovery, development, and manufacturing company. Begun in
1991 and now employing approximately 850 employees, AMRI focuses
on tools and processes for the discovery of new small-molecule prescrip-
tion drugs. Many of its clients are large pharmaceutical companies that
are offshoring innovative drug discovery and development work. Realiz-
ing that its customers needed more cost options, AMRI recently opened
state-of-the-art chemistry innovation facilities in Hyderabad, India, and
in Singapore, two leading global innovation hot spots. Now, when quot-
ing work, AMRI offers its pharmaceutical company clients a three-tiered
price structure, typically with the United States as the highest price, Singapore in the middle, and India at the bottom. Customers choose the price
that they are willing to accept based on such factors as sophistication of
the workforce relative to the work at hand, cultural and legal protections
for innovations, ease of communication, and others.

The recent economic revitalization of Silicon Valley has been at-
tributed in part to the expansion of global innovative capabilities. One
evidence of the influence of globalization on Silicon Valley is the number
of patents originating there with inventors from other locations around
the world. The Silicon Valley Index reports growth in the number of
patents naming Silicon Valley inventors along with inventors from other
countries.[12] According to the Index, this "co-patenting" by valley employees and foreign collaborators increased sixfold from 1993 to 2005.
Most foreign coemployees are from India, China, Italy, Hong Kong,
Finland and Taiwan. A Scripps News article observed that "Globalization is helping to expand the valley's economy, rather than threatening
it."[13] Thus, competition and collaboration with global innovation hot
spots appear to be having a positive effect on innovation in Silicon Valley. Scripps News concludes that "[d]espite some predictions that Silicon

Valley would lose out because of globalization, the region is keeping its lead as a capital of technology investment and employment."[14]

iProperty Risks and Opportunities

The rapid global spread of innovation provides companies with low-cost sources of innovation that never existed before. But companies are also more likely to face competitive risks from places that would not have been considered 10 years ago. These threats may result from two facts: (1) competitors are moving their own centers of innovation to less expensive hot spots around the globe, and (2) new homegrown competitors are arising out of these innovation hot spots. For example, iProperty threats may arise from:

- Outsourcing or offshoring strategies that locate critical technology in countries lacking sufficient legal protections or an employee culture that values iProperty, with a resulting risk of iProperty loss
- Competitor setting up manufacturing operations to make a copy-cat product in a country where the innovator has no meaningful iProperty protection
- Competitor selling products in markets in which the innovator has passed up the opportunity to obtain patents
- Escape of valuable trade secrets, know-how, and other iProperty from an offshore operation when employees leave to work for a local competitor or to start their own company
- Litigation, such as a patent infringement suit, initiated in your country by a company from a distant innovation hot spot

These and many other potential threats are increasing in probability due to economic globalization, the increasingly global expansion of innovative capabilities, the high mobility of brain power, and the increasingly densely populated global patent landscape.

In 2005, a record year for international patent applications at the World Intellectual Property Organization, South Korea surpassed the Netherlands in the number of international applications filed, and China surpassed Canada, revealing a definitive shift to the East.[15] Companies competing for the future based on their innovative products and services cannot afford to dismiss the importance of this change. The world's patent landscape is being dramatically reshaped as it is rapidly being populated by patents originating from companies in a new set of countries with growing innovative capacity. Companies that are comfortable looking only in their own backyards for iProperty competition are likely to be surprised, to say the least. These issues are explored in more detail in Chapter 2.

Lagging Legal Standardization

Businesses now operate in an economic world in which political and geographic boundaries are increasingly devoid of meaning. Generally speaking, innovative goods and services and the funds that buy them flow freely from country to country. But, with a few exceptions, the legal systems that protect the ideas embodied in those goods are still firmly fenced in. There is no global system of intellectual property rights. Intellectual property systems come in all shapes and sizes. And even where the legal standards apparently are similar, the cultural contexts in which those laws are enforced continue to vary widely.

In 1994, the World Trade Organization (WTO) proactively (with pressure from western countries) and profoundly changed the future of global intellectual property standards with its Trade Related Aspects of Intellectual Property Rights Agreement (TRIPS). As described in the TRIPS preamble, the objectives of the agreement are threefold:

1. Reducing distortions and impediments to international trade
2. Promoting effective and adequate protection of intellectual property rights
3. Ensuring that measures and procedures for enforcing intellectual property rights do not themselves become barriers to legitimate trade

The TRIPS agreement is widely recognized as the most significant intellectual property accord of the twentieth century.[16] Among other things, TRIPS requires countries to treat nationals and foreigners equally when it comes to obtaining and enforcing intellectual property laws. The result of TRIPS has been the increasing standardization of availability, acquisition, scope, maintenance, and enforcement of iProperty rights in countries large and small around the globe. For example, India and China both made conforming, though not complete, changes to their patent systems in 2005, and China is planning another extensive overhaul in 2007.

When was the last time you had a discussion with your patent counsel about international iProperty developments and their impact on your organization?

───────────── ∼≫ ─────────────

Having the laws on the books is one thing. Actually enforcing them is another. Among the tools that the U.S. government has to encourage, push, cajole, and manipulate countries into improving their intellectual property systems is a yearly report card, affectionately referred to as the Special 301 Report.[17] China, for example, always gets failing grades in all subjects. The 2007 Special 301 Report retains China on the Priority Watch List, a distinction that identifies China as a member of the world's iProperty axis of evil. Priority Watch List countries have failures in "IPR [Intellectual Property Rights] protection, enforcement, or market access." In the understated language of diplomatese, the listed country is "the focus of increased bilateral attention concerning the problem areas." In the most recent report, Argentina, Chile, Egypt, India, Israel, Lebanon, Thailand, Turkey, Ukraine, and Venezuela are singled out for special attention.

Because the enforcement problems are often more immediate at a local level (especially in China), the U.S. Trade Representative has recently started giving attention in the Special 301 Report to local protection and enforcement through a special local review. The goal of local scrutiny is to single out pirate hangouts and to pressure responsible governments to start doling out penalties for pirating that are sufficiently serious that they actually serve as a deterrent—rather than the insignificant hand-slapping that is often the result of intellectual property litigation in China today. The 2007 report lists a variety of pirate hangouts from around the globe, from Silk Street Market, Beijing, China, to the triborder region in Paraguay, Argentina, and Brazil.

Another important tool for handling differences in intellectual property standards among countries is the dispute resolution mechanism created by TRIPS. WTO members can bring cases alleging violation of TRIPS provisions by other countries before the WTO. If the case is proved, the losing country may be required to pay damages and/or change its laws. If the losing country does not pay the damages, the winner may impose tariffs on imports from the losing country and pay the proceeds of those tariffs directly to companies that have been damaged by the losing country's violation.

The United States has rarely used the dispute resolution procedures, but there are signs that the U.S. government is turning up the heat. In June 2006, the Trade Representative created a new Office of Intellectual Property and Innovation and appointed a Chief Negotiator for Intellectual Property Enforcement to enhance its focus on protecting and enforcing intellectual property rights. In 2007, the Trade Representative further ramped up the pressure on China by requesting dispute settlement consultations, in part over deficiencies in China's legal regime for protecting and enforcing copyrights. The 2007 Special 301 Report indicates that the United States will consider dispute settlement consultations where countries do not appear to have fully addressed their TRIPS obligations.

Since the mid–1980s, the United States and China have considered intellectual property issues of such critical importance that, in addition to myriad lesser diplomatic efforts, these issues have frequently been addressed in discussions between the chief executives of the two countries.[18] Support appears strong on both sides for strengthening cooperation on intellectual property protection. In a recent meeting with the director of the U.S. Patent and Trademark Office, Chinese officials emphasized that China attaches great importance to U.S. experience in the area of intellectual property protection.[19] The countries have even designated special liaison officers to deal with intellectual property projects, and the United States plans to send experts to train Chinese intellectual property officials. In July 2006, China published revised patent examination guidelines to significantly improve its patent system in such areas as software and chemical patents and the requirement for novelty. Yet China's rhetoric indicates that it is resentful of western meddling in its internal intellectual property affairs. And despite many improvements in its intellectual property systems aimed at improving and harmonizing the relevant laws, many deficiencies remain.

Increasing Global Economic Output

Finally, while a detailed discussion of the important policy topic of increasing global economic output is outside of the scope of this book, we wish to mention here that globalization of innovation capabilities plus improved intellectual property protections around the world can be expected to accelerate an upward economic spiral. Improved legal, political, and cultural protections for intellectual property will stimulate further investments in innovation, which stimulate further innovations, which increase productivity, which yields economic growth, which stimulates further investment in innovation. In the words of one commentator, "It is by means of enforcing such standards that governments bolster their innovative capacity . . . and not by a propensity to resort to shortcuts."[20]

For example, consider Avesthagen, a company in Bangalore, India, that makes generic versions of biotech drugs. The company has built more than 30 alliances and partnerships with industry and government organizations in India and elsewhere, relationships it has leveraged with a growing portfolio of iProperty, including 140 patents and patent applications. In 2007, this record enabled Avesthagen to attract into India a $32 million investment funded in part by Fidelity International.[21]

In another example, Aptuit, Inc. and Laurus Labs Limited teamed up in 2007 to develop a new drug development company in India, named Aptuit Laurus. The new company will be backed by a $100 million investment in development, manufacturing, and informatics capabilities. In addition to a significant investment in infrastructure, the deal will add hundreds of high-paying jobs in medicinal chemistry, solid-state chemistry, large-scale pharmaceutical dosage form manufacturing, clinical packaging, and logistics. The companies saw the intellectual property issue as significant enough to mention it in their press release; pointing to the importance of the recent Indian patent law reforms, the press release stated:

> The security of IP in the region is further supported by the implementation of the World Trade Organization (WTO) Agreement on Trade-Related Aspects of Intellectual Property Rights (TRIPS) and other steps taken by the Indian government to protect product patents.[22]

How the world's developing economies implement intellectual property policies is not a simple issue. We agree with many commentators that while India, China, Singapore, and other developing countries may be ready for full-fledged intellectual property systems, it would be detrimental, if not impossible, for many of the poorest countries to implement the intellectual property policies of the developed world. However, the value of an effective intellectual property system for attracting investment, creating jobs and valuable products and services, will motivate insightful leaders in developing countries to implement effective policies appropriate to their country's stage of development. As elegantly stated by journalist David Warsh in his work on the economics of knowledge, *Knowledge and the Wealth of Nations*, "If the intricate system of incentives to create new ideas is underdeveloped, society suffers from the general lack of progress (most of all, the poor). So, too, if these incentives are too lavish or closely held."[23]

FUELING THE GLOBAL SPREAD OF INNOVATION

So far we have outlined the interactive relationship among a variety of trends, including technology innovation, the globalization of innovation, the urgency of innovation, change and stagnation in intellectual property laws and enforcement systems, and the relationship of these trends to global economic health. In addition to these trends, six factors are both influenced by and contributing to the globalization of innovation:

1. The rise of a global "creative class" of knowledge workers
2. Business process outsourcing and offshoring trends
3. The increasing cost of innovation in developed countries
4. The improvement of economies and infrastructures in developing countries
5. The globalization of education
6. The development of government and private initiatives designed to support entrepreneurial businesses

The "Creative Class"

In his book, *The Rise of the Creative Class*, economist Richard Florida introduced the concept of the "creative class."[24] This class, sometimes referred to as "knowledge workers," includes those creative individuals who become the scientists, engineers, artists, and entrepreneurs who drive innovation-based economic growth. Members of the creative class are the key players in the globalization of innovation. Individuals in this often free-spirited group are motivated by creative opportunities and locations that offer unusual and diverse lifestyle opportunities. In his latest book, *The Flight of the Creative Class*, Florida describes how a discussion with a group of international graduate students about their postcollege plans influenced his thinking about the global redistribution of the creative class:

> The more we probed the issue, the more concerned we became. These young people were only the tip of the iceberg. Not just for them, but for established scientists and engineers, for entrepreneurs and employees, for artists and cultural mavens, America was no longer the only place to be. This was doubly true of our foreign-born students, on whom we depend to help build our scientific enterprises, and of immigrant employees and entrepreneurs, who power so much of our growth. The balance of the world's creative brainpower was shifting.[25]

What is your company doing to attract and retain its share of the global creative class?

Countries around the world have for years been losing talent to the United States and Europe. A study by Viveck Wadhwa of Duke University and others highlights the contribution that these immigrants have made to the U.S. economy in particular.[26] According to Wadhwa, the percentage of patents filed by foreigners (non–U.S. citizens) living in the U.S. tripled in the past decade. A large proportion of patent applications listing at least one foreign national for large patent holders list at least one foreign patent applicant, for example:

- Qualcomm Inc., 72%
- Merck & Co., 65%
- Exxon Mobile Corp., 48%
- The U.S. government, 41%

These same countries are now growing their own high-tech and biotech sectors, and they are also working hard to lure their expatriates back home. Both China and India have a diaspora of millions of expatriates who can serve as a resource for their countries' development in terms of capital, business know-how, education, and advanced technological knowledge.[27] The Chinese Academy of Sciences has started awarding "fellowships" to attract Chinese expatriates back home in a program called "the hundred talents program."[28] The National Association of Software & Service Companies estimates that about 25,000 Indian techies returned home between 2001 and 2005.[29] One report indicated that in a survey of Indian executives in the United States, 68 percent were looking for opportunities to return to India. A similar study of graduates of the All India Institute of Medical Sciences found that 40 percent of graduates living abroad were ready to return.[30]

Immigration problems in the United States are also forcing many high-value immigrants back home. About 1 million foreign nationals were awaiting decisions on permanent residency in 2006, including 500,000 highly skilled immigrants, but, for example, one important type of permanent visa, the EB visa, is capped at 120 per year.[31] According to Wadhwa:

We've brought in highly skilled people and given them training in American business and marketing savvy, and then forced them to go back home and start competing. Companies lose talent, and workers are resentful and angry. It's a lose-lose situation.[32]

And the more expatriates return home to start and grow technology companies, the more jobs are created for other highly educated scientists and engineers who want to return or stay at home. The net effect is a further redistribution of the capacity to produce sophisticated innovations to a broader group of countries around the globe.

Outsourcing

Outsourcing and offshoring of skilled and unskilled jobs is also contributing to the spread of innovation hot spots. A recent survey of 700 companies by Enterprise Systems found that more than 33 percent of respondents are currently outsourcing some or all of their applications, services, or operations and about 43 percent are currently evaluating outsourcing providers.[33] This important trend results in the channeling of money into developing economies, where it often funds infrastructure and builds communities that are attractive to creative workers. Moreover, creative workers are needed to develop and maintain the technologies that make it possible to connect low-skill outsourcing centers to their customer base, largely in the developed world. Outsourcing operations are training a new class of creative workers and contributing to the redistribution of creative capacity around the world.

Cost of Innovation

An important and more recent trend is the outsourcing or offshoring of innovation jobs. As innovation hot spots emerge in low-cost labor markets around the world, businesses have more options than ever for outsourcing or offshoring innovation. The cost of human talent is typically much less in developing economies. For example, an Indian graduate typically costs about 12 percent of the cost of an American graduate.[34] As a recent article in *The Economist* stated: "The bottom line is that you can buy almost 10 Indian brains for the cost of one American one."[35] We recently spoke with a Ph.D. biotech scientist who moved back to India after working at a U.S. biotech firm for several years. His Indian salary is about one-fifth the amount he was paid in the United States. In India, he has the same skills, access to the same high-tech equipment, and he is surrounded by the same quality of scientists as he was when working in the United States. His innovative capacity is available in India for a fraction of the cost of those same skills in the United States. And his salary enables him to maintain an acceptable standard of living in his home country, where he can be closer to his family and raise his children within his preferred culture.

Growing Infrastructure

As already suggested, outsourcing and offshoring trends are enabling local economies to build attractive work environments for their creative workers, thereby enticing educated expatriates back home. Infosys Technologies Limited (ITL) is one of many examples. The company is headquartered in Bangalore, India, another innovation hot spot, where magnificent metallic structures housing global businesses are built amid the remains of an ancient civilization and surrounded by abject poverty. Thomas Friedman describes ITL's global conferencing center as "ground zero" of the Indian outsourcing industry: a cavernous wood-paneled room with cameras in the ceiling for teleconferencing and a massive super-size flat-screen TV that can pull together ITL's entire supply chain—New York, London, Boston, San Francisco, Singapore—all at once, all live.[36] As compared with locations in other countries, companies in outsourcing hot spots have better access to building materials, such as steel and concrete, as well as better roads, cleaner water, more reliable electricity and communications, and other components of infrastructure. The infrastructure that underlies and is enabled by the economics of outsourcing is also a fundamental enabling technology for the global distribution of innovation.

Improving Education

The universities of the United States and Europe have traditionally been the key destinations for top students from developing economies, such as China and India. After leaving school, many of these students remained in the West to enjoy the standard of living, and many created companies, raised venture capital from here and abroad, and built companies that added new products and services to the economy. But now higher education is "going global."

Universities in developing nations, such as the Indian Institutes of Technology, often referred to as the MIT of India, are earning top ratings, and many have close ties to top U.S. and European Union universities. At the same time, western universities are offering creative local options for overseas students. For example, Duke University in Durham, North Carolina, and the National University of Singapore opened a medical school in Singapore, its first graduate medical school, and Duke plans to open a second medical school in Beijing. Moreover, the cost of education in developing economies is much less than that in developed economies.

One measure of success in a nation's efforts to improve its homegrown innovation capacity is the increase in the awards of doctoral degrees, particularly in the sciences, from domestic institutions.[37] China, for example, moved from essentially zero in 1985 to almost 7,500 domestically awarded doctorates in 2000. South Korean awards increased from 128 to almost 3,000 in roughly the same period. A related measure is the number of scientific papers published in peer-reviewed journals. In 2003, for example, authors from China, Singapore, South Korea, and Taiwan published 55,300 papers in the American Chemical Society's journals, up from 7,200 papers in 1998.[38] Because it is no longer necessary for students to travel to the United States and Europe for top-rated educations or to put those educations into use, many of the world's best minds are comfortable staying right at home.

Governmental and Nonprofit Initiatives

In view of the economic gains created by centers of innovation, governments are spending their nations' hard-earned cash to create their own centers for attracting creative workers from around the world. Biotechnology centers are representative of this trend. The *Chicago Tribune* recently reported that biotech centers are springing up across the globe, from Australia to Toronto and Singapore to Amsterdam.[39] Until recently the United States accounted for most of the world's biotech investment, but countries around the world are using government subsidies to attract biotech companies and the investments and jobs that go along with them. Interestingly, venture capital funds are starting to flow to these new hot spots (e.g., in China and India), to take advantage of the low cost of R&D.

PLAYING THE GLOBAL iPROPERTY GAME

Participating in this global competition, although a serious business endeavor, is in many respects a game: the iProperty game. Innovator companies must make an expensive investment in iProperty chips. Players place the chips, technology and market bets, in a strategically selected set of countries on a worldwide playing board. Once chips are placed, they can be removed, but they cannot be moved to other countries (i.e., protection efforts can be abandoned, but if not initiated in other countries in a timely manner, the opportunity for protection in those countries may be lost). The usefulness of a specific placement of chips is subject to a high degree of uncertainty. Attempts to place a chip are not always successful (i.e., the expected protection may not materialize despite the investment or the technology may fail). Even when a chip is successfully placed, it may not have its intended effect (e.g., legal protections may be established but not successfully enforced). An iProperty chip may be trumped by a superior chip placed by another player (e.g., even if a patent is granted, a competitor may have superior patent rights that block the company from exploiting its own patent). Threats will arise in countries where no patent chip was placed (i.e., unless all economically viable countries are protected, copying *will* occur in countries where the company has not invested in protecting its ideas). The most successful companies in this economic game will be those that innovate well; they will have more chips to play with than their less innovative competitors. And among companies that innovate well, those companies that are masterful at protecting the resulting ideas in the complex global arena will have a competitive advantage (i.e., ownage) over those that are not.

NOTES

1. Thomas Friedman, *The World Is Flat: A Brief History of the Twenty-first Century* (New York: Farrar, Straus and Giroux, 2006), 8.

2. See Kenichi Ohmae, *The Next Global Stage: The Challenges and Opportunities in Our Borderless World.* (Upper Saddle River, NJ: Wharton School Publishing, 2005).

3. The 2007 State New Economy Index, The Kauffman Foundation with the Information Technology and Innovation Foundation (2007), 4–5.

4. Baruch Lev, *Intangibles: Management, Measurement, and Reporting* (Washington, DC: Brookings Institution Press, 2001), 14–16.

5. Bruce Greenwald and Judd Kahn, *Competition Demystified: A Radically Simplified Approach to Business Strategy* (New York: Penguin Books, 2005), 5.

6. Lester Thurow, *Fortune Favors the Bold: What We Must Do to Build a New and Lasting Global Prosperity* (New York: HarperCollins, 2003), x–y.

7. Walter Willigan, "Leveraging Your Intellectual Property: A Proved Path to Value Extraction," PricewaterhouseCoopers LLP, 1998.

8. "The Myth of Commoditization," *MIT Sloan Management Review* [0](Winter 2007), 10–14.

9. See Michael Porter, *The Competitive Advantage of Nations* (New York: The Free Press, 1990), 580.

10. "Thinking for Themselves: India and China Aim to Challenge Western Tech Firms Through Innovation, Not Just Cheap Labour," *The Economist* (October 22, 2005), 15.

11. Organization for Economic Co-operation and Development, "China Will Become World's Second Highest Investor in R&D by End of 2006, Finds OECD," press release, April 12, 2006,www.oecd.org/dataoecd/37/18/37770382.xls.

12. Joint Venture Silicon Valley Network, "The Silicon Valley Index" (San Jose: Joint Venture, 2007).

13. Caroline Said, "Silicon Valley Hits Another Boom Cycle," ScrippsNews, February 2006, www.scrippsnews.com/node/19085.

14. Ibid.

15. World Intellectual Property Organization, "Exceptional Growth from North East Asia in Record Year for International Patent Filings," press release, February 3, 2006.

16. For a helpful account of the events leading up to TRIPS and its impact on intellectual property policy, see Pat Choate, *Hot Property: The Stealing of Ideas in an Age of Globalization* (New York: Alfred A. Knopf, 2005), chapter 8. In fact, despite the somewhat misleading title, the entire book is well worth reading for anyone who wishes to understand the evolution of intellectual property laws in the twentieth century.

17. See William Alford, *To Steal a Book Is an Elegant Offense: Intellectual Property Law in Chinese Civilization* (Stanford, CA: Stanford University Press, 1995), for a review of the history of how the United States used the Special 301 Report to pressure Taiwan to improve its intellectual property laws in the 1980s.

18. See William Alford, ibid., chapter 6, for an excellent review of the history of these interactions. Alford persuasively argues that the U.S. approach of using external pressure to force domestic legal changes in China is "deeply flawed in both its methodology and objectives, and ultimately self-deluding as to the process and implications of legal change."

19. "China, U.S. Vow to Deepen Co-op on iProperty Protection," *China View* (November 13, 2006).

20. Bright Simons, "Drug Patents Don't Kill Poor Patients," Ohmy News, June 4, 2007, http://english.ohmynews.com/articleview/article_view.asp?at_code=414276.

21. Seema Singh, "Avesthagen Closes $32.5M Funding," *Red Herring*, January 24, 2007, www.redherring.com/PrintArticle.aspx?a=20912&sector=Briefings.

22. Aptuit, Inc. and Laurus Labs, "Aptuit to Invest More than $100 Million in Laurus Labs (India); Dr. Satyanarayana Chava Named Aptuit Laurus CEO, Joins Aptuit Board," joint press release, viewed on PharmaLive,www.pharmalive.com/News/index.cfm?articleid=451980&categoryid=54#.

23. David Warsh, *Knowledge and the Wealth of Nations: A Story of Economic Discovery* (New York: Norton, 2007), xvii.

24. Richard Florida, *The Rise of the Creative Class: And How It's Transforming Work, Leisure, Community and Everyday Life* (New York: Perseus Books Group, 2002).

25. Richard Florida, *The Flight of the Creative Class: The New Global Competition for Talent* (New York: HarperCollins, 2005), 95.

26. Vivek Wadhwa, Guillermina Jasso, Ben Rissing, Gary Gereffi, Richard Freeman, "Intellectual Property, the Immigration Backlog, and a Reverse Brain-Drain: America's

New Immigrant Entrepreneurs, Part III," *Social Science Research Network*, August 22, 2007, http://papers.ssrn.com/sol3/papers.cfm?abstract_id=1008366 (accessed September 9, 2007).

27. Oded Shenkar, *The Chinese Century: The Rising Chinese Economy and Its Impact on the Global Economy, the Balance of Power, and Your Job* (Boston: Wharton School Publishing 2004), 55.

28. "Opening the Doors," *The Economist* (October 7, 2006), 13.

29. Ibid.

30. Ibid.

31. Rachel Konrad, "'Reverse Brain Drain' may Hurt Patent Filings," *The Raleigh News & Observer* (August 24, 2007).

32. Ibid.

33. Dian Schaffhauser, "Outsourcing Survey, Part 1: Who and Where," www.esj.com/enterprise/print.aspx?editorialsId=1701.

34. "The World Is Our Oyster," *The Economist* (October 6, 2006), 9.

35. Ibid.

36. Friedman, *The World Is Flat,* 5–6.

37. Committee on Prospering in the Global Economy of the 21st Century: An Agenda for American Science and Technology, National Academy of Sciences, National Academy of Engineering, Institute of Medicine, *Rising Above the Gathering Storm: Energizing and Employing America for a Brighter Economic Future* (Pre-publication Copy, 2005), 3–9.

38. Michael Heylin, "Globalization of Science Rolls On," *Chemical Engineering News* (November 27, 2006), 28.

39. Jon Van, "The Rush Is on for Biotech Bonanza," *Chicago Tribune* (June 22, 2005), Business Section, 1.

~ 2 ~

iProperty World

Assessing iProperty Risk in a Changing Global Environment

The changes in the economics of global innovation discussed in Chapter 1 provide opportunities and challenges for companies large and small to use iProperty strategies for competing in the new global economy. The global distribution of technologically sophisticated idea–generating capability means that the locus of innovation is quite likely to be situated in one of the many developing countries around the world where, more often than not, adequate legal protections are lacking and where managers and employees typically are not sufficiently trained or motivated to protect intellectual property.

It is now possible, for example, to buy innovation on a massive scale and at a greatly reduced price in India, China, and Singapore, but how are companies to assess whether the benefits of inexpensive innovation can be obtained without undue damage to the legal rights that result from and protect that innovation? Rapidly changing technologies also impact the ability of innovators to protect their ideas by making it easy to leak and transmit valuable information across the globe in seconds. iProperty companies must understand and address these risks head on. And innovator companies must grapple with infringement risks arising out of these innovation hot spots, whether the innovator is operating globally or not. We divide the challenges into four categories:

1. **Institutional risks** include, for example, inadequate laws and/or lack of predictable enforcement in many countries.

2. **Infringement risks** result from a globe that is increasingly populated with enforceable iProperty rights.

3. **Management risks** include, among other things, lack of iProperty management knowledge and lack of iProperty culture among employees.

4. **Technology risks** include, for example, risk of electronic transmission or extinction of iProperty rights by Internet publication of iProperty information.

These risks conspire to undermine the usefulness of iProperty for sustaining competitive advantage.

INSTITUTIONAL RISKS

The spread of centers of innovation to low-cost labor markets provides companies with opportunities to reduce the cost of innovation. However, in many low-cost labor markets, laws for protecting intellectual property remain inadequate. Even where laws are improving, enforcement often remains unpredictable. Shifting work from countries with strong systems to those with weak or nonexistent systems can come at a huge cost for innovators, particularly where companies do not address the increased risk or employ protective tactics to guard against loss of valuable iProperty. The employers' ability to protect against the loss of valuable iProperty depends literally on where the employee sits.

While the forces of globalization contend for the harmonization of laws for protecting iProperty, local social and cultural forces continue to ensure that national patent laws remain unique in many respects. For example, laws relating to patentability of computer software, business processes, new uses of pharmaceutical compounds, and methods of medical treatment vary widely. The reach of patents is still limited to specific territories: There is no truly international patent. The need to file separate patent applications in multiple countries dramatically increases patent costs. As a result, companies must carefully analyze and make strategic decisions about how and where to protect their innovations. Trade secrets may be less expensive to protect, but in many countries, enforcement ranges from extremely difficult to virtually impossible. Lack of appreciation among employees for the value of intellectual property can further undermine the effectiveness of otherwise adequate intellectual property laws.

India's New Patent Law

India, for example, passed a new patent law in 2005 to bring its system into line with TRIPS, which was discussed in Chapter 1. The new law provides for, among other things, the patenting of previously unpatentable subject matter, such as foods, medicines, and chemicals. The law also opens the door to the patenting of software in certain circumstances, moving India's practice closer into alignment with European standards but still short of the liberal software protection standards of the United States. However, political forces continue to make the lasting impact of the new law uncertain. Patents appear to be viewed as an international bogey man by much of India's population who cannot see how patents benefit the interests of anyone except global corporate giants. In India's current political climate, it is unclear to what extent the new patent law will reduce iProperty losses to domestic and foreign companies and how quickly any expected benefits may accrue.

Just prior to the two-year anniversary of India's new patent law, Novartis AG sued the Indian government due to alleged insufficiencies in the law. The suit relates to the rejection of Novartis' patent application for a new use of its cancer drug Glivec. Under the patent law, new forms of a drug, such as salt forms or novel crystalline forms, are patentable only if the applicant for a patent can demonstrate that they have significantly better efficacy than the known forms of the drug. The Indian government argues that the Novartis application claims a new form of an old drug without the required showing of enhanced efficacy and is therefore not patentable under Indian law. In its defense, Novartis argues that the Indian patent law is not compliant with TRIPS.

This conflict has incited the involvement of international relief groups, such as Medicines Sans Frontiers, that do not want to see the law enforced. These groups fear reduced ability to get drugs to impoverished people in India. Supporters of Novartis argue that the Indian government retains the right under the new law to grant a compulsory license permitting other companies to make and sell the drug if Novartis prices the drug in a way that denies access to the Indian people. The government's opportunity to use this "safety valve" will not be diminished even if Novartis is granted its patent.

Despite these uncertainties, new patent law in India has already fueled new investments in the development of a growing Indian research and development (R&D) drug industry. Prior to its implementation, the inability of Indian firms to recoup their investments stymied the investment in Indian pharmaceutical R&D. Following implementation of the new law, Avesthagen, a Bangalore biopharma and agricultural biotech company, closed the $32 million investment discussed in Chapter 1. With a public market valuation of about $1.5 billion, Avesthagen is reported to be growing at 40 percent per year and is predicted to reach $5 billion in revenue by 2010.[1] Turning back the iProperty clock now could deter the further development of companies like Avesthagen.

An innovative Indian pharmaceutical industry investing in the development of new drugs targeting local health issues and accounting for local economic realities is the best way to guarantee continued improvements in the health of the Indian people. But without a sufficiently robust intellectual property regime, an innovative pharmaceutical industry will struggle to develop, and the firms that succeed will be those whose focus is outside India in countries that recognize and protect their investment. Furthermore, India is in an intense competition with China when it comes to attracting international pharmaceutical firms, and the latest polls appear to suggest that India is losing the race.[2] Failure to provide adequate protection for intellectual property is not likely to help this problem; it will have long-lasting effects as pharmaceutical companies take their knowledge, investments, and jobs to China rather than India.

Who in your company is responsible for looking into the future to predict changes in intellectual property laws and cultures in key countries around the world?

While the 2005 act opened the door to greater legal protections for iProperty, the Indian infrastructure has yet to catch up and uncertainties remain about enforcement. Like many aspects of the Indian government, the Indian patent office is a hopelessly entrenched bureaucracy. For example, obtaining a copy of a patent can be accomplished for free in the United States and Europe via the Internet; obtaining an Indian patent requires an advance payment and a personal visit to the specific patent office where the application was filed.[3] Even with the payment, there is a waiting period before a copy of the patent may be obtained. The lack of a searchable database for Indian patents has prompted XB Labs to invest in developing such a database, called "BigPatents India."[4]

Staffing is also a problem for the Indian system. There were about 3,500 patent examiners in the United States, 4,000 in China, and just 275 in India. It is simply impossible to support a working patent system with this kind of worker shortage. Adding another layer of complexity to these issues is India's multiple-office patent system. Each office interprets the laws differently, which means that the outcome of a particular patent application may vary depending on the office in which it is filed.

Educational programs have been established to help bring the Indian system up to speed. For example, the George Washington University Law School established the India Project in 2004, which includes programs and conferences that facilitate interaction among American and Indian scholars, judges, practitioners, and businesspeople.[5] The law school has also worked with the prestigious Indian Institute of Technology–Kharagpur to assist in the development of the new Rajiv Gandhi School of Intellectual Property Law in Kharagpur. However, some Indians view these projects as a biased parade of self-interested parties seeking to advance their own interests in India in a manner that is incongruous with the realities of the Indian economy.

China: The World's Biggest iProperty Pirate

Like India, China is a member of most major treaties, including the World Intellectual Property Organization (WIPO) and the Berne Convention, and has laws on the books designed to protect iProperty. Nevertheless, China remains the world's largest iProperty pirate. Levels of piracy in China for copyrighted products have been estimated at 85 to 93 percent. For example, business software losses to the United States in 2005 were estimated at $1.27 billion. Importantly, the share of infringing product seizures of Chinese origin at the U.S. border increased to 81 percent in 2006, up from 69 percent in 2005 and 63 percent in 2004. China's share of infringing goods seized at the U.S. border is more than 10 times greater than that of any other U.S. trading partner.[6] These are just losses to U.S. companies; extrapolating losses to other countries around the globe suggests staggering numbers.

Some scholars believe that the issue in China is more fundamental than in India. India has an independent common law legal system that is based on the English system. It is questionable whether China will ever move to a law-based system. At present, neither domestic nor foreign firms can rely on China's legal system to uphold the legal rights of an individual or organization. Due largely to institutional weaknesses and self-interest, the norms written into the laws have not been assimilated into an effective system of enforcement.[7] The U.S. Trade Representative has complained that China's poor record extends to virtually every form of intellectual property and has pointed in particular to the rampant counterfeit and piracy problems that plague China's domestic market and the fact that China has become a leading exporter of counterfeit and pirated goods to the world.

At a recent U.S. Patent & Trademark Office conference on protecting intellectual property in China,[8] Stanford McCoy, the U.S. Trade Representative's Chief Intellectual Property Negotiator for Enforcement, illustrated the tenacity of Chinese pirating with a story from one of his visits to China. While touring a public market, a man approached McCoy's group offering to sell counterfeit golf clubs. McCoy agreed to accompany the man to his warehouse, but the police appeared and chased the man away. McCoy's group assumed this display was a show to demonstrate Chinese efforts to police piracy. But as the group boarded an elevator on their way out, the pirateer, having escaped his pursuers, dashed into the elevator, where he repeated the offer. Apparently those Chinese who are willing to make their living selling pirated goods are not easily dissuaded, a fact that compounds the challenge for those companies that wish to protect their iProperty in China.

The Good News

The issues faced by India and China are illustrative of the many growing pains experienced by developing nations as they seek to obtain the economic benefits of a modern intellectual property system while avoiding harms that may be caused by a system that is more suitable for a developed economy than a developing one. These intellectual property battles involve clashes between national and international political forces and powerful international organizations, each of which is struggling to impose its own view of the proper balance between incentives for innovators and the public's access to important innovations. Our purpose here is not to solve this important dilemma but to emphasize, for innovator companies deciding where to innovate and where to protect their innovations, how the tide can change.

Our opinion is that while progress is slow, the changes are encouraging. Countries that wish to compete in the global knowledge economy must recognize the need for effective protection of intellectual property and take steps to implement effective systems or they will be left behind. As observed by MIT economist Lester Thurow, companies will not invest in R&D spending unless they "see a system of intellectual property rights where they believe they can recoup their investments and make good returns."[9] It will take some time for important developing nations to realize the gains in wealth brought about by innovation that is stimulated and expanded by improved intellectual property laws. But as people working in innovation hot spots continue to increase the wealth and standard of living of their local communities, the obvious value of innovation and legal protections for iProperty will encourage governments to invest more in the development and enforcement of patent laws.

Enforcement successes are becoming more common. For example, in 2006, Motorola settled an intellectual property lawsuit against Korean manufacturer KBT Mobile Company, Ltd.[10] The lawsuit, filed under Korea's Unfair Competition Prevention Act, cited infringements of patents, trademarks, and designs for Motorola's RAZR mobile phone. The conflict between Motorola and KBT began with consumer inquiries about Motorola RAZR lookalikes available in Asia. KBT was marketing a RAZR lookalike called the V500 in China, Hong Kong, and Taiwan.

Yvonne Verse, vice president of Global Intellectual Property Management and Licensing for Motorola's Mobile Devices business, commented:

> We are very pleased that KBT has acknowledged Motorola's legitimate and protected rights to Motorola RAZR-related patents, trademarks and designs....To create competitive advantage, Motorola invests extensive human and financial resources to bring compelling innovations to market. Around the world, we are committed to protecting our investments—and we are prepared to vigorously defend our innovations through enforcement of our intellectual property rights.[11]

As a result of the settlement, KBT has agreed to cease to manufacture, sell, offer to sell, export, and/or display any RAZR-like products. KBT also agreed that it will not enable other companies to manufacture a RAZR-like product, and has committed to stop using Motorola patents and trademarks. We expect the number of stories like this one to increase dramatically in coming years.

Mark Cohen is an official at the U.S. Patent & Trademark Office who has been posted as a diplomatic attaché to China. In this role, Cohen's goal is to pressure the Chinese to improve intellectual property protections there. For all the negativity that surrounds the topic of protecting ideas in China, Cohen is not pessimistic. He emphasizes that companies can take steps to protect their intellectual property in China.[12] As described by Ted Plafker in *Doing Business in China*, according to Cohen, it is a fundamental mistake to approach protecting intellectual property in China as if it were defined and enforced the same as it is in the United States Companies must take advantage of local intellectual property options, like China's design patents. They should also carefully select the location of their legal responses and coordinate with local industry to enhance pressure on the legal system. The target of the effort is also important. For example, it may be more effective to go after landlords than companies selling pirated goods. The U.S. Embassy in Beijing maintains an intellectual property toolkit on its Web site with information about protecting intellectual property rights in China: http://beijing.usembassy-china.org.cn/ipr.html.

INFRINGEMENT RISKS

So far we have been discussing institutional risks created by the unpredictability of obtaining adequate application and enforcement of patent and other intellectual property laws in innovation hot spots. These risks, however, are offset by a paradoxical increased desirability for and value of patent protection in these countries. Despite the unpredictability of enforcement, increasing numbers of innovators are willing to bet that enforcement is likely to continue to improve during the life of patents filed now. Further, many patent applications originating in new innovation hot spots are finding their way into the developed countries via an international patent application procedure established by the Patent Cooperation Treaty. As a result, the global landscape is becoming more and more populated with patents, and infringement risks are increasing everywhere.

Risks in Developing Countries

China still hosts the world's largest concentration of iProperty pirates, and companies can expect to see dismal reports out of China for years to come. But iProperty enforcement in China is not what it was five years ago, and we expect to see dramatic improvements in the next five years. The Patent Office of the People's Republic of China (the CPO) was established in 1980 "to protect intellectual property, encourage invention and creation, help popularize inventions and their exploitation, promote the progress and innovation in science and technology, and meet the needs of socialist modernization."[13] The Patent Law of the People's Republic of China was passed in 1984 and went into force in 1985. In 1998, CPO was renamed the State Intellectual Property Office (SIPO).

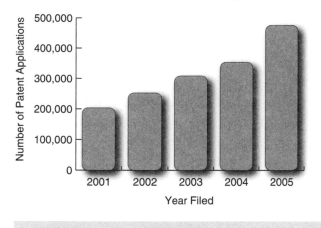

EXHIBIT 2.1 Number of Chinese Patent Applications Filed Each Year, 2001 to 2005

China's efforts to improve its system have been validated by a growing number of companies that are willing to invest in obtaining Chinese patents. As illustrated in Exhibit 2.1, from 2001 to 2005, the number of Chinese patent applications filed per year more than doubled, from 203,506 in 2001 to 476,264 in 2006.[14] Chinese companies filed the vast majority of these applications, but as shown in Exhibit 2.2, the number of Chinese patent applications filed by foreign companies is also rapidly increasing, more than doubling from 37,800 in 2001 to 93,107 in 2005.

Some developed countries are more willing than others to gamble on the value of aggressive patenting in China and in other developing countries more quickly than others. For example, as reported by the *People's Daily Online*, in 2006, China's neighbor, Japan, applied for 37,848 patent

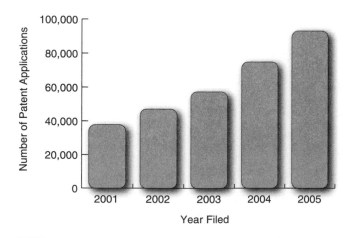

EXHIBIT 2.2 Number of Chinese Patent Applications Filed by Foreign Companies Each Year, 2001 to 2005

applications in China, more than any other country.[15] According to the article, Japanese companies accounted for half of the top foreign enterprises filing in China. The United States and South Korea ranked second and third. The increasing number of Chinese patent applications filed by foreign companies suggests a growing confidence that the Chinese patent system will continue to improve. The growth in Chinese patents increases infringement risks for companies doing business in China.

> How does your company track global patenting trends in your field of competition?

In contrast to the Chinese system, the Indian patent system was established in colonial times by an 1856 act based on the British patent law of 1852 and, until recently, the system changed little. As already noted, the 2005 Patent Act made substantial improvements to India's patent system and brought the Indian system into closer alignment with international standards. As in China, improvements in the Indian patent system have stimulated a growing number of patent applications. Approximately 30,000 applications were filed in 2006,[16] as compared with 23,000 patent applications filed in 2005 and 6,000 patent applications in 2001. Seventy percent of the Indian patent filings are by foreign companies, attesting to, among other things, the value of Indian markets, expanded opportunities for obtaining patents afforded by the 2005 Patent Act, and an expectation by outsiders that patents filed in India are likely to be enforced.

In one industrial sector, the Indian drug industry, which grew up based on its ability to copy drugs from around the world, now has the opportunity to protect its own innovation. In addition to motivating investment in domestic R&D, the new patent law helps to create an environment in which companies in developed countries are more comfortable outsourcing R&D to India. Indian companies still lag behind when it comes to protecting their own intellectual property; however, this problem has not gone unnoticed,[17] and it is likely that the number of patents filed will increase dramatically in the next few years as companies see their more forward-looking counterparts benefiting financially and competitively from their patents.

Companies operating in China, India, and other developing countries, whether via outsourcing or offshoring operations or marketing and sale of products or services, must place their bets on whether these patents will be enforced. It is important to keep in mind that patents provide 20 years of protection. With increasing international diplomatic pressure, countries whose enforcement mechanisms are now only starting to show some improvement may have significantly better enforcement before the expiration of the 20-year patent term. For potentially expensive losses, such as investment in manufacturing facilities, even a growing probability of enforcement resulting from improved laws, changing legal cultures, and diplomatic interventions may sufficiently deter would-be infringers, even if the country in question does not have a strong history of enforcing intellectual property rights.

A global landscape crowded with patents will fuel more intellectual property litigation, but it will also spur more intellectual property deals. For example, Color Kinetics Inc., a U.S. company that designs and sells lighting systems, recently announced a global licensing agreement with Neo-Neon International Ltd. Global licensing agreements are signed every day, but this one stands out because Neo-Neon is a Chinese company. Under the agreement, Color Kinetics granted Neo-Neon access to its complete patent global portfolio, with hundreds of patents and patent applications pending in countries around the world. Color Kinetics' press release indicated that the license is "allowing the continuing development and sale of [Neo-Neon's] LED lighting products worldwide," suggesting that this was not a regular outlicensing deal, but the settlement of a dispute between the companies.

The deal illustrates the growing value of building a global patent portfolio, as well as the risk of being hijacked by a patent portfolio in unexpected regions of the world. In all likelihood, the revenues Color Kinetics earns as a result of the deal do not require any significant investment in infrastructure. In effect, Color Kinetics is legitimately exploiting an opportunity to benefit from the earnings of its Chinese competitor, without substantial further investment. Whether doing business locally or globally, companies must not overlook the opportunity to profit from protecting their inventions in other countries.

As stated by Bill Sims, Color Kinetics' president and chief executive officer, "This agreement marks another strong win for our growing licensing business, which leverages nearly ten years of investment, research and development as the foundation of our intellectual property."[18] Color Kinetics also recently inked a deal with Robe Show Lighting, a Czech Republic company making lighting systems for theatrical, touring, television, and other entertainment applications. Companies, like Color Kinetics, with iProperty foresight are profiting from iProperty protection strategies in countries around the globe.

Many companies in developing countries now have an incentive to protect their ideas in their own countries and regions, but lack the resources to protect their ideas in developed countries. For example, while India has risen on the list of countries targeted for patent protection by non-Indian companies, Indian companies lag behind in protecting their ideas in developed countries. The failure of Indian companies to protect their novel ideas is probably due in part to the high cost of protection. In the old days, patent infringement research in developed countries would reveal most of the risks that reside in developing countries, because most patents filed in the latter originated in the former. Today, however, the patent systems in developing countries are providing a greater incentive for homegrown companies to protect their novel ideas in their own countries, even if they cannot afford protection in the developed countries. As a result, companies wishing to establish operations or markets in global hot spots outside the developed countries must expand their infringement research efforts to include these countries or risk infringement of a growing number of hidden patents. This issue is made all the more difficult and expensive in China and Taiwan, for example, where patent applications are in local languages.

Risks in Developed Countries

As China, India, and other developing countries improve their patent systems, and more companies patent their inventions there, outsiders doing business there will face greater risks of patent infringement. This much is obvious, but what may not be as apparent is that increased numbers of patent filings in China, India, and elsewhere will also lead through Patent Cooperation Treaty patent applications to patents back in the United States, Europe, Japan, and other countries with traditionally strong patent protection. U.S. companies, for example, are accustomed to Japanese and European companies using U.S. courts to enforce their U.S. patents against U.S. companies. However, they are not accustomed to infringement suits based on patents originating from China and India.

Chinese companies, for example, are beginning to enforce their patent rights aggressively against U.S. companies. Apple is currently fending off a patent infringement suit alleging that the iPod product infringes a patent filed by a solo inventor in Taiwan. Netac, a Chinese flash memory maker, recently sued a New Jersey rival in a federal court in Texas.[19] The number of companies from developing countries suing companies in developed countries will increase dramatically in coming years. WIPO reports that international patent applications originating from China have increased sevenfold in the past 10 years. Many of these international patent applications will eventually become legally enforceable patents in the United States, Europe, and elsewhere. No company whose position in the market is defined by its innovative technology can afford to ignore this growing source of risk.

MANAGEMENT RISKS

In many countries in which laws and legal systems protecting iProperty are improving, companies have the opportunity to execute novel iProperty strategies to protect important ideas. While unskilled laborers may be abundant in these countries, managers with basic iProperty skills are hard to find, and managers with revolutionary iProperty vision are rare. Two of five firms in China report difficulties finding qualified senior managers of all types.[20] Managers and employees in countries in which iProperty protections have not traditionally been strong rarely have training or experience in how to protect ideas or manage the strategic development of an iProperty portfolio. For example, such managers often lack critical skills necessary to:

- Recognize potentially valuable and patentable ideas when they arise
- Develop iProperty strategies for protecting ideas
- Prevent loss of iProperty by activities such as publications and offers for sale that can destroy iProperty rights
- Prepare patent applications suitable for obtaining foreign patent protection in the United States and Europe
- Manage the cost of these processes

In fact, as we emphasize throughout this book, managers in developed countries often lack some or all of these skills. Companies innovating in, or obtaining innovation services from, the new innovation hot spots must invest the time and effort to instill in managers and employees the vision and skills essential to strategically deploy iProperty for protecting the resulting ideas.

TECHNOLOGY RISKS

In addition to the institutional, infringement, and management risks already discussed, important iProperty challenges arise from the ease and rapidity of the spread of technology. The first challenge relates to extinguishing iProperty rights by publication. In most countries, publication of an invention before filing a patent application is an automatic bar to patentability (i.e., the patent rights are extinguished the minute the publication hits the press). The United States differs from the rest of the world in that it provides a one-year grace period after a publication during which a patent may be filed to protect a published invention. Publication on the Internet is becoming more problematic for many companies even in the United States, Europe, and Japan, in which iProperty knowledge is relatively well understood by managers and employees. When combined with the lack of appreciation of the value of iProperty by managers in emerging centers of innovation, the ease of Internet publication poses a particularly high risk for the loss of iProperty rights.

What kinds of electronic protections do you employ to prevent loss of your trade secrets?

The spread of the Internet around the world also means that companies can quickly lose control of valuable trade secrets. Publication on the Internet eliminates secrecy and thus eliminates the possibility of trade secrets. Technology facilitates communication, but it also makes companies "leaky." In the time it takes to press "send," whether intentionally or accidentally, critical technology information can be transmitted to virtually any country in the world, and the e-mail can be sent to 1,000 people as easily as it can be sent to one person. Moreover, tiny and highly portable storage devices, such as memory sticks and flash drives, are now inexpensive and readily available and can be used to download and carry large amounts of data. The risk of information theft is particularly high in countries where legal and social standards have not evolved to value iProperty.

Risks from outside the company walls are also becoming more prevalent. Most information systems are now accessible via the Internet from anywhere on the globe. Today's hackers are more sophisticated than ever before, and the least lapse in security can lead to intrusion and loss of valuable information.

MINIMIZING GLOBAL RISKS

Companies seeking to understand iProperty risks in the global economy must consider the four primary sources of risks discussed in this chapter: institutional risks, infringement risks, management risks, and technology risks. Infringement risks pop up more frequently, both in developed countries, which are granting more and more patents to players from around the globe, and in developing countries, where the promise of improved systems is now attracting large investments in iProperty portfolios. Managers in all countries must strive to be forward-looking, and, in developing countries lacking strong iProperty cultures, companies must help managers and employees to develop an appreciation for the value of iProperty and implement policies and processes designed to yield strategically targeted portfolios. Finally, all companies must continually be aware of technology risks that threaten easy loss of iProperty.

Companies with the foresight to consider these risks and execute strategies that take advantage of iProperty strengths, while at the same time using good business judgment to reduce the risks, will have a unique and decided advantage over their competitors who do not. In the next chapter, we discuss how strategic planning can be applied to the deployment of iProperty, just as it is for other areas of business, to provide a framework in which management can create, control, and sustain a portfolio that protects, strengthens, and expands the company's business opportunities.

NOTES

1. Seema Singh, "Avesthagen Closes $32.5M Funding," *Red Herring*, January 24, 2007, www.redherring.com/PrintArticle.aspx?a=20912&sector=Briefings.

2. "Indian Government Warned over Pharma Competitiveness," *Pharma Times*, July 21, 2006, www.pharmatimes.com/WorldNews/Articles/9255-India-manufacturing.aspx?src=PTNews-11033.

3. Sapna Dogra, "The Patent Challenge," Express Pharma Online, July 16–31, 2006, www.expresspharmaonline.com/20060731/market01.shtml.

4. XB Labs corporate Web site, http://xblabs.com/static/xblabs (accessed August 27, 2007).

5. George Washington University Law School, India Project Web site, www.law.gwu.edu/Academics/India+Project/India+Project+Overview.htm (accessed June 8, 2007).

6. U.S. Trade Representative, "Special 301 Report," 2007, www.ustr.gov/Document_Library/Reports_Publications/2007/2007_Special_301_Review/Section_Index.html.

7. See United States Congress, Joint Economic Committee, *China's Economic Future: Challenges to U.S. Policy* (Armonk, NY: M.E. Sharpe, 1997), 224.

8. Author's notes from Conference on Protecting Your Intellectual Property in China and the Global Marketplace, presented by the United States Patent and Trademark Office, Boston, MA, September 2006.

9. Lester Thurow, *Fortune Favors the Bold: What We Must Do to Build a New and Lasting Global Prosperity* (New York: HarperCollins, 2003), 172.

10. Motorola, Inc., "Motorola Stops RAZR Copycat in Korea," press release, May 10, 2006.

11. Ibid.

12. Ted Plafker, *Doing Business in China: How to Profit in the World's Fastest Growing Market* (New York: Warner Business Books, 2007).

13. State Intellectual Property Office of China, "Introduction," http://www.sipo.gov.cn/wipo_new/english/neirono3/gywipo_wipojj_01.htm (accessed August 25, 2007).

14. State Intellectual Property Office of China, "Applications for Three Kinds of Patents Received from Home and Abroad, 1985–2005," www.sipo.gov.cn/sipo_English/statistics/200607/t20060725_104689.htm (accessed June 25, 2007).

15. "Japan Files Most Foreign Patent Applications in China," *People's Daily Online*, May 31, 2007, http://english.people.com.cn/200705/31/eng20070531_379726.html.

16. V. Hemamalini "Advantage Pak Over India in 301 Watchlist War," *Economic Times of India*, December 21, 2006, http://economictimes.indiatimes.com/Advantage_Pak_over_India_in_301_watchlist_war/articleshow/877918.cms.

17. See J. Bhagwati. "It Is Technology, Stupid," *Business Standard*, May 29, 2007, www.business-standard.com/common/storypage.php?autono=285917&leftnm=4&subLeft=0&chkFlg=.

18. Color Kinetics Inc., "Color Kinetics Announces Licensing Agreement with Neo-Neon," press release, December 18, 2006.

19. Netac, Inc., "Milestone of China Company to Enforce Its Patent Rights Overseas," press release, February 16, 2006.

20. "The World of Work," *The Economist* (January 6, 2007), 57–58.

Part Two

iProperty Strategies
for a Flat World

~ 3 ~

Global Strategy

iProperty for Protecting, Strengthening, and Expanding Business Opportunities

In his book, *The 33 Strategies of War*, Robert Greene describes how Napoleon defeated his enemies, the Prussians, because they lacked imagination.[1] They failed to respond to the new strategies Napoleon employed and continued to rely on worn-out tactics that had been successful in the past. Their failure was all the more pathetic because they had the opportunity for 10 years to study Napoleon's innovative strategies. Instead of learning and adapting, however, they tenaciously held on to established dogma. In contrast, Napoleon had no respect for past traditions and chose to fight in a new way. He adapted his strategy to fit the situation at hand and won a decisive victory. According to Greene:

> When Napoleon was asked what principles of war he followed, he replied that he followed none. His genius was his ability to respond to circumstances, to make the most of what he was given—he was the supreme opportunist.[2]

Failing to deal with reality and adapt to it is a fundamental strategic blunder. Every battle is different. Technology, tactics, and circumstances change. One cannot assume that what worked in the past will work today in war. In this same way a "business-as-usual" approach to managing intellectual property can be so very dangerous to companies. As described in Chapters 1 and 2, the world is not what it was even 5 years ago. Global changes are affecting the way the whole world competes, and companies that do not adapt will go the way of the Prussians. Companies

41

cannot rely on yesterday's strategies; they must grapple with and adjust to the way things are today and develop strategies that will work for tomorrow.

STRATEGIC CONTEXT

Economic globalization creates the ultimate environment for heating up competition. Hot competition for products without distinctive advantages leads to commoditization, loss of market share, and diminishing profits. Greenwald and Kahn, introduced in Chapter 2, emphasize that where there is

> a universe of companies seeking profitable opportunities for investment, the returns in an unprotected industry will be driven down to levels where there is no "economic profit," that is, no returns above the costs of the invested capital.[3]

Generating greater than sustainable economic profits requires distinctive products and services, ones with communicable advantages to the purchaser. But in the global economy, no product or service remains distinctive for very long unless it is protected in some manner. In the words of Greenwald and Kahn: "Being able to do what rivals cannot is the definition of a competitive advantage."[4]

iProperty companies that are masterful at creating *and* protecting differentiated products and services have the ability to more consistently achieve above-average returns compared with those that are not. Forward-looking companies recognize both the urgency to innovate for competitive advantage *and* the urgency to protect that innovation to sustain the competitive advantage.

Companies structuring iProperty portfolios are faced with a plethora of decisions in the iProperty arena: how to purposefully generate ideas, identify valuable ideas worth protecting, decide what forms of protection make sense for each particular idea, avoid wasting resources on unnecessary protection, and so on. Virtually all innovator companies now have opportunities to employ iProperty options which come in myriad shapes and sizes: utility patents, design patents, trade secrets and copyrights, as well as practical and contractual protections. The availability, cost, and effectiveness of each approach can differ in each country.

Successful companies must pay attention to all of these strategic options and more. Inattention is risky because an inadequate iProperty portfolio or a surprise competitor portfolio can result in a torpedoed multimillion-dollar deal, an expensive infringement suit, an injunction shutting down a factory, customs problems with a major product shipment, or an important product that is vulnerable to easy competition, rendering it impossible for the company to recoup an investment in a costly research and development program.

If iProperty is such a risky business, it is natural to assume that companies would invest significant resources into managing and developing their iProperty strategies and portfolios. After all, few companies would invest comparable resources in the development of a new product, for example, without significant forethought and strategic evaluation. Yet while companies invest many millions of dollars in the development of an iProperty portfolio, they often give precious little thought to designing strategies for maximizing the effectiveness of that portfolio. Too often they either rely on an entrenched internal patent silo or periodically "lob ideas over the wall" to outside patent counsel rather than expending the time and energy necessary to develop an effective strategy.

Does your company have a documented iProperty strategy that is driven by your business strategy and guides the development of your iProperty portfolio?

Many companies simply dismiss altogether the potential value of iProperty based on assumptions about what can be protected or the effectiveness of potential protections. This is especially the case in industries in which innovations have not traditionally been considered to be patentable. But in today's world, virtually all innovator companies now have opportunities to employ iProperty strategies for protecting their ideas. Some sectors, such as banking, are rapidly catching on. Others have been slow to realize the need to pay attention. A related problem is that leaders who think iProperty is not valuable in their own hands seriously underestimate the value of iProperty in the hands of competitors. Such leaders are susceptible to plunging their companies headlong into costly infringement disputes.

SPENDING MONEY AND GETTING NOWHERE

Many companies realize that they are not achieving their full iProperty potential but are not sure where to turn for help. Consider the frustration expressed by Andrew Watson, general counsel of Thirdspace, a developer of video server systems, when he started looking for an advisor to assist him with developing an iProperty strategy:

> We quickly realized that we needed some specialist help. This was by far the most frustrating part of the process, as it took me several months to find the right person. It surprised me that none of the big consultancies in Europe could talk with any degree of knowledge about commercial IP strategies. Neither could the law firms and patent attorneys, none of whom are focused elsewhere in the IP world (and to be honest, practice based lawyers are simply not businessmen). . . . What surprised me even in the U.S. was that our supposed IP boutique U.S. legal practice knew even less than me on the subject.[5]

Patent Attorney as Guru

Companies are often susceptible to the "patent-attorney–as–guru syndrome." According to Steve Menton, managing consultant at IP&AM, a U.K. intellectual asset management company, while most business leaders argue that their success depends on the strength of their iProperty, "Intellectual property management is invariably treated as 'someone else's problem,' a specialty that should be dealt with by a central function with minimal input from the rest of the organization."[6] Marcus Reitzig of the Copenhagen Business School in Denmark echoes this sentiment in *MIT Sloan Management Review:*

> [Intellectual property] management cannot be left to the technology managers or corporate legal staff alone . . . [it] must be a matter of concern for functional and business-unit leaders as well as a corporation's most senior officers.[7]

Patent attorneys and agents are usually highly skilled at obtaining legal protection for intellectual property, but rarely are they focused on tightly integrating the company's business strategy and its iProperty strategy. From the company perspective, information about potentially novel ideas is fed into an intellectual property black box with a foggy expectation that what emerges from the box will provide adequate coverage; after all, "We are spending a lot of money." The result is often an inefficient use of resources, a misaligned intellectual property portfolio that does not adequately support the company's business or product strategy, a misaligned business strategy that does not account for the reality of the company's intellectual property position, and a never-ending series of surprises as competitive patents randomly float to the surface.

Management Misunderstandings

Compounding the black box problem is the fact that executives and managers rarely understand their own iProperty portfolios. Many times their beliefs are based on inaccurate assumptions about iProperty realities. For example, often executives boldly pronounce that their patents cover a certain technology improvement, when in fact no one has even considered protecting the technology improvement in question. Executives often believe that software or business methods or natural products are not patentable . . . yet *all* are patentable. And many executives hold unsupported opinions about the usefulness of patents: "We could spend a bunch of money patenting it, but the patent wouldn't do us any good." "You can always get around a patent." "I heard about a company once that had a patent and . . . *yada yada yada*." These opinions commonly result from a story in which a patent was shown to be unenforceable for a very understandable reason of which the storyteller is unaware. The story then takes on a mythological significance as an illustration of why no reasonable person would rely on a patent to protect an innovative technology.

Business leaders who are comfortable repeating worn-out mantras and holding on to outmoded beliefs cannot be expected to develop iProperty strategies that will succeed in today's global competition. Of course, iProperty protections are not worthwhile investments in every situation. And most, if not all, of the common complaints include at least a seed of truth. Many patent applications, for example, are filed based on poorly conceived inventions with unjustified expectations that the resulting patent will be enforceable. Nevertheless, despite the fact that patents and other forms of iProperty are not always used correctly or with the desired effect, they are used successfully in many cases and should be thoroughly considered as strategic options, not dismissed out of hand.

Worst Possible Timing

Companies also frequently seek to understand their iProperty portfolios at the worst possible times, such as when deal negotiations are in progress. In other words, managers often fail to justify the expense of proactively mapping out the strengths and weaknesses of their portfolios and identifying strategic problems until the pointed questions of a potential investor or partner bring the issue to a crisis. Often this point occurs too late in the process to repair the problems, when the decision makers are under immense pressure to understate, ignore, or even bury the problem. Investors, partners, and acquirers considering such deals are keenly interested in how companies use iProperty to sustain competitive advantage. They understand that the value of an innovator company is intimately related to the sophistication with which it operates in the iProperty arena. The corollary is that strategic deployment of the iProperty portfolio creates leverage in relationships with investors, partners, and acquirers because the more secure the company's ideas, the less likely the investor, partner, or acquirer is to have other suitable options.

Changing Course

Not surprisingly, the combination of black box patent practices, management misunderstandings, and bad timing can have devastating results. The iProperty portfolio that grows out of such circumstances can range from slightly malformed to totally inadequate for the company's strategic needs. The solution is a documented iProperty strategy and an effective team for executing the strategy. Starting with business strategy and proceeding to iProperty strategy, all players on the field must be proactively tied into, and their decisions must be guided by, a rational strategy that is soundly based in current realities and a sense of future trends.

Having an iProperty strategy is helpful only if the strategy is shared by all of the key players in the company's iProperty processes. One way to ensure a shared vision and effective execution is a working iProperty team that is responsible for developing and implementing the company's iProperty strategy, a tactic we discuss in detail in Chapter 9. Developing and executing an iProperty strategy requires a multidisciplinary approach involving technical, business, and legal expertise. Team members collaborate on decisions affecting the iProperty portfolio and make these decisions in a manner that comports with the company's vision, mission, and goals. The multidisciplinary approach can seem like a large investment of time and personnel resources. However, in the long run, a fully functioning, forward-thinking iProperty team guided by a well-constructed iProperty strategy actually saves time and money and is a requirement for any company that desires to overthrow the old norms and re-imagine the use of iProperty in its business.

iPROPERTY ORDER FROM IDEA CHAOS

The bottom line is that managing the protection of ideas is a messy business. Valuable ideas do not flow in a smooth, orderly manner from

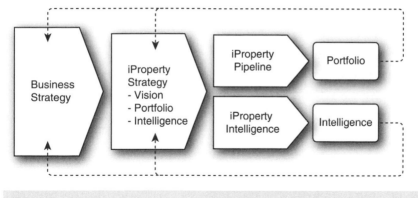

EXHIBIT 3.1 Core Components of an iProperty Strategy Process

inventive minds. They come in fits and starts. They are hammered into useful products by a process that can be characterized only by pain, suffering, and persistence. Likewise, the transformation of ideas into a valuable iProperty portfolio is an exercise in the management of chaos. Bringing order to this chaos requires strategies and tactics for separating valuable ideas from the dross, developing and executing strategies for orderly growth of iProperty portfolios, and minimizing the risk of infringing the iProperty of others.

Exhibit 3.1 illustrates the components of any iProperty program that seeks to overcome these challenges:

- A business strategy that employs iProperty for strategic advantage
- An iProperty strategy, including an iProperty vision, that allocates resources in a manner calculated to achieve the strategic advantage required by the business strategy
- An iProperty pipeline to guide the development of the iProperty portfolio
- An iProperty intelligence process for gathering and understanding iProperty opportunities and risks

The remainder of this chapter provides an overview of the business and iProperty strategy components. Chapter 5 focuses on the iProperty intelligence component, and Chapters 8 and 9 develop the concept of an iProperty pipeline.

Precipitating Strategic Decisions

David A. Aaker, vice chairman of Prophet Brand Strategy and professor emeritus of the Haas School of Business at the University of California at

Berkeley, emphasizes that the goal of any process of setting strategy is to "precipitate as well as make strategic decisions." According to Aaker, "the identification of a strategic response is frequently a critical step. Many strategic blunders occur because a strategic decision process was never activated, not because a wrong decision was made."[8]

The same is true for the iProperty strategy process. The most serious blunders usually occur because the issue was never identified and surfaced for a decision, not because the wrong decision was made. Consider bacteriologist Alexander Fleming, who discovered penicillin while working at St. Mary's Hospital in London in 1928. St. Mary's simply failed to patent the discovery. Andrew Moyer, working for the U.S. Department of Agriculture, later patented the process for making penicillin, which permitted U.S. companies to reap the benefit of mass production. Either St. Mary's had no strategy for raising the patenting question or it made a serious strategic blunder. The world got penicillin anyway, but St. Mary's received no financial credit, which it could have invested back into its charitable mission.

How many companies have donated valuable ideas to competitors because they simply failed to realize that iProperty protection is available? How many have been blindsided by a patent infringement suit simply because no one thought to check publicly available databases for competitor patents *before* putting a product on the market? How many have watched competitors in foreign countries copy their products without any ability to stop the copycats simply because they lacked the foresight to obtain patent protection in those countries? How many deals have failed because the iProperty turned out to be technically flawed or legally unenforceable?

Strategy Inputs

Aaker divides the inputs of a business strategy into external and internal analyses. External analyses, he says, include analyses of customers, competitors, markets, and business and legal environments. Internal analyses include performance analyses, such as profitability, sales, employee capability, and performance, as well as determinants of strategic options, such as past and current strategies and organizational capabilities and constraints. Likewise, the analyses required for the development of an iProperty strategy that fulfills the goal of clarifying issues and making strategic decisions are subsets of these internal and external analyses.

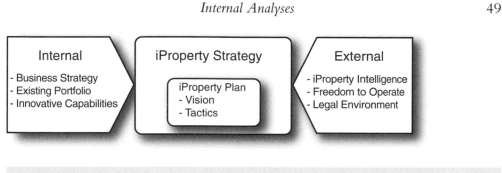

EXHIBIT 3.2 Inputs for iProperty Strategy Analysis

INTERNAL ANALYSES

As illustrated in Exhibit 3.2, internal analyses of relevance to the iProperty strategy process include:

- **Business strategy.** An understanding of how iProperty fits into and supports the company's business strategy
- **Existing iProperty portfolio.** A sophisticated understanding of the company's own iProperty portfolio
- **Innovative capabilities.** An evaluation of the company's iProperty-generating capabilities

Business Strategy

We used to say that developing an iProperty strategy begins with an understanding of the business strategy. However, in the ideal world, this is not the case. For a forward-looking innovator company intent on competing for the future, iProperty strategy must be one of the major components of the business strategy. No business strategy for such a company is complete without considering how the company will innovate and how the resulting innovations will be protected.

The business strategy in turn must define at a high level how the company will use iProperty. For example, will the company

- Use iProperty defensively to keep others out of its space?
- Use patents at all, or will it rely solely on first-mover advantages?
- Aggressively pursue infringers of its iProperty?
- Need iProperty for use as bargaining chips to trade with others?

- Use iProperty to establish credibility in the market for its products or develop a powerful portfolio for the purpose of deterring other entrants or gaining prestige?

- Focus its iProperty on its own products or seek to develop a broad portfolio that permits it to outlicense core or noncore iProperty to others?

- Outlicense its iProperty only to noncompetitors, or outlicense its iProperty to competitors on appropriate terms?

- Participate in open-source iProperty strategies or work with others in its industry to develop patent pools?

- Have the resources (cash and people's time) to execute the desired strategy?

When the business strategy addresses these high-level questions, a company can develop an iProperty strategy that puts the required machinery into action to effect the uses of iProperty required by the business strategy. One of the most common problems in developing an iProperty portfolio is the failure to connect each component (i.e., each patent, trade secret, publication, etc.) of the developing portfolio with the business strategy. As a result, resources are spent to protect iProperty that may not support the business strategy; even worse, companies fail to provide adequate protection for critically important iProperty.

Properly designed, an iProperty strategy creates these connections. Simply stated, for *any* company whose revenue stream is based on technological innovation, a documented iProperty strategy is essential for weaving iProperty into the fabric of the business strategy. Among other things, this strategy must detail how the company will obtain and deploy iProperty to create, sustain, and/or enhance the competitive position of its products or services. The iProperty strategy must also establish how the company will avoid being shut down or even slowed down in its business pursuits by the iProperty of others. And in a global economy, the iProperty strategy must account for opportunities and threats on a global basis.

Existing Portfolio

An army cannot develop a strategy for fighting a battle without an understanding of its arsenal. A strong arsenal will lead to one kind of strategy; a weak arsenal will lead to another. Likewise, an innovator company cannot adequately develop a strategy for protecting its competitive turf without understanding the strengths and weaknesses of its existing portfolio, the products and technologies that it protects, and the breadth and strength of that protection.

Can you map your iProperty portfolio against your company's products and services? Can you identify a purpose for each unit of iProperty in your portfolio?

―――――――――――――― ⁓ ――――――――――――――

It has been our experience that very few executives really understand the iProperty portfolios of their companies, even at a general level. Frequently, when we are recommending communication tools for educating high-level executives on their companies' own iProperty portfolios, the patent counsels and managers with whom we are working respond: "You don't understand; I can't even get their attention to discuss iProperty even for a few minutes. They have much larger issues to be concerned about."

Senior executives can often describe the company's tangible assets, where they are located, how they are staffed, and their capabilities. But rarely can these same executives do the same for their valuable iProperty assets: what they protect, where they provide protection, and how the company is using them to boost its bottom line. It is old news now that the value of intellectual assets for most companies far surpasses the value of physical assets, so why is it that most senior executives can tell you so much more about the company's real estate than its iProperty? In order to create an iProperty strategy, executives must understand their iProperty portfolios and how they fit into their company's overall strategy, financing, markets, and the like. To achieve this understanding, patent attorneys and the executives who manage them require new ways of communicating iProperty information, such as visually mapping the company's iProperty portfolio against its technologies, products, and markets, and explaining how the portfolio fits into the competitive iProperty landscape in which the company operates. Chapters 5 and 8 include examples of approaches to visualizing iProperty.

Innovative Capabilities

Innovative capability is a function of a company's idea-generating and idea-executing ability; it involves personnel, systems, culture, and structural resources. Ideas spring from minds and, at least for the present, minds are embodied exclusively in people. Developing an iProperty strategy requires consideration of what innovative capability is needed to achieve the company's business objectives, taking inventory of available innovative capability, and determining how to address the difference between the two. What inventive capabilities does the company need? Who are the employees? What are their abilities? Who are the key innovators? What resources are available to them?

The experience, skill, and resources of a company's employees determine what problems the company can solve and what technologies it will use to solve them—that is, what kinds of innovations the company will generate. For example, a biochemist, a physiologist, and a geneticist will all approach the problem of a heart defect from very different perspectives. Ensuring innovative outside-the-box thinking requires outside-the-box capabilities. How, for example, would an electrical engineer approach the heart defect problem?

Inventive capabilities can be ramped up by training, motivating, and incentivizing employees and by creating an outside-the-box culture. Jerry Yang, co-founder of Yahoo, states: "We value engineers like [we value] professional athletes. We value great people at 10 times an average person in their function."[9] How do you value your employees? How do you provide them with incentives to innovate?

The challenge is compounded in a world in which the meaning of the word *innovation* is being diluted by overuse. Hewlett Packard added the word *invent* to its logo. Alone, the revised logo would have meant very little, but HP has also facilitated the development of a new culture that is characterized by radical ideas, inventiveness, and synthesis of the old guard and the "young Turks."[10] The company promotes an environment in which unorthodox ideas can flourish and be developed quickly. Apparently throwing money at the problem is not enough. Ford topped Booz Allen Hamilton's list of top spenders on innovation in 2006, in the same year that it had record losses of $12.7 billion.[11]

Does your company just talk about innovation, or does it actually have a corporate culture that rewards outside-the-box, innovative thinking?

Getting a product to market, however, requires more than just thinking outside the box. Paradigm shifters may help to establish a new strategic direction, but they are not likely to be able to handle the focused attention required to scale up manufacturing and actually place the product in the hands of consumers. The paradigm shifters must be supported by focused, action-oriented thinkers who can handle the myriad incremental developments required to refine and perfect the new concept and turn it into a real product.

The relationship among business strategy, iProperty strategy, and innovative capabilities is iterative. A company's business strategy identifies the kinds of problems it will solve, the kinds of solutions it will seek, and the kinds of innovative capabilities it needs to generate those solutions. Analysis of inventive needs versus innovative capabilities elucidates the kinds of innovations a company is likely to generate, given its current staff, and what inventive capabilities it may need to add. The iProperty strategy may also become a driving factor in how a company fills those missing needs. Relying on outside contractors for core needs, for example, can be risky, leading to lost iProperty opportunities and even to education of competitors if the outside firm works for or becomes a competitor. In some circumstances, it may make sense to consider bringing that expertise in-house to maintain ownership and control.

EXTERNAL ANALYSES

In addition to internal analyses, companies must understand and account for a variety of external factors in the development of an iProperty strategy. Such external factors include:

- **iProperty intelligence.** A high-level survey of the patent landscape surrounding a particular product or technology space
- **Freedom-to-operate analyses.** For determining whether key products and technologies infringe or are likely to infringe competitor patents
- **Legal environment.** An understanding of the global legal environment governing the acquisition and enforcement of the iProperty portfolio

iProperty Intelligence and Freedom to Operate

"The necessity of procuring good intelligence is apparent and need not be further argued"—this according to George Washington. As in war, the absolute necessity of competitive intelligence holds true for the iProperty arena. Yet getting a grip on competitive iProperty is one of the most overwhelming aspects of iProperty management. When we mention iProperty intelligence, managers and patent counsel immediately focus on the freedom-to-operate (FTO) process. Yet the FTO process is only a subset of iProperty intelligence and generally occurs late in the development of a specific product. The FTO process drills down on the details of patent infringement in an effort to reduce the risk that products or services near to commercialization will infringe the rights of others; iProperty intelligence also mines the patent databases of countries around the world for information about business, technical, and iProperty strategies of competitors. Both of these aspects of iProperty are discussed further in Chapter 5.

Legal Environment

A crucial aspect of preparing an iProperty strategy is an understanding of the legal environment in which the company is operating. Laws in each country are different and are constantly changing. The kinds of innovations that can be protected are changing, typically expanding to include protection for more types. A surprising number of executives do not realize that business methods can be protected. Yes, business methods really *are* patentable, and companies such as Netflix, Google, and Amazon.com are protecting their competitive advantages using business method patents. Consider the following patent claim from Netflix:

> A computer-implemented method for renting movies to customers, the method comprising:
>
> providing electronic digital information that causes one or more attributes of movies to be displayed;
>
> establishing, in electronic digital form, from electronic digital information received over the Internet, a movie rental queue associated with a customer comprising an ordered list indicating two or more movies for renting to the customer;
>
> causing to be delivered to the customer up to a specified number of movies based upon the order of the list;
>
> in response to one or more delivery criteria being satisfied, selecting another movie based upon the order of the list and causing the selected movie to be delivered to the customer; and
>
> in response to other electronic digital information received from the customer over the Internet, electronically updating the movie rental queue.[12]

Yes, Netflix owns the business process that it uses to help customers maintain a movie rental queue.

The kinds of protection that can be obtained in various countries are also changing. Tactics that were in the past used by only a few companies are coming into their own. For years, IBM used publications to block competitors from patenting inventions in its space; now any company can use IP.com to create road blocks for its competitors (see Chapter 12). More and more companies use open-source strategies to ensure that users of a flexible platform technology do not create a morass of patents that block each other. And new uses of old forms of iProperty are becoming established tactics, such as design patents for protecting a nonfunctional cartridge shape for a uniquely shaped pen and copyrights for protecting computer software.

The iProperty portfolio decisions made today will determine the shape of the portfolio for many years, so all decisions must be forward looking. As a result, not only must the strategy team track the current state of iProperty protections in relevant countries around the globe, it must look into the future and predict the state of legal systems in countries around the globe in years to come. No iProperty team is complete without a member who owns these complex legal issues.

iPROPERTY STRATEGY

The internal and external factors just presented provide inputs for the iProperty strategy. The strategy, which should be expressed in a documented iProperty plan, typically includes vision and mission statements for the iProperty portfolio, as well as specific iProperty objectives that define how the company will invest its time and resources to develop an iProperty portfolio that will, along with the business and product strategies, help to maintain a sustainable competitive advantage. An effective iProperty strategy provides guidance (without being too restrictive) to the company's innovators regarding the kinds of ideas that are likely to provide the most value to the company. It also establishes the framework that guides evaluation of those ideas by the iProperty team and provides direction for the team's decisions about where and how to invest in protecting them. The iProperty strategy also maps out the use of other iProperty tactics, such as the use of defensive publications for weakening its competitors' iProperty positions, the use of trade secrets to protect various appropriate kinds of information and technology, and licensing strategies for monetizing the iProperty assets.

Importantly, a documented iProperty strategy prepared by a functioning iProperty team that has patent counsel as a member can eliminate the communication logjam created by traditional defensive legal practices. Early in co-author Bill Barrett's career as a patent attorney, during a visit to a client's office, he noticed a stack of paper over two feet tall in the corner. The stack consisted of Bill's letters to the client, which were routinely tossed into the corner with an idealistic intention to get back to them soon. This approach was the client's strategy for dealing with the standard patent firm process of papering clients to death by forwarding form letters with copies of each document received from domestic and foreign patent offices and agents. The process is tailored more toward risk reduction for the attorney than meaningful communication with the client. When Bill saw the stack, he realized that in addition to causing the death of a small forest of trees, his letters were not an effective way to communicate with the client. Although most of the letters were routine, several very important requests for information were buried among them. Bill's client did not get to the important requests because they were lost in a flood of trivial communications.

Further, each of these letters costs the client $75 to $100 in attorney fees, an expense that can add up dramatically. For example, some law firms send a cover letter conveying a foreign agent's request for instruction to pay a $170 annuity in a foreign patent application,[13] several reminders about the annuity, a cover letter conveying a letter to the agent with instructions to pay the annuity, a letter conveying the agent's acknowledgment that the instructions were received, and a letter conveying confirmation that the annuity was paid. In most cases, the letters are generated automatically by an electronic docketing system. By the time the letters stop flowing, the client has paid $350 to $500 just to get a $170 annuity paid. Multiply this by the hundreds or thousands of foreign patents and patent applications in a portfolio!

Are you getting papered to death by your law firm?

A written strategy that includes instructions to the patent counsel about committing to and paying, as well as communicating payment of, annuities could eliminate this expense. The iProperty plan, formulated in advance by the iProperty team, provides the guiding principles and key decisions affecting the development of an iProperty portfolio and empowers iProperty counsel to make day-to-day decisions without the need for a tower of unnecessary paper. Many of the warnings, admonitions, and requests for decisions included in the plethora of computer-generated form letters can be incorporated into the iProperty plan and communicated to an iProperty team on a regular basis to make communications and decision making more effective.

Creating a Vision

In their study of visionary companies, James Collins and Jerry Porras identify three components of a business vision: core values, a core purpose, and one or more Big Hairy Audacious Goals (BHAGs).[14] Likewise, an iProperty vision describes the core values that guide the vision and the core purpose that drives the vision and includes one or more visionary BHAGs. The vision addresses opportunities, accounts for internal capabilities and changing external realities, inspires commitment, and is aligned with the company's overall business vision. A sample iProperty vision might state:

> Our people will be masterful innovators. The speed and effectiveness of our iProperty process will make our investors want to check us for performance enhancing drugs. Our iProperty portfolio will not contain junk. It will dwarf our competitors' portfolios in strength if not in numbers. Without requiring litigation, it will make them fear to tread on our space. Yet we will always be prepared to litigate if necessary. We will know more about our competitors' iProperty than anyone else in our industry.

Detailing Tactics

The iProperty plan sets forth the guiding principles and details specific tactics that must be realized to achieve the vision. Thirdspace, mentioned earlier, made and executed an iProperty plan. According to Watson, "We presented ourselves from top to bottom as a patent and [intellectual property] savvy company, with [intellectual property] as chapter five in our business plan." Thirdspace's approach involved these strategies and tactics:

- Use patents for leverage in the sales field, identifying competitor products that appear to infringe company patents.
- Arm the sales team with the skills needed to react to patent concerns from customers, mainly in the United States.
- Address iProperty concerns in a manner that raises the perception of Thirdspace as a sophisticated company and an effective partner.
- Use patents to attract a second round of investment.

- Work with engineers to improve patents by filing continuation applications.
- Abandon less important patent filings and focus efforts and budget on the most commercially valuable filings.
- Use patents as leverage in partnership and collaboration discussions with influential global partners.
- Present patents as a core asset in the Thirdspace business plan.

The strategy was a success, Thirdspace raised its next round of financing, and the investor cited the iProperty portfolio as one of three key reasons for making the investment. Watson points to the Thirdspace patent portfolio as one of the two core reasons why the company was sold and not liquidated.

Tactical Considerations

An iProperty plan must account for a wide variety of tactical decisions. An observant tactician will always be on the lookout for new tactical options as they arise. Examples follow:

- **Portfolio breadth.** Will the iProperty investment be focused on a core set of iProperty that directly supports very specific business objectives, or will it be used to build a portfolio that broadly protects multiple product and/or technology spaces?
- **Global reach.** Will the portfolio broadly protect the company's ideas in an extensive set of countries around the globe, or in a more restrictive set of countries?
- **Information access.** How will the company make crucial information about its iProperty portfolio and landscape known to business leaders at the right time and at the appropriate level of detail needed to facilitate effective decisions? How will the company facilitate accurate communication of iProperty information to partners and customers?
- **Infringement risk.** Will the company try to avoid infringement risks at all costs? Is this even possible? How will the company respond to allegations of infringement?
- **iProperty enforcement.** How will the company respond to infringement of its own iProperty by others? Will it resort quickly to litigation or seek to negotiate a deal? Is the goal to stop all infringers or extract a payment from infringers?

- **Rights preservation.** How will the company avoid unnecessary loss of iProperty, for example, due to public disclosures, offers for sale, and the like?

- **Corporate culture.** Does the corporate culture understand and respect the role and value of iProperty? If not, what specific steps will it take to influence positive changes in the culture? Is the current level of employee participation sufficient? Are innovations coming only from a small group, or are they broadly distributed across the employee base? How will the company stimulate improved participation?

- **Value chain.** Will the company's iProperty focus on its segment of the product value chain (see Chapter 4), or will the iProperty strategy provide for protection upstream and/or downstream from the company's present position?

- **Due diligence.** Is the goal to sell the company to a third party, out-license a product or technology, enter a codevelopment relationship, or the like? How will the company prepare for the due diligence that will precede such a deal? Has the company implemented best practices in due diligence preparation?

- **Resources.** Have the appropriate, adequate resources (people and money) been allocated to achieve the set of activities in the plan?

Measurable Results

In addition to strategic issues, an effective iProperty plan will include specific, measurable short-term iProperty objectives. These are steps that the company must take in the next year to keep moving closer to realization of the iProperty vision. Ideally, the steps are measurable to permit the company to track progress. Examples include:

- **Number of patent applications filed.** How many new patent applications will the company file in the next year? Similarly, how many trade secrets will it identify and document?

- **Areas covered by patent applications.** What new areas of the company's technology space will the company protect by filing patent applications in the next year? Where are the weaknesses in the iProperty portfolio across the value chain? For example, a company might extend its protected space by filing new patents related to methods of manufacture, methods of use, new formulations, packaging, and the like.

- **Number of iProperty management meetings.** In a busy company, it is easy for any group to push back meetings and even eventually stop having them. How many times will the iProperty team meet this year to manage the execution of the company's iProperty strategy? What key topics will be covered at these meetings?

- **Number of notebook audits.** Do employees use laboratory notebooks to record valuable data and innovations? How many random audits will the company conduct to ensure proper use of notebooks? How (and how often) are the notebooks backed up?

- **Number of competitive patent studies.** Which technology or product patent spaces will the company seek to understand? The areas selected will influence the company's awareness of competitive patent activity. How many electronic patent watches will the company institute and in which areas? Who will review and evaluate the strategic implications of patents identified by these electronic watches?

- **Number of FTO opinions.** When and how many freedom-to-operate studies will the company conduct to assess infringement risks prior to investment in key technology or product patent spaces?

- **Outlicensing revenue.** Will the company generate revenue from outlicensing some or all of its patent portfolio? How much? Which aspects of the portfolio will be available for outlicensing? How many deals will the company close? What resources will the company use to ensure success of its outlicensing efforts?

- **Number and topics of educational presentations.** In which iProperty topic areas are employees deficient? What educational opportunities will the company offer to remedy these deficiencies? Will they be voluntary or mandatory? What forums will be used?

- **Number of implemented iProperty policies.** What iProperty policies does the company have in place? Are they generally adhered to? Are they well understood by employees? How will the company educate employees about iProperty policies? What new policies will the company develop and implement?

When developing an iProperty plan, it pays to include specific measurable goals. The point is not to be pedantic but to create a plan with actions that can be assessed and managed.

STRATEGIC iPROPERTY MINDSET

Given that competition is now global, companies of all sizes must focus their time, money, and energy on building shareholder value by developing and implementing profitable business models, moving products closer to all accessible parts of the global market, and gaining market share. In the shadow of these primary goals, the long-term investment in time and resources needed to ensure the development of a strategically aligned global patent portfolio can be forgotten. Many companies accumulate patents in an ad-hoc manner, rushing to file patent applications when innovations happen to surface, omitting patent applications on potentially valuable innovations because their value is not understood, rushing to make patent investment decisions at the last minute, and seeking to understand the output of this process only when the pressure is on. Other forms of protection, such as trade secrets and employee retention, are frequently overlooked altogether.

The minimalist approach to iProperty planning and process is clearly out of touch with the critical importance of iProperty to companies competing in the new global economic environment. iProperty strategy, tactics, and management techniques must infiltrate the technology company from the business strategy to the product teams, from the boardroom to the bench scientist. Managing iProperty requires the implementation of a visionary strategy with specific objectives and measurable standards that control the development of the iProperty portfolio. Just as a company would never leave the development of its product pipeline open to chance, so it must actively and strategically manage its iProperty pipeline to ensure maximum return on its investment.

NOTES

1. Robert Greene, *The 33 Strategies of War* (London: Penguin Books, 2006), 18.
2. Ibid., 22.
3. Bruce Greenwald and Judd Kahn, *Competition Demystified: A Radically Simplified Approach to Business Strategy* (New York: Penguin Books, 2005), 5.
4. Ibid., 6.
5. Andrew Watson, "From Virgin to Evangelist—Seeing the IP Light," *IAM* (December–January 2004).
6. Steve Menton, "Placing IP Management at the Heart of a Business," *Les Nouvelles* 39 no. 3 (September 2004), 112–116.
7. Markus Reitzig, "Strategic Management of Intellectual Property," *MIT Sloan Management Review* (Spring 2004), 35–40.

8. David Aaker, *Developing Business Strategies*, 5th ed. (New York: John Wiley & Sons, 1998), 18.

9. "Scenes from a Conference: Comments from 'Riffing with the Masters,'" *Business 2.0* (January 1, 2001).

10. Hewlett Packard, Inc., "Carly Fiorina, Comdex 99, Las Vegas, Nevada, Keynote Highlights," corporate Web site, November 15, 1999, www.hp.com/hpinfo/execteam/ speeches/fiorina/ ceo_comdex_short.html?jumpid=reg_R1002_USEN.

11. Reena Jana, "The Innovation Backlash," *BusinessWeek*, February 12, 2007, www. businessweek.com/print/innovate/content/feb2007/id20070212_728732.htm.

12. Reed Hastings, Marc Randolph, and Neil Hunt, "Approach for renting items to customers," U.S. Patent No. 7,024,381, April 4, 2006, claim 1.

13. An annuity is an official payment required by the patent offices of many countries in order to maintain a patent application.

14. James Collins and Jerry Porras, "Building Your Company's Vision," *Harvard Business Review* (September–October 1996).

~ 4 ~

Global Business

Integrating iProperty Strategy and Business Strategy

Companies that want to surpass their competitors must view iProperty as a proactive business tool. As such, they should view iProperty as an investment—of time and money—and apply the same quality of analytical and assessment criteria as would be used for, say, a marketing budget. Simply put: What is the return on investment? At least one study has reported that "implementation of a patent strategy in the R&D [research and development] department together with a corresponding patent management process almost doubles the profit margin of a company."[1] Careful iProperty development can also facilitate forays into nontraditional product and geographical markets and help to build stronger relationships with buyers and suppliers.

In *Edison in the Boardroom*, Julie Davis and Suzanne Harrison discuss the hierarchy of expectations that companies may have regarding the value of intellectual property to their business.[2] They observe that a company's iProperty goals and sophistication can range from a purely defensive level, in which patents are used specifically to protect a product stream and to promote freedom of action, to the visionary level, in which iProperty becomes a strategic tool for identifying business trends, leveraging markets, and enhancing profit margins.

Viewing iProperty in purely defensive terms is shortsighted. Companies that fail to envision more strategic roles for iProperty will fail to obtain the full value that strategic deployment of iProperty can provide. It is clear that, as a company's iProperty expectations move from defensive to visionary, it must use more sophisticated business processes to view, strategize, and track the development of its portfolio. One important but rarely used tool for envisioning and evaluating potential iProperty strategies makes use of a value chain analysis. Viewing a company's iProperty options through the value chain lens can bring to light a variety of strategic options that may not otherwise be readily apparent. When properly applied, value chain analysis can produce strategies that result in greater market leverage, greater revenue, and enhanced innovation.

DEFINING THE VALUE CHAIN

A value chain is a strategic business map.[3] The value chain follows the flow of product manufacturing, typically showing each stage in the manufacturing process from the raw materials to introduction of the product to the market. Value chain analysis may also include aftermarket stages, such as repair, recycling, or reconditioning of used products. Each stage in the value chain correlates to a certain level of profit margin/revenue that a company can expect when engaging in business activities at that stage. Each stage of the value chain also may be associated with a specific set of countries in which such activities take place, a specific set of competitors, and specific sets of customers and suppliers. A company's own position on its value chain reflects the business activities in which it has elected to participate and the value the company can obtain for its investment.

Exhibit 4.1 illustrates a simplified value chain framework for a company that manufactures and sells personal computers. The stages of the value chain begin with raw materials and end with aftermarket repair. Companies that participate in the raw materials stage of the value chain may be involved in the production of integrated circuits, wire, sheet metal, and so on. Companies operating within the components stage integrate these materials into circuit boards, disk drives, power supplies, mechanical assemblies, and the like. Companies in the systems stage assemble together modules, assemblies, and subassemblies. In these first three stages, value

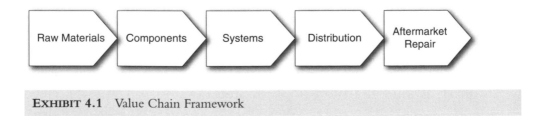

EXHIBIT 4.1 Value Chain Framework

is added by designing and producing more complex physical assemblies through successive levels of integration. Next come the distribution and aftermarket repair stages, in which value is added by providing a service that facilitates the delivery of the product to the consumer and by assisting the consumer in maintaining and servicing the computer system.

A value chain framework can be created for any industry, product market space, or individual company. By understanding its value chain framework, a company can readily visualize where value, and the market leverage it brings, exists in its business environment and strategy. The value chain is also an outstanding visual construction for developing and under-standing of a variety of iProperty risks and opportunities and facilitating strategic iProperty moves for competing in the global economy.

VALUE CHAIN STRATEGIES FOR iPROPERTY

Assume that Acme, Inc. traditionally produced products that fall into the component and systems stages of the value chain, as illustrated in Exhibit 4.2. Acme would therefore want to invest in becoming a more effective competitor in these market spaces. Its investment in R&D has yielded innovative and competitive products. Many of these ideas are patentable inventions, and Acme has expended resources to file patent ap-plications to protect those inventions that distinguish its products. Some ideas are internal process tweaks and know-how that are readily pro-tected by trade secrets. Acme has documented these trade secrets and

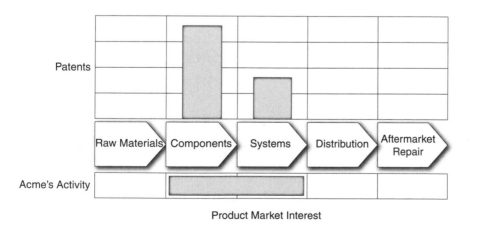

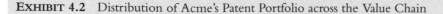

EXHIBIT 4.2 Distribution of Acme's Patent Portfolio across the Value Chain

has made high-resolution videos of important process tweaks and created a confidential video catalog of these process-oriented trade secrets that is accessible only to those employees who have a definitive need for access.

But like so many other companies, Acme's view of iProperty is purely defensive—as bargaining chips for ensuring freedom of action for itself if it is sued by competitors and/or as a barrier to entry for its competitors. As shown in Exhibit 4.2, this defensive posture is evident in the distribution of its patent portfolio. Acme has invested in patents only in the component and systems stages of its value chain. Most of these patents concentrate on the more detailed innovations relating to unique variations on individual components rather than on the broader innovations relating to the systems that Acme builds.[4]

Assume that Acme decides that it wants to explore more strategic uses of iProperty in its business. What lessons can it learn from the value chain analysis? We focus here on three of the most effective strategies:

1. Protect high-profit stages of the value chain.
2. Expand downstream on the value chain.
3. Expand upstream on the value chain.

Protect High-Profit Stages of the Value Chain

In any value chain, certain stages are likely to be more valuable than others. This value difference may be a result of the size of a market, the higher profit margins for that market, or a favorable combination of the two. Exhibit 4.3 illustrates the relative value of the stages of Acme's value chain. The value curve indicates that the market value of the products produced rises as the product moves toward the end consumer. In this case, Acme currently produces products in the lower-value stages of the value chain.

Although it is important for Acme to pursue iProperty protection for its own products, it may be uniquely suited to develop iProperty in the higher-value stages of its value chain due to the company's industry experience and know-how. Acme should map out the value of each stage of its value chain and identify the high-value stages. The company can then assess whether to invest resources in developing novel ideas for products and services that satisfy market needs at the high-value stages, and it can develop an iProperty for protecting those ideas.

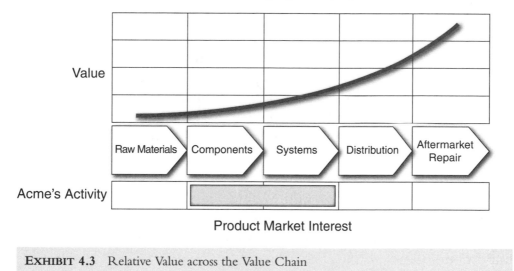

EXHIBIT 4.3 Relative Value across the Value Chain

For example, Acme may be able to position itself to extract value from the high-profit aftermarket repair stage of its value chain. Value in this scenario could come in the form of licensing dollars from deals with companies that distribute and/or repair products like the ones made by Acme. In addition, Acme may be able to develop and license iProperty for the aftermarket repair stage to Dell. Acme could then receive a small percentage of the profits of the very large market served by Dell. Because the value of a patent portfolio is related most directly to the size of the commercial profits that can be obtained through the sale of products protected by the portfolio, the potential revenues to Acme from the right licensing play could be a significant addition to or even outstrip the revenues from sales of traditional products in its own market space.

In some cases, the capture of valuable stages in the value chain is simply an exercise in the drafting of patent claims. In fact, value chain mapping should be a typical part of the process of developing a claiming strategy for a patent application. Once the patent counsel understands the value chain, he or she can draft the application and patent claims to capture valuable stages.

When was the last time your company mapped out its value chain from an iProperty perspective?

Although value curves will differ between value chains for different market segments, the basic principle remains the same. Companies that want to participate in other high-value segments of their marketplace can do so through strategic ownership and use of iProperty. To identify opportunities for such participation, the company must invest time and resources in mapping its value chain and developing an understanding of the relative value distribution across that chain. In the global economy, companies must identify the key countries that participate in various stages of the value chain as well as the iProperty opportunities in each country that are relevant to that stage in the value chain. Once opportunities are identified in various countries, strategies targeted to those countries can be prepared and implemented to capture value chain stages in economically important regions.

Expanding Downstream

As shown in Exhibit 4.4, the direction associated with the flow of the development, production, and commercialization of the product is commonly referred to as *downstream*, while *upstream* encompasses the precedent activities including raw material and component production. These terms are also useful in describing the relationship between companies participating in the same value chain. For example, the fictional Acme produces product in the component and systems value chain stages. Therefore, companies that participate in the distribution and/or aftermarket repair stages can be said to be downstream of Acme and are likely to be its customers. These companies are buying product from Acme, adding value by developing new applications or by distributing Acme's products (as Wal-Mart has amply demonstrated, even this distribution step can involve valuable ideas that can be protected by iProperty). Acme can

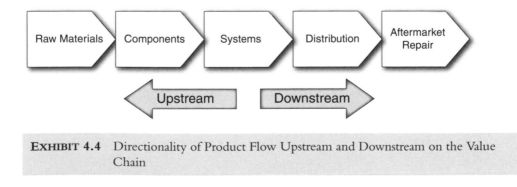

EXHIBIT 4.4 Directionality of Product Flow Upstream and Downstream on the Value Chain

extract value by executing R&D strategies that yield iProperty in the company's downstream areas and then properly protecting the resulting innovations.

Acme can gain strategic insights by conducting a targeted patent search and mapping patents of its customers. Doing so will reveal many of the most important issues confronting its customers. Understanding its customers' key technical problems may lead to innovative solutions that Acme can incorporate into its products, saving its customers time and resources. If Acme is particularly insightful, it will use its customer's iProperty to predict future problems and will develop solutions before those problems even arise. In addition, downstream innovation protected by iProperty may leverage Acme's negotiations with its partners and thus enable the company to capture even more value from its value chain.

Protecting Against Customer iProperty

By understanding issues related to its downstream iProperty, Acme can protect itself against customers who would patent broad uses of Acme's products and block Acme's other customers from using them. Such protection could take a variety of forms, such as protective terms in a license agreement that is associated with a purchase of the product; publication by Acme of defensive publications (see Chapter 12) that serve as "prior art," which interferes with customers' ability to obtain blocking patents; or even a "quasi-open-source" community strategy under which every customer agrees to contribute improvements and uses of a technology to a collective open-source community.

Acme can also use the information it obtains from a study of customer patents to develop patents and patent claims that protect customers' uses of its products and technologies. These patents can be licensed to the customer with the sale of a product, or certain rights in the patents can be reserved so that the customer will need to acquire a license to do certain things with the products and technologies. Acme can access revenues from downstream stages in its value chain by including licensing restrictions on sales of its platform technologies. For example, E.I. DuPont de Nemours and Company (DuPont) uses such an approach with its Teflon® products. Each sale of Teflon includes an agreement that the purchaser will not use Teflon as claimed in any of a listed set of DuPont patents without authorization from DuPont. If the purchaser wishes to use Teflon commercially in a manner that is claimed in one of DuPont's patents, the purchaser must return to DuPont for a license, and, of course, pay a royalty to DuPont.[5]

Dow Chemical Protects Its Downstream Value Chain

Dow, a manufacturer of chemical, plastic, and agricultural products, is about as far upstream in its value chain as one can get. The company supplies raw materials to a huge collection of downstream companies, including component and system manufacturers in a variety of application spaces. Dow clearly understands the importance of the value chain from a strategic iProperty point of view. A prime example is the way in which Dow capitalized on the downstream iProperty of its XLA elastic fiber product. According to Bruce Story, intellectual capital director of the Polyolefins & Elastomers Business Divisions of Dow during the time that this product was being newly commercialized:

> Although Dow is a basic materials supplier, we embarked upon a new business model in which we would capture more value downstream with this product. The most critical part in being successful with this strategy is in owning the intellectual assets of raw materials, components and systems and having a strong trademark strategy. As a result, we are beginning to establish ourselves as facilitating innovative fashion fabric performance. We are finding a ready receptivity among leading fashion clothing designers as our material allows new freedoms in design and use.

When asked about the possibility of alienating Dow's customers by securing patents in their technology space, Story focused on building stronger relationships with the customers:

> There are various reasons why you would want to patent in [your customers'] space. A key reason for us is to protect our customers from their competitors. Our goal in developing new polymers is to be able to sell them to a wide variety of customers. If a particular customer were to broadly patent the use of that material in a particular application space, they would be able to keep the rest of their competitors from participating in the market. This would be bad for the industry and bad for Dow, as we would have a very small market, and it might not make good economic sense for us to make the product. So, we are trying to patent, or publish, in such a way as to create freedom of action in the broad end-use so as to protect all the customers.[6]

In terms of its iProperty value chain, Dow asks three questions:

1. Which stage of the value chain should we participate in?
2. Which stages need to be protected?
3. What approaches should be used to achieve this protection?

The stages in which Dow does *not* actively participate are particularly important for iProperty protection strategies. Dow's development and implementation of new internal processes for iProperty and clear understanding of its position in its value chain have demonstrated proven value and delivered a positive impact on innovation within the company.

Expanding Upstream

Returning to the Acme model, companies that participate in the raw materials stage can be said to be upstream of Acme, typically vendors of materials used by Acme. Often companies like Acme enter into joint development efforts with upstream companies during the course of product development. These joint development efforts take different forms, ranging from very informal conversations over coffee to formal programs with contractual agreements in place. In any form, these efforts can be very productive and may generate potentially patentable ideas.

In fact, innovations that result in improved performance of the raw materials supplied to Acme may be the key market differentiators for the products it produces. Unfortunately, while ownership and patenting of inventions arising out of joint development efforts often receive detailed treatment in joint development agreements, such agreements usually lack a formal process for identifying, documenting, and properly determining ownership and how economic exploitation of such inventions will occur. Failure to identify and protect ideas arising out of such collaborations can lead to iProperty leakage, whereby ideas become incorporated in products of the upstream companies and then sold to companies that may be in competition with the originating company.

Suppliers Taking Hostages

Acme should be wary of sophisticated suppliers who may want to use an iProperty strategy to expand downstream into Acme's space. By anticipating the company's needs and using iProperty to protect the solutions to those needs, Acme's suppliers may gain leverage to extract a higher price from Acme. Can you say "hostage"? If Acme does not anticipate this problem and head it off, a shrewd supplier may patent an important input to Acme's products. With no alternative supplier for the patented input, Acme will indeed be a hostage. This situation is not uncommon. And surprisingly, buyers are often unwitting collaborators, supplying critical information leading to the patent during deal negotiations without any agreement in place protecting them from suppliers' iProperty plays.

Are you ensuring that your suppliers do not use iProperty to hold you hostage?

What kinds of strategic options does value chain analysis suggest with regard to upstream iProperty? First, Acme is at risk from suppliers and should be diligent in signing contracts that restrict use of Acme's confidential information and clearly define the terms for how ownership of any iProperty relating to Acme's technology space should be handled. Acme should hold regular meetings to discuss and capture innovations generated by any joint development effort. By clearly defining iProperty ownership before the relationship begins and by diligently identifying and documenting iProperty during the course of the relationship, Acme can prevent sensitive iProperty from being sold to competitors and avoid conflicts that may arise over iProperty ownership. Alternatively, Acme can license the technology it has diligently protected to its competitors in exchange for a revenue stream. An additional benefit for supplier and buyer alike is a closer, more secure, and longer-lasting supply relationship.

Motorola and P&G Work Upstream on their Value Chains

The company that develops a technology may not always be best suited to commercialize it.[7] For example, Motorola, Inc. developed a new display technology that made cell phone displays less expensive and brighter. Motorola is not in the business of selling displays, and it couldn't manufacture and sell enough displays to fully capitalize on economies of scale, so it licensed its iProperty covering the technology to its supplier. The move ensured that Motorola would have access to low-cost displays and presumably a revenue stream on sales of the displays sold to others by its supplier.

The Procter & Gamble Company (P&G) designed a new packaging for its deodorants, used iProperty to protect the packaging, and licensed the iProperty to its competitor. At first, P&G was reluctant to license an innovation that gave it a competitive advantage. But after further analysis, the company concluded that the loss in business would be minimal, and the reduction in production costs would be significant. By combining its volume requirements for the packaging with its competitor's requirements, P&G lowered its own costs of procuring the packaging. According to Jeff Weidman of P&G:

[T]he supplier liked the packaging so much that he asked if he could also license the design and sell it to his other customers. So our competitor paid us a royalty. And the combined volume of all those additional packaging molds saved us a lot of money in supply costs and lowered our capital requirements.[8]

COMPETITIVE VALUE CHAIN ANALYSIS

As suggested, companies can gain insights into their competitors' activities by conducting targeted patent searches and mapping patents of competitors, customers, and suppliers across the value chain. In fact, failure to understand competitor patents in the Internet age, with easily available and often free databases and other information, is strategically irresponsible. Because every patent application is published 18 months after the initial filing (with a few exceptions), patents constitute publicly available documentation of key technical problems and solutions to those problems, as well as competitive positions and trends and best practices for preparing and obtaining effective patents. Nevertheless, companies rarely survey the publicly available patents and patent applications of suppliers, customers, and competitors. Closing this gap in intelligence gathering is easier and more important than ever as the global economic playing field intensifies the competitive environment.

A variety of iProperty approaches can be used to protect any technology area and invention type. The approaches are, within certain broad rules, limited only by the imagination of the iProperty strategist. Best practices in various technology areas are constantly evolving and are publicly available for all who are willing to take the time to look. In some countries and regions, such as the United States and Europe, the published information even includes the interactions between the patent applicant and the patent examiner, showing what approaches worked or failed and even revealing the types of arguments that wcre effective at overcoming examiner rejections. Any company that wants to protect a valuable product or technology should first obtain a deep understanding of this readily available information.

MASTERING THE VALUE CHAIN

Like Dow, Motorola, and P&G successful iProperty companies pay attention to how their iProperty portfolios map out against their supply chains. In doing so, they make use of iProperty at Davis and Harrison's visionary level. iProperty becomes a strategic tool for identifying business trends, leveraging markets, and enhancing profit margins. The value chain technique requires companies to:

1. Define their value chains for each product area.
2. Identify the value of each step.
3. Identify where the company operates on its value chain.
4. Decide how it could benefit from iProperty in stages in which it does not participate.
5. Determine the stages it will protect with iProperty.

In particular, companies should look upstream and downstream for revenue-generating opportunities that iProperty ownership may facilitate and focus on using iProperty to capture high-value stages in their value chains. Moreover, layering geographical information onto the value chain can provide important insights about when, where, and how to protect and exploit ideas in a global iProperty strategy. It also pays to remember that competitors view your company from the perspective of their own value chains. Pay attention to potential competitor strategies and consider proactively blocking them to avoid being held hostage by a supplier or having one of your customers tie up your market space using an iProperty position to block their competitors from using your products.

NOTES

1. Malte Köllner, "Patents for High-Tech Start-ups," *IAM* (October/November 2005): 42, citing N. Omland, "Patentmanagement und Unternehmenserfolgeine empirische Analyse," Mitteilungen der Deutschen Patentawälte (2005); 402.

2. Julie Davis and Suzanne Harrison, *Edison in the Boardroom: How Leading Companies Realize Value from Their Intellectual Assets* (Hoboken, NJ: John Wiley & Sons, Inc., 2001).

3. Interested readers can learn more about the basis for, and more traditional uses of, value chain analysis by reading Michael Porter's *Competitive Advantage: Creating and Sustaining Superior Performance* (New York: Free Press, 1998).

4. In some cases, counting of patents may be misleading, since each patent may include a different number of patent claims, typically ranging from a few to hundreds. Further, it is not uncommon for individual patents to include both components and systems claims. In such cases, a more accurate analysis may involve counting of claims or counting of major (independent) claims in the patent applications.

5. See "DuPont™ Teflon® AF License Agreement," www2.dupont.com/Teflon_Industrial/en_US/contact/teflonaf_licenseapp.html.

6. Quoted in Tom Hunt, "A Value Chain Approach to IP Management," *IAM* (November 2003), 14.

7. David Kline, "Sharing the Corporate Crown Jewels," *MIT Sloan Management Review* (Spring 2003), 89–93.

8. Ibid.

~ 5 ~

Global Navigation

Mapping the iProperty of Competitors

In 2006, a court ordered Internet phone service provider, Vonage, to pay $58 million and royalties for infringing patents owned by Verizon. Vonage's meteoric rise to success is chronicled in an interactive timeline available on its Web site.[1] For our purposes, the story starts with the appointment of founder Jeffrey Citron as chief executive officer (CEO) and a $12 million round of venture financing in 2001. In 2003, Vonage raised a $15 million round of financing. In 2004, the company raised another $145 million, and another $200 million was raised in 2005. By mid-2006, Vonage had 1.9 million subscriber lines and a very large bill for patent infringement.

The day Vonage received the check for the first $12 million of venture investment, three of the seven patents that Verizon would use to sue Vonage were granted and publicly available on the Internet from the U.S. Patent & Trademark Office Web site. By the time the next $15 million was invested, all seven of Verizon's patents had been granted and were available on the Internet. By the time of the $145 million and the $200 million investments, the Verizon patents had been granted for years, long enough to collect a significant layer of dust. In 2006, soon after Vonage made its public offering, Verizon decided to roll up its sleeves, dust the patents off, and put them to competitive use.

While all the facts are not available to us, and we do not wish to be dogmatic in our conclusions, presumably at each of these major investment points, investors conducted significant due diligence on the Vonage business plan to identify risks. It appears that at each stage, the warnings were there and could have been found in readily accessible databases. A thorough investigation of Vonage's patent landscape for risks would have cost a small fraction the hundreds of millions invested in Vonage.

In addition to apparently venturing blindly and headlong into a patent infringement suit, Vonage also appears to have failed to procure its own patents, making it an easy target. Presumably other major players in the VoIP (Voice over Internet Protocol) space have significant patent portfolios that can be used to potentially leverage a settlement with Verizon that would at least include a cross-licensing deal. As an example, when IBM sued Amazon.com in 2006, Amazon.com was able to strike back with a lawsuit of its own, accusing IBM of infringing Amazon's patents.[2] Similarly, when Japan's Sanyo Electric Co. sued Taiwan's MediaTek Inc. in 2005 for patent infringement,[3] MediaTek countersued, claiming Sanyo's electronics products infringed MediaTek's patents. The case was settled with a cross-licensing deal in 2007.

Yet Vonage's Web site indicates that it acquired VoIP patents from Digital Packet Licensing Inc. only in 2006.[4] As of April 29, 2007, when we searched the U.S. Patent & Trademark Office's patent applications database, we were unable to identify any pending Vonage patent applications.[5] The first related patent application we identified was filed by Vonage's CEO, Jeffrey Citron, and others in September 2006. Again, while we are not privy to Vonage's decision-making process or any actions it may have taken in light of the Verizon patents, it seems to us that if Vonage had been assessing risks and thinking ahead, not only would it have been aware of the Verizon patents but it would have taken steps to avoid infringement to proactively prepare itself to deal with any infringement litigation that might arise.

Patent attorneys, particularly those serving the high-tech sector, often complain that the patent landscape is too complex to bother with. There is no way to understand the landscape with sufficient clarity to avoid the risk of infringement. While we agree that in many cases the landscape is too complex to avoid infringement completely, the case usually is overstated. The potential damages for infringing the patents of others can be enormous. In same year that Vonage was chastened for patent infringement, Microsoft got slammed with a $1.5 billion damages award for infringing Alcatel-Lucent patents relating to MP3 technology. In addition to monetary damages, court-ordered injunctions in patent infringement cases can shut down factories, stop product shipments, and otherwise wreak expensive havoc. Moreover, identifying and reducing infringement-related risks is just one component of what we call "iProperty intelligence," a comprehensive approach to mining valuable technical and business information from the publicly available iProperty data to develop an understanding of the landscape in which a company operates.

iPROPERTY INTELLIGENCE

Like any landscape, the patent landscape must be visually mapped to be understood. Mapping involves developing a database of the relevant patents and patent applications (patent documents) and using the database as the basis for producing a variety of textual and graphical outputs that elucidate relationships among the patent documents and between the patent documents and other available technical and business information. The kinds of relationships that can be mapped are limited only by the imagination and insightfulness of the analyst. Examples include relationships involving technical fields, product categories, invention types, inventors, owners, chronologies, and the like.

We will focus our discussion on mapping information found in publicly available patent databases. Such databases include a wealth of knowledge about the activities of competitors, including, among other things: which competitors are playing in which technology spaces; what problems they consider important enough to invest their valuable research and development capital to solve; what technologies they are using to solve those problems; and which protection strategies have been successful and which ones have failed.

Often, the development stage of a company and its level of investment in a specific field can be deduced by examining the quality of the detail with which the company describes and illustrates the related technology in patent applications. For example, developing highly detailed design drawings and specifications requires expensive resources, and their presence in a patent application suggests that the invention being described arose out of a more advanced development effort. On the other hand, simple, high-level conceptual description and illustrations may suggest inventions arising out of early stage efforts or even out of the inventors' spare time. Similarly, elaboration in a patent application of the results of a thorough and expensive research program may evidence the degree of scientific and financial commitment by a company to the field of the research. Lack of such research results can imply that the idea did not result from a full-fledged research program. Of course, for every rule there is an exception. Interpretation of a patent landscape requires good judgment and insightful analysis, not the rote application of general rules of thumb.

Mapping the distribution of competitors' patent documents in countries around the world can yield important insights. Building a global portfolio is expensive, and companies typically reserve the most geographically expansive strategies to the inventions they consider the most important. Concentrations of patent filings in specific countries may suggest outsourcing, offshoring, or marketing targets: If one is planning to manufacture or sell significant quantities of a product in Singapore, the relevant inventions must be protected there. Given the wealth of technical and business information that is freely available by searching patent databases on the Internet, we wonder how it is that companies understand so little about their competitors' iProperty.

Have you mapped out the iProperty space in which your company is doing business?

Superior iProperty intelligence provides competitive advantages. When a company understands its patent landscape it can often avoid forging into a heavily patented area in which the risk of infringement is high. If the crowded region cannot be avoided, effective iProperty intelligence can help the company to devise a route through the region that carefully skirts specific problem patents to avoid infringement. Alternatively, a proactive program of new ideation and innovation may illuminate a fresh pathway that avoids infringement.

Understanding the patent literature of key competitors can provide insight into the strengths and weaknesses of their portfolios and suggest approaches to avoid or defend against their strengths and exploit their weaknesses. For example, a company with a deep understanding of the technology trajectory and patent strategies of its competitor can often invent in front of its competitor and patent technologies that the competitor will need. As an example, as a company develops a new technology, it often fails to anticipate problems scaling up production until it has actually begun to develop manufacturing processes. An insightful competitor, knowledgeable of scale-up and manufacturing challenges in the space, can often anticipate these challenges, identify key solutions, and patent them.

In this way, a company can shape its own patent portfolio for use as a defensive weapon. By building a portfolio of patents that potentially block important activities of its competitors, a company can, first, improve the odds that if sued for patent infringement, it will have patents that enable a countersuit, as in the Amazon.com and MediaTek examples discussed above. A second, and potentially more profitable, opportunity is the chance for a partnership between a company and its competitor. Finally, companies can use iProperty intelligence to evaluate the iProperty portfolios of technology licensors/licensees and potential merger/acquisition targets. This knowledge can be used to shape the company's own portfolio to create leverage for the anticipated deal. Even inexpensive provisional patent applications can be utilized to increase the value of one or both sides of a transaction.

Companies are often reluctant to tackle the problem of understanding their patent landscapes due to the sheer volume of the world's in-force patents and pending applications. In the United States alone, the world's innovators file over 400,000 patent applications each year. Patent filings are on the rise in all economically important countries. Developing a thorough understanding of a company's patent landscape requires the company to account not only for patent documents of direct competitors but also for patent documents of suppliers, customers, competitors of suppliers, and companies in adjacent technology areas that may be relevant.

Due to the size and complexity of the task, competitive iProperty intelligence is most effective when it is accompanied by the development of a database for cataloging and characterizing competitor patent documents. Although this may seem an obvious solution to a complex information problem for businesspeople, the idea of developing a database of knowledge about competitor patents makes litigators uneasy. Such a database provides material that, if not appropriately managed, can be misinterpreted and may cause problems during litigation. In particular, when a company knows about a patent and willfully infringes it, the damages awarded in a patent infringement suit can be tripled. Some attorneys conclude that it is better not to understand the landscape than to risk a judgment of willful infringement. In *Rembrandts in the Attic*, Kevin Rivette and David Kline refer to this position as "the ignorance myth."[6]

The solution to the willful infringement problem is not to put your head in the sand but to do the task right. Study the patent landscape so that you can avoid infringement, and keep a knowledge base so that you do not have to reinvent the wheel each time someone in your organization looks at a patent. But keep the process under the control of and managed by the legal department. Although the data is publicly available, conclusions about the interpretation of patents and whether a patent is infringed or invalid are highly confidential and should, to the extent possible, be maintained as privileged information (i.e., protected by the attorney–client privilege from disclosure during litigation). Finally, when you identify a problem patent, don't just bury it. Do something about it!

As we discussed in the introduction, iProperty "ownage" implies freedom to take action in your space. Rich West, serial entrepreneur and chief executive officer of Advanced Liquid Logic, Inc., an early-stage medical device company in Research Triangle Park, North Carolina, emphasizes that when competitive patent documents are identified, degrees of action include "understanding, marginalizing, licensing, and owning." Understanding a competitive patent position requires significant time and effort. The researcher must clear away mounds of irrelevant material and drill down into the relevant details to identify strengths and vulnerabilities. This process often requires a team approach in which potential positions are suggested, tested, and kept or discarded for scientific, business and/or legal reasons. Marginalizing involves understanding and then changing product designs to avoid them, establishing a reasoned case for the patents' invalidity, and/or developing a portfolio of patents that blocks the use of the problem patents' technology in commercially important areas. Finally, where a company cannot marginalize a patent or a portfolio of patents, the company should consider whether there is value in owning or licensing the patents.

ASSESSING THE PATENT LANDSCAPE

Exhibit 5.1 illustrates a patent landscape assessment process. The process is divided into three phases. In Phase I, the researcher conducts searches of the patent databases for one or more countries or regions of interest, screens the results of the searches, builds a database of patent documents that are *generally relevant* to the field of a proposed product or service, and identifies patent documents within the database that are *specifically relevant* to the product or service under consideration. For example, if the product is a fuel injection system for an automobile, *generally relevant* patent documents may include those describing technical approaches to delivering fuel into an internal combustion engine. The generally relevant patent documents form the basis for broad examinations of technology and industry trends. *Specifically relevant* patent documents may include only patent

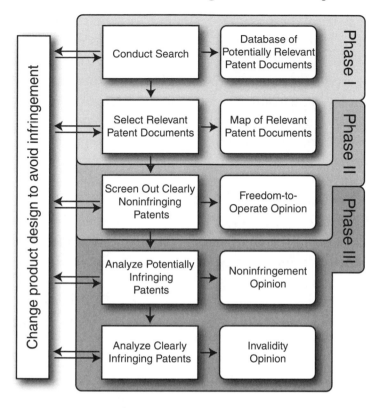

EXHIBIT 5.1 Simplified Patent Landscape Management Process

documents for fuel injection systems, excluding all other approaches to delivering fuel into an internal combustion engine. The specifically relevant patent documents provide a basis for identifying and dealing with infringement risks. The researcher can use the completed database to develop maps of both generally and specifically relevant patent documents for visually evaluating the landscape at both extremes of analysis: high-level assessments of SWOT (strengths, weaknesses, opportunities, and threats) and detailed analysis of specific claims.

Phases II and III of the process involve legal and technical analyses that should be done by skilled patent counsel with expertise in the technical field of the evaluation. In Phase II the patent counsel compares the claims in the specifically relevant patent documents with the proposed product or service. Based on this comparison, the counsel can prepare a legal freedom-to-operate (FTO) opinion describing valid and persuasive reasons why each of the included patents is not infringed.

Phase III involves more detailed analysis that is required when the patents cannot be dismissed based on a cursory review. The counsel performs the same comparison between the patent claims and the product or service as in Phase II, but also engages in a more extensive research effort to identify limitations on the meaning of the claims not apparent from a simple reading of the patent. Phase III may also include an analysis of whether there are reasons to believe that the patent is simply invalid. Determining invalidity involves conducting a search of the patent literature and other sources of technical information, such as professional journals and the Internet. The results of Phase III are documented in extensive legal opinions establishing the technical and legal reasons for noninfringement or invalidity. Of course, Phases II and III are only as effective as the quality of the work done in Phase I. If the search misses important patent documents, they will remain as hidden land mines that could unexpectedly damage the company if, as in the Verizon example, their owners decide to enforce them.

As iProperty researchers progress through the phases of the landscape management process, they are systematically identifying risks and should formulate strategies to reduce the risks. Generally speaking, with each phase, the process becomes more complex and more resource intensive. Likewise, as the product development effort progresses, business decisions loom larger, such as when to make larger investments (e.g., signing a large supply contract), and the decisions become more difficult to reverse (e.g., building a factory). There is an inherent tension between the need for early iProperty research results to avoid unnecessary product development costs, and the need to control the cost of the landscape process itself. Identifying an insurmountable patent early in the process can prevent wasted resources pursuing designs that the patent blocks.

On the other hand, early in the product development process the number of possible product designs can be so large that effective Phase II and III analyses would be too expensive to undertake. At this early stage, the number of patents potentially blocking any of the numerous hypothetical product designs is so great that the serious infringement analyses of Phases II and III are far too time consuming and expensive. Moreover, many potential aspects and configurations of the product may not have been finalized or even invented, making infringement analysis premature. However, even at an early product development stage, the relatively high-level analyses of Phase I are generally useful to establish an overview of the patent landscape and flag any obvious problem areas. As the company narrows potential product configurations to a manageable number of alternatives or a proposed final product, the detailed FTO analyses of Phases II and III become more practical and cost effective. The expense of the FTO analysis can thus be controlled by appropriate timing of the process to coincide with the development of clarity around the desired product design.

As illustrated in Exhibit 5.1, each step in the patent landscape assessment process should be tightly coupled directly into the product development process. The invaluable information obtained in an FTO program can shape the product strategy to ensure that it proceeds through the patent landscape in a manner that avoids infringement and billion-dollar damages awards, like the one in the Microsoft case. We now proceed to discuss each of the three phases of the process in more detail.

PHASE I: MAPPING THE PATENT SPACE

If you have worked with patent attorneys long enough, you have seen the standard aggregation of patent data: a table of application numbers, patent numbers, titles, filing dates, issue dates, countries, inventors, and the like. While the organization may vary, the content is essentially the same. Imagine studying such a table of competitive patent documents that is 10 or 20 pages long. What can you learn from such a table? How long would it take to absorb sufficient data to see trends?

Although such tables are always useful and will be required for certain purposes, such as specifying rights in a licensing transaction, studying patent tables is an inefficient approach to developing a high-level understanding of the myriad technical and business relationships among a group of hundreds of patent documents. Further, it is virtually impossible to use these tables to communicate important information about iProperty to executives, investors, potential partners, and others with limited attention spans.

In contrast, patent mapping is about transforming data into a visual form to render trends and relationships within the data readily perceptible. The practice of visualizing information about a company's patent space is emerging as a common, everyday tool.

As an example, Aureka Themescape® provides "a birds-eye view of the most common concepts in [a set of patent documents], laid out in a topographical map."[7] The Themescape map shows concentrations of documents and their relationships to one another. When the Procter & Gamble Company (P&G) merged with Gillette, a Themescape analysis of the merger revealed visually how Gillette's patent portfolio neatly filled a void in P&G's patent portfolio. Specifically, Gillette's oral care patent portfolio (i.e., under the Oral-B® brand name) complemented

P&G's current patent estate supporting the CREST® brand name. More important, Gillette's patent portfolio for the men's razor/skin care business and the Duracell® and Braun® businesses helped fill a void in P&G's patent estate. Eric Wagner, patent counsel at Moore & Van Allen, notes: "The Themescape® visual analysis showed the P&G patent portfolio forming a U shape with Gillette's patents fitting right in the gap, thus suggesting that this merger, from a patent portfolio point of view, was a very good move for P&G."[8]

According to Wagner, the more important result of the analysis may have been the information that could be extrapolated when combined with competitive intelligence data and publicly available data regarding P&G's business strategy. For example, the Duracell technology would be helpful because P&G has a lot of products that require a battery. Wagner explains further how analysis based on the visual Themescape map yielded important insights:

> One can envision P&G now including a Duracell battery in these product packages, and I would imagine the acquisition of Duracell people will help P&G move that platform forward. Braun makes coffee makers, so that acquisition will complement the Folger's brand (e.g., special coffee maker for special Folger's coffee packets maybe?). Braun also makes hair dryers, which could complement all of P&G's hair care products. And, probably most important, P&G already has a huge women's skin care business, not so much with men's skin care. Based on the analysis, I think the market for men's skin care is P&G's next move, and of course the Gillette brand and products give P&G a huge leap in market share and brand recognition for men's care.

Wagner emphasized that the output of this type of analysis is not self-evident and that significant background work is required to prepare the data for analysis. However, "with the proper homework and information at hand, this approach can provide a unique and informative analysis into the relationship (and potential relationship) of two different patent portfolios."

Visualizing the Landscape

As suggested by the P&G/Gillette example, visualization of patent data alone or with other publicly available data (publications, Internet, marketing literature, etc.) can reveal strategic insights about the technologies and products of a company or a group of companies that would not be apparent from a stack of patent documents. The visual cortex of the human brain is the largest single functional area, and humans process complex visual information rapidly and efficiently. Colin Ware, director of the Data

Visualization Research Laboratory at the University of New Hampshire, describes the goal of visualization as the transformation of data into a "perceptually efficient visual format."[9] Patent visualization transforms patent data into such a perceptually efficient visual format. Ware describes a four-stage process for visualizing data, which we have adapted to patent landscaping as follows:

1. Collecting and storing data
2. Preprocessing to transform the data into something understandable
3. Creating a visual representation using software and algorithms
4. Interpreting the visual representation using the human perceptual and cognitive system

Next we describe how to use this framework to develop a visual understanding of a company's patent space.

Collecting and Storing Data

An understanding of a target patent space begins with a patent search to gather the relevant patent data. Prior to conducting a search, it is critical to set some parameters, the search guide, around the target set of patent documents. From a business perspective, the search guide may be designed to obtain a set of patent documents suitable for learning about competitors' activities in a generic technology or product space. Or the search may be targeted toward identifying any patent that could be a source of risk to a specific product development path.

From a technological perspective, the search guide might focus on a specific grouping of technologies, such as "all mold-resistant construction materials." For a company making mold-resistant paints, it might be useful to learn how other companies are making a wide variety of mold-resistant products. Or the search might be more narrowly focused on "mold-resistant exterior paints for houses." The parameters may also include, in this case, specific paint companies known to have patent documents that are of particular interest. A broad patent landscape analysis of the patent documents of close competitors may identify new technology or product directions that competitors are taking.

Once the target patent space has been defined, a search strategy can be developed. The quality of a patent visualization effort depends completely on the quality of the initial patent searching efforts. An effective search strategy will identify all relevant patent documents. However, given the inaccuracies inherent in searching, it pays to cast a broad net, capturing many relevant patent documents together with some percentage of irrelevant patent documents that will be ruled out later in the process. The use of multiple search engines and multiple strategies (e.g., keyword searches, company searches, tracking down patent documents cited in key patents) can improve the comprehensiveness of the search results.

A variety of quality search engines are available for patent searching. The U.S. and European patent office Web sites have excellent search capabilities. Commercial fee-based search engines are also available. Examples include Nerac.com, Micropatent.com, Derwent.com, LexisNexis.com, and Delphion.com. We like the flexibility of Micropatent and its capability for downloading patent data into a spreadsheet that can be used to manage patent document review. One advantage of the fee-based services is the capability to institute ongoing patent watches in which the search system automatically notifies the searcher by e-mail of new patent documents satisfying the search criteria. In the fast-moving iProperty world, staying informed in real time is imperative. Professional searchers are also available. For some kinds of innovations, such as complex organic molecules, a manual search by a professional, scientifically trained searcher is still indispensable.

Preprocessing the Data

Once the searching strategy has yielded a body of potentially relevant patent documents, the next step is to review the patent documents manually to identify specifically and generally relevant ones. This step can be a quick, high-throughput process in which the title, abstract, and claims of each patent are reviewed to identify patents that could possibly encompass aspects of the company's product, processes, or services. Patent documents with potential relevance are retained for further analysis, and only those that are clearly irrelevant are excluded.

Until the world's patent offices agree on a method of data validation, companies doing research on the databases must wrestle with numerous inconsistencies in the data. For example, a significant amount of effort is required to determine the current assignees (owners) for any group of patent documents. First, the names of original assignees may vary in spelling, spacing, and commas: for example, "Glaxo Inc." versus "Glaxo, Inc." Patents often are assigned subsequent to the granting of the patent, so the owner named on the patent may not be the true owner or assignee.

The full collection of patent documents owned by GlaxoWellcome Inc., for example, includes many patent documents that were originally assigned to a variety of companies that have been purchased by or merged with GlaxoWellcome Inc. and its predecessors. Effective preprocessing of the patent data includes research into the current owners of the patent documents identified in the search. Information on current owners is available on the U.S. Patent & Trademark Office's Web site.

Creating a Visual Representation

Once the body of relevant patent documents has been identified, the documents can be visually mapped to reveal strategic information. Mapping involves the preparation of charts that permit visualization of patent data. The data being visualized is of two types: electronic data available from patent databases and data added by human analysis of the documents. An example of electronically available data is information such as the document's filing date, grant date, title, inventors, and the presence of various search terms. Human-added data includes technology categories, product categories, applications of the innovation, and the like.

Have you ever seen a visual representation of your company's patents or the patents of your competitors? In the United States? In major-market countries? In emerging economies?

Interpreting the Visual Representation

The final step in the visualization process involves interpreting the visual data. Different kinds of visualization lead to different kinds of interpretation. For example, Exhibit 5.2 shows a branching patent map of players in the somatostatin space according to the categories in which they are operating. Somatostatin is a peptide hormone naturally found in the body, and various somatostatin-based products are on the market, including a modified version of somatostatin sold by Novartis under the brand name Sandostatin®. We conducted a search on patent documents relating to somatostatin to see what we could learn about the somatostatin space.

First, hold the map at a distance and view its general layout, focusing only on high-level categories and ignoring the other details. Looking at

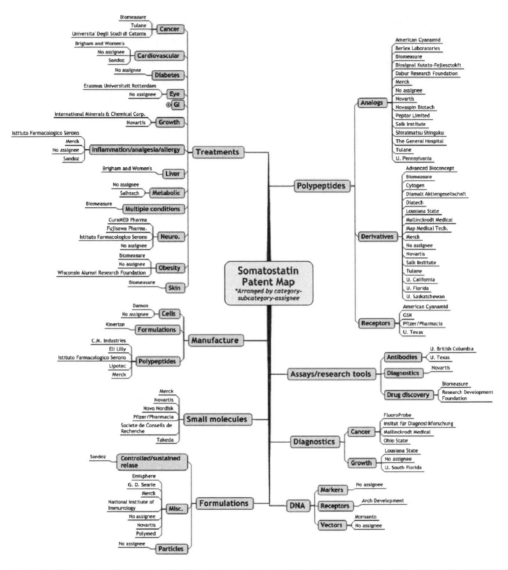

EXHIBIT 5.2   Branching Patent Map Showing Players in the Somatostatin Space

the somatostatin map from this high level shows that the greatest activity in terms of numbers of players is in the space of polypeptide analogs and polypeptide derivatives. Similarly, the small molecules (made of organic, not peptide molecules) section of the map also reveals significant patent activity. This is to be expected, since once a polypeptide has been shown to have a likely pharmaceutical utility, a typical next step is to identify peptide analogs and derivatives that have improved properties relative to the natural version. As knowledge about the natural peptide and its analogs and derivatives grows, companies develop small organic molecules that have the same kinds of pharmaceutical utility. The small molecules are usually less expensive to manufacture and easier to deliver into the patient as a medicine than the peptide versions. At the time this map was made, Merck, Novartis, Novo Nordisk, Pfizer, Takeda, and Societé de Conselis de Reserche were all working on small molecule mimics of somatostatin.

The formulation (e.g., the liquids, tablets, capsules taken by the patient) is usually the final optimization step of a drug product. Thus when R&D drug companies have significant patent portfolios protecting formulations for a drug, this suggests that the company may be farther along in the development path than other companies who lack such patents. Companies focused on formulation technology may also file formulations patents that seek to capture value downstream on their value chains by providing formulation solutions to drug developers. A quick scan of the map can suggest a variety of these patent tactics to a person who is familiar with the industry and its practices.

Companies working in this example somatostatin space must be concerned about infringing the patents of others. After all, the landscape includes numerous patents and a large number of companies to be concerned about. One particular area of concern would be broad fundamental patents that protect techniques used in everyday research that almost everyone working in the area could potentially infringe. On the somatostatin patent map, examples of such fundamental patents are receptors and assays, which may be required by almost any company developing a somatostatin-related drug product. A company might not automatically look for patents in these areas, but the patent map brings them to light and highlights them as possible risk factors.

A variety of patent maps can be made using the branching map approach. Patent maps are easy to make. For example, they can be made using Excel® pivot tables and mind-mapping programs such as MindManager® software. While shown here in black and white, the addition of color adds a new dimension of information. For example, individual patents can be color coded to reveal their age so that newer patents with longer terms are distinguishable from older patents with shorter terms. Patent documents owned by universities can be flagged as potential inlicensing candidates. Problem areas can be highlighted, as can patents with extensive global patent filings. Other techniques for communicating visually on a patent map include spatial relationships, icons, shapes, fonts, and the like.

Exhibit 5.3 shows a simplified patent filing rate chart showing activity of key players over time. Filing rate charts like this one can provide a variety of strategic insights into the activities of the players in a space over

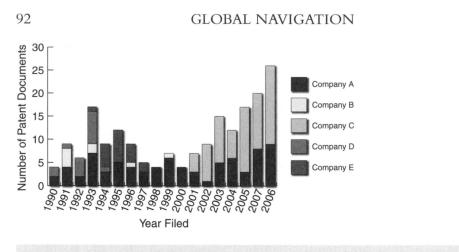

EXHIBIT 5.3   Patent Filing Rate Chart Showing Activity of Key Players Over Time

time. This chart shows, for example, that Company A has been actively filing patent applications in this area for many years. Company B and Company D were active in the 1990s but have not been heard from since. Company C has been very active in the space since 2001. This chart has been simplified for publication, and so the number of observations is limited. However, in many cases, such charts include hundreds of patent documents and many companies and nonprofit organizations. When a group of people work together to analyze one of these charts, the insights can be quite revealing.

Exhibit 5.4 is similar to Exhibit 5.3 but shows technologies over time. Charts like this one can help a company to discern changes in technology focus over time. In the example, Technology A was the subject of significant activity in the late 1990s, but interest appears to have tailed

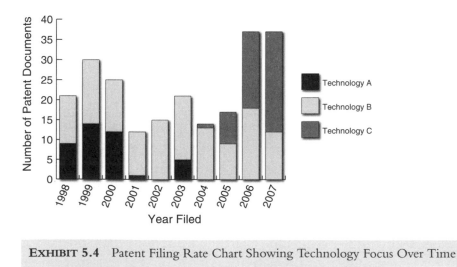

EXHIBIT 5.4   Patent Filing Rate Chart Showing Technology Focus Over Time

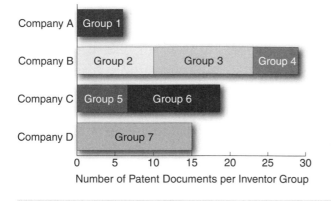

EXHIBIT 5.5   Comparison of Key Inventor Groups by Company

off. Technology B has been the subject of consistent attention from 1998 to 2007. Technology C appears to be an important new technology, as evidenced by significant recent investment in patent protection. Imagine a chart showing the technology trends in your patent space over the last 20 years. What do you think you would see?

Exhibit 5.5 shows a comparison of key inventor groups by company. This kind of analysis suggests which company's inventors are pushing the technology space forward and/or capturing iProperty ground more quickly. The map reveals that Company A has only one key inventor group in the space, in contrast to company C, which has two, and Company B, which has three. If you are company A, you have to ask how are you going to compete with Companies B and C, which appear to have developed significantly more idea-generating power in your space. Similarly, if Company A's Group 1 revolves around a single person, the company's idea-generating potential is at risk: It is subject to significant loss if the key inventor leaves to go to another company. Its Group 1 appears to be less productive on average than the other groups represented. Company A needs to ask itself how it can increase the productivity of Group 1, and it may want to consider whether there are key inventors in the other groups that it would like to recruit. On the other hand, Companies B and C may identify key inventors that they must retain and take steps to ensure their retention.

Do you know how your company's inventors are performing in comparison with your competitors' inventors?

Companies can also use patent mapping to identify the inventors that Lee Fleming and Matt Marx have termed *gatekeepers*.[10] The pair studied relationships among more than 2 million inventors in U.S. patents and identified a group of key inventors who "span organizational boundaries and accelerate the process of invention by contributing to and capitalizing on inter-firm spillovers of important knowledge." Companies can identify their own gatekeepers and those in their industries at large by studying clusters of inventors in their patent landscapes. As pointed out by Fleming and Marx, these individuals can be very valuable to an organization, but they typically pose management challenges. Moreover, like star athletes, they can be difficult to retain. These issues can be addressed once gatekeepers are identified. Can you identify the gatekeepers in your company? How about the gatekeepers in your industry? In other countries? The global mobility of inventors and innovators combined with their social relationships with other inventors and innovators creates a greatly enlarged dynamic system of linkages among people at the forefront of creating value and poses additional iProperty-related risks.

These are just a few of the many kinds of visual representations that a company might develop to gain a better understanding of the iProperty space in which it is operating. A variety of other approaches are possible. Our coauthor Tom Hunt likes to create a visual framework for the searches first, along the lines of the frameworks shown in Chapter 8, to provide boundaries for the search and to organize the output in a way that makes business/technical sense. According to this approach, the framework fits the company's understanding of its business. Therefore, when search results are mapped against it, the data will take on immediate meaning to that business. Coauthor Bill Barrett likes to focus the search on topics of relevance to the company's strategy, and then develop the framework for displaying the data through an iterative interaction with the data itself. This approach permits a company to identify important questions and issues that it may not identify if it is too rigorous in shaping the output from the outset. Coauthor Chris Price loves the presentation, regardless of the method used, to facilitate decisions of his iProperty teams.

Visually represented data facilitates strategic observations that would not be possible with a traditional patent table or a stack of patents. It also teases out insights that patent counsel are not typically looking for when they delve into the details of a set of patents to conduct a freedom-to-operate study. Keep in mind that the visual representation of the data is never the final word. It does not give answers; it only raises questions and suggests answers. It is up to smart people to use good judgment and dig more deeply as needed to find the right interpretation.

PHASE II: FREEDOM TO OPERATE

Assume that you have mapped out the patent data in your particular technology or product space. You have a better understanding of the players in the space, who is doing what, which ones are the hot new entrants and which ones are heading for retirement, and the kinds of technologies that various players are using to solve the problems you are solving. You have gained a number of strategic insights based on high-level information and have adjusted your strategy accordingly. And you have identified groups of patent documents that are highly relevant to your plans. Now you must move to the next level of detail and analyze the highly relevant patents to determine whether it is likely that you will infringe.

FTO Is a Difficult Problem

FTO is about avoiding infringement. Infringing someone else's patent can result in legal expenses, money damages, and even court orders to stop selling a product or cease operation of a manufacturing plant. The consequences can be devastating, as Microsoft found out in the Lucent case discussed earlier. The amount of money spent on legal fees alone to defend such a case is a major imposition for a large company and can bankrupt a small company.

FTO management is a thorny business for a number of reasons. First, any aspect of a product or process could be the infringing actor. For example, in something as simple as a drug product, the active ingredient, various crystalline forms of the active ingredient, any of the formulation components, a specific ratio of formulation components, coatings, capsule materials, treatment methods, and even the packaging could infringe. Second, the complexity is compounded by the fact that more and more patents are granted every year. According to the U.S. Patent Office's Web site, since 2000, the office has issued an average of about 164,000 patents per year.[11] The number of U.S. patents issued has climbed on average by about 7,000 patents per year since 2000, with 196,404 patents issuing in 2006. Factor in the need for FTO in multiple countries around the world, and the analyst clearly has a full-time job.

Why not create an iProperty intranet dashboard through which all key decision makers in your company can access information about your iProperty and your competitors' iProperty at the level of detail that makes the most sense for them?

Screening Out Clearly Noninfringed Patents

As indicated in Exhibit 5.1, Phase II of the patent landscape assessment process involves screening out clearly noninfringed patents. This screening step starts with the set of specifically relevant patents identified during the searching and screening steps. Experienced patent counsel must be consulted for a detailed analysis of the patent claims and the descriptive portions of the patents in light of relevant legal principles. The patent counsel's job is to assess whether the planned product or process appears to infringe the claims. He or she divides the patents into two sets: one set of patents that will clearly not be infringed and a second set of patents that are in a gray zone; that is, it is difficult to be certain whether they would be infringed. For the first set of patents, the patent counsel can prepare a formal FTO opinion. The FTO opinion lists relevant claims from the clearly noninfringed patents, compares them to the proposed product or process, and explains why they will not be infringed. Patents in the gray zone are moved to phase III for a more in-depth analysis.

PHASE III: THE HARD PART

In a best-case scenario, all patents are dealt with in Phase II, and no patents remain in the gray zone for further analysis. For patent documents requiring Phase III analysis, the patent counsel must often dig through thousands of pages of legally and technically detailed documents to identify whether there is an acceptable path forward. The first step is to identify any remaining patents that are, upon further analysis, not infringed. Then, if any patents remain that appear to be infringed, the patent counsel conducts research to determine whether the patents are valid and enforceable.

Analyze Potentially Infringed Patents

In this step, the level of detail in the analytical process becomes excruciating, as the patent counsel conducts a formal infringement analysis. The counsel must carefully analyze the meaning of the patent claims in light of the description of the innovation in the patent specification, the file history of the patent, and the relevant legal principles. The file history is a detailed record of the back-and-forth debate between the patent office and the applicant over whether the innovation claimed in the patent application is patentable. Because file histories are usually hundreds and often thousands of pages in length, this process is time consuming and expensive. If the conclusion of this infringement analysis is that the product does not infringe, the appropriate output is a noninfringement opinion clearly explaining the legal and technical rationale for this conclusion. A well-reasoned noninfringement opinion has evolved as the standard under U.S. patent law to show that the infringer had a good faith belief that it would not infringe the patent in question. This good faith belief protects the infringer against charges of willful infringement and can induce a court to forgo awarding enhanced damages if the company is later found to infringe the patent.

Analyze Clearly Infringed Patents

By this step, which concludes Phase III of the patent landscape assessment process, there should be no more patents to analyze. The relevant legal opinions have established that the product strategy will not result in infringement of any patents. If necessary, the company has modified its strategy to avoid infringed patents and/or licensed or purchased necessary patent rights. However, if a patent remains that would clearly be infringed by the company's product or process, and acquiring the patent or a license is not an option, the only remaining choices are to change the product design or ditch the product altogether to avoid infringement, knowingly infringe and risk a painful patent lawsuit, or show that the patent is invalid. If the company has waited too long in the process and has scaled up a manufacturing process, making changes in the product design can be incredibly expensive. But knowingly infringing a patent is not a good idea unless the company has millions in unwanted cash—willful infringement can result in triple damages in patent lawsuits.

Yet demonstrating that the patent is invalid can be difficult and risky. Courts operate under the presumption that the patent office has done its job properly in issuing the patent, and this presumption can be overcome only by clear and convincing evidence of facts to the contrary. This standard stacks the deck against one who would challenge the validity of a patent. Nevertheless, the patent office does make mistakes—lots of them, actually. Establishing a case for invalidity is often appropriate, especially where issued claims are unduly broad and prior publications can be found describing products or processes that fit within the scope of the patent's broad claims.

The process of analyzing the validity of a patent and preparing an invalidity opinion requires an independently thinking, technically savvy and creative patent counsel who can conduct an exhaustive search of all relevant information that was publicly available prior to the filing date of the patent in question. Examples of information that must be reviewed include patents and scientific literature. The analysis also requires detailed review of the file history and may require extensive legal research to elucidate various relevant points of law. For the law firm writing the opinion and its client, the damage caused by an inadequate or inaccurate opinion is high. Consequently, the amount of analysis and hand wringing by the law firm preparing the opinion is correspondingly high and correspondingly expensive.

Finally, while we have described the steps of Phase III with specific reference to the U.S. landscape, which usually requires the greatest analytical and documentary detail, the analysis should include the patent landscapes of other economically important countries, particularly countries where the company plans to set up manufacturing or distribution operations and/or sell a significant amount of product.

MASTERING THE PATENT LANDSCAPE

There is much more to analyzing the patent landscape than just identifying and dealing with the worst land mines. The world's patent databases provide extensive repositories of competitive information rich in strategic and technical details and available to anyone who takes the time to look. A systematic approach to mastering the patent landscape starts with planning and searching to create a living, breathing database stocked and consistently updated with information about competitors' patent portfolios. This database can be used to create visual representations of the patent landscape that reveal strategic facts that would otherwise be hidden in hundreds or thousands of pieces of data. Information about the extent to which a company is investing in various problems, technologies, and products can shed light on company strategy well in advance of product launches. Visual representations also can be used to help senior management quickly gain a high-level understanding of the company's own patents as well as how those patents stack up against the patent portfolios, practices, and strategies of competitors, suppliers, customers, and potential licensees.

In addition to developing a high-level understanding of the patent landscape, companies must analyze infringement risks and adjust product designs as needed to avoid infringement of patents of hungry competitors with well-funded war chests. In some cases, companies can purchase or in-license required patent rights. The earlier in the product development process that a problem patent is identified, the easier and less expensive it is to formulate a response. No executive wants to see his or her company embroiled in expensive patent litigation, much less pay expensive damages or see a valuable factory shut down by a court order. For small companies, the cost of litigation alone can be enough to bury them. Even Bill Gates must flinch at a $1.5 billion damages award. It may not be impossible to eliminate the risk of a patent infringement suit completely; however, with an effective, systematic process, companies can analyze risk and take action to significantly reduce and manage the risk.

NOTES

1. Vonage, Inc. corporate Web site, "Timeline," www.vonage.com/corporate/about_timeline.php.
2. Ben Charney, "Amazon Strikes Back at IBM with Lawsuit," *Wall Street Journal Online* (December 15, 2006).
3. MediaTek, "Sanyo Agree to End Patent Disputes," *Wall Street Journal Online* (June 7, 2007).
4. Vonage "Timeline."
5. Note that there is an 18-month blackout period during which pending patent applications are not publicly available. Thus, lack of patents in the database in April 2006 means that there were no pending applications as of October 2005. Any subsequently filed Vonage patent applications would not be publicly available.
6. Kevin Rivette and David Kline, *Rembrandts in the Attic: Unlocking the Hidden Value of Patents* (Boston: Harvard Business Press, 2000), 104–105.
7. Thomson Scientific, "Products," scientific.thomson.com/products/aureka/ (accessed August 30, 2007).
8. Eric Wagner, interview and e-mail communications with the author, May 2007.
9. Colin Ware, *Information Visualization: Perception for Design*, 2nd ed. (San Francisco: Morgan Kaufmann Publishers, 2004), 23.
10. Lee Fleming and Matt Marx, "Managing Innovation in Small Worlds," *MIT Sloan Management Review* (Fall 2006), 8–9.
11. U.S. Patent & Trademark Office, "Patent Statistics Chart Calendar Years 1963–2006," www.uspto.gov/web/offices/ac/ido/oeip/taf/us_stat.htm.

~ 6 ~

Global Protection

Selecting the Fields of Engagement

In this chapter and Chapter 7, we focus in on a particularly challenging area of iProperty strategy, the global patent strategy. Companies today have numerous opportunities for executing business strategies that are made possible or more effective by patent protections in countries around the world. For example, business opportunities may involve conducting innovation in one of the new innovation hot spots, manufacturing in a low-cost manufacturing center, protecting target markets in foreign countries, or outlicensing protected technologies to companies that can service distant markets. These opportunities are often available in countries where the reliability of patent protection is uncertain, which complicates assessments of risks and benefits of patent protection.

It may be difficult, if not impossible, to know whether a patent will be granted, how broad it will be if granted, how long will it take to obtain a granted patent, whether the granted patent will be enforced, and whether the patent will survive scrutiny in a litigation. Patent costs are also a significant consideration, as they are high and difficult to predict. The costs associated with obtaining and enforcing patents vary widely from country to country, and determining the timing and amount of specific costs depends on factors that cannot be readily ascertained, such as the personal attributes of the examiner assigned to review the application in a specific country.

Like it or not, companies entering the international patent arena must contend with a multinational, messy conglomeration of systems, each with its own peculiar deviations from international standards, and each with its own aggregation of individual decision makers exercising personal judgments that affect the timing, cost, and outcome of the process. How is a company to develop a cost-effective and strategically targeted global patenting strategy in this difficult context? We begin to answer this question here by examining some of the key challenges confronted by companies patenting internationally, exploring issues involved in the development of a global patenting strategy, outlining a global patenting strategy decision-making paradigm, and introducing the evaluation of ideas for investment in international patent protection. In Chapter 7, we tie these concepts together in a tool we refer to as the Global Patent Strategy Matrix.

GLOBAL PATENT STRATEGY CHALLENGES

How does your company make decisions about patents? Who has the responsibility for deciding whether to protect an innovation in 5 countries or 50 countries, whether to spend $50,000 or $500,000, or how many innovations to protect at the selected investment level? Most managers would not spend $500,000 on a research project or a piece of equipment without significant forethought and planning; however, it is easy to commit to a $500,000 patent strategy without making a rational assessment as to whether the strategy selected is the best use of the money.

In the Trenches

Here is how costs get out of hand. Patent counsel dispatches a series of letters or e-mails over several months informing you of the deadline for filing patent applications in foreign countries. Failure to adhere to this important deadline will result in significant loss of iProperty rights. The letters accumulate on that special stack in the corner of your office with all the other letters from the patent counsel—or the e-mails become lost in the thousands you keep in your inbox because you do not want to archive anything. Two weeks before the deadline, after a string of phone calls and desperate e-mails, your faithful but now frantic patent counsel stalks you to your office. He or she pleads, "You're going to lose all your foreign patent rights if you don't make a decision!" To avoid further embarrassment, you pony up a list of countries.

Your trusty patent counsel then sprints back to his or her office and posts an assistant at the fax machine and/or e-mail system to manage the process of sending huge faxes and e-mails (with attachments large enough to tax the capacity of almost any system) to foreign agents around the world requesting the filing of a last-minute patent application and ensuring that those communications are actually received and acted on before you lose your rights in the respective countries. In some countries you will accrue exorbitant translation fees as translators work through the night to accurately translate the patent application before the deadline.

You may not realize it, but your patent attorney has now hired on your behalf patent agents in all the countries you selected. These agents are diligently working for you, communicating with their countries' patent offices and with your attorney, prosecuting your application, and billing you by the hour. Not only that, but your attorney is now busy receiving all these communications, writing cover letters interpreting the communications for you, preparing responses to the agents' letters, and, of course, billing you by the hour. You are paying attorney fees, foreign agent fees, translation fees, examination fees, maintenance fees, and so on. The bills will not stop coming in for years.

The fact remains that for innovator companies, obtaining appropriate patent protection is almost always a crucial component of an iProperty strategy. Substantial patent costs are inevitable. But companies can take steps to ensure that the money invested in protecting innovation is targeted toward protecting the most valuable set of countries where the patents will provide the greatest benefit. The key to this complex patent game is developing a strategy for placing the right chips on the right countries on the worldwide patent playing board.

Staggering Costs

In a July 2003 General Accounting Office (GAO) report assessing the key factors that small businesses should consider in making foreign patent decisions, a panel of experts concluded that "[t]he cost of obtaining, maintaining and enforcing foreign patents is the most significant foreign patent impediment that small businesses encounter."[1] Small companies with more modest international patenting strategies may quickly find themselves on the path toward spending millions as they pursue protection for multiple ideas in countries around the world. Even for large companies, the costs can be staggering. For example, using the Global IP Estimator® software,[2] we estimate the cradle-to-grave cost at $2.5 million for obtaining and maintaining patent protection for a single invention in every country in the world. Considering that most innovative products and services are protected by whole fleets of patents, it is clear that the cost of a complete global patenting strategy is prohibitive for most companies and daunting for even the largest companies.

Of course, cost is one of the most fundamental considerations in making any economic decision, but it is surprising how many companies fail to consider the cost of foreign patent decisions thoroughly. Failure to evaluate this cost accurately leads to two different but critical errors: (1) underestimating the cost and committing to a strategy that is too expensive for the company to sustain, and (2) overestimating the cost and unnecessarily forgoing valuable protection. Either error can have significant negative consequences.

The first error leads to wasted resources that could be better invested elsewhere, say invested in other more valuable iProperty, in research and development, or in important purchases of capital equipment. Patent applications are not like many other investments, such as real estate or equipment, that can readily be sold to help alleviate the cost of making a mistake. When a patent application has to be abandoned because it cannot be supported, its intrinsic value goes to zero. There is no value left in an abandoned patent application.

The second error, overestimating the cost and forgoing valuable protection, leads to lost opportunities, such as an Asian licensing deal that never comes to fruition because there is no iProperty protection for the product in Asia; in other words, no Asian deal is needed, since the product can be freely copied and sold in the target Asian countries without requiring a license.

Unexpected Cost Spikes

Unwary companies may not only experience significant patent expenses, but in any particular year, the expenses can spike through the roof. Exhibit 6.1 shows a simple profile of costs each year for 20 years for supporting a single patent application that is filed in a small group of countries around the world. The costs reflect a modest strategy in which the U.S. provisional, Patent Cooperation Treaty (PCT) and European Patent Office (EPO) procedures are used to obtain patents in the United States, Japan, Canada, Australia, France, Germany, Italy, Netherlands, Poland, Spain, and United Kingdom (see Exhibit 6.5 for a depiction of these pathways).[3] Exhibit 6.2 shows a cost profile for a 20-year budget based on the assumption that the company starts in year 1 filing two provisional patent applications per year and ultimately files each patent application in this same group of countries.

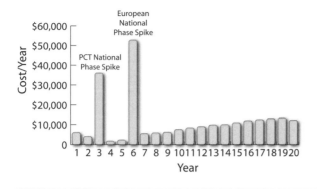

EXHIBIT 6.1   Cradle-to-Grave Costs for a One-Patent Application Filed in a Standard Set of Countries

As illustrated in Exhibit 6.1, the cost profile includes extreme spikes that can come as a big surprise to the unwary. The spike in year 3 occurs when the *international* PCT application becomes *national/regional* (i.e., the single international application must then be filed in multiple national or regional patent offices in order to mature into a portfolio of national patents). This means that, according to our sample strategy, the international PCT application from a U.S. company is filed in national patent offices of Japan, Canada, and Australia and in Europe's regional patent office, the EPO. A global patenting strategy that includes more countries or one that includes the same countries but multiple patent families protecting multiple ideas would result in a larger cost spike.

The second spike, in year 6, is caused by the entry of the EPO application into the National Phase in Europe, at which time the granted application is registered in each of the selected European countries. Much of this cost is based on the requirement that the application be translated into the various national languages of the selected set of countries. Like the PCT National Phase, our sample European National Phase includes a limited set of European countries: France, Germany, Italy, the Netherlands, Poland, Spain, and United Kingdom. Filing in a larger set of European countries or filing multiple patent applications in Europe would result in a larger spike. While the first spike is highly predictable, the time between filing the EPO patent application and the EPO National Phase is unpredictable, so the six-year spike could come in years 4, 5, 6, 7, and so on. Note that as we are writing this book, the European Commission is considering reducing or eliminating the translation burden, which would help to reduce the size of the European National Phase spike.

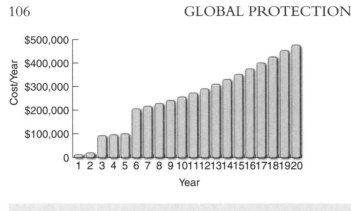

EXHIBIT 6.2 Cumulative Cradle-to-Grave Costs for Filing Two Provisional Patent Applications per Year Followed by Filing in a Standard Set of Countries

Assume that the company is a startup company. It cruises along, as shown in Exhibit 6.2, for the first couple of years with expenses in the range of $10,000 to $25,000 per year. Then suddenly in the third year, the company's expenses jump up to the $70,000 to $90,000 range. And then around year 6, the expenses jump to almost $200,000. This amount covers only two new applications per year using the filing strategy described above. Many startup companies need to file more than two applications per year and/or they need to protect their innovations in more countries than those included in our modest list. The cost listed also leaves out the many continuation applications that are typically necessary to fully protect a technology (and the U.S. Patent & Trademark Office is currently attempting to implement new rules that would make continuation applications even more expensive). If not carefully controlled, in just a few years, patent expenses can overwhelm the budget of a small company. Even large companies filing tens or hundreds of new patent applications per year are not immune to the pain of overwhelming patent costs.

Cost-Benefit Analysis

Clearly, given the cost of protecting an innovation in multiple countries, developing a patenting strategy is no trivial matter. Failing to patent in a critical country can exact a significant cost in lost opportunities because ideas can be freely copied in countries where there is no patent protection. However, no company can afford to patent an idea in every country. It is tempting to decide whether to file a patent application in a specific country based on whether investment in that specific country is expected to yield an increase in profit (compared to the profit, if any, that would accrue in the absence of the investment) that exceeds the cost of protecting the idea. Even the GAO report discussed earlier characterized the cost issue as hinging on "whether the range of benefits that foreign patents may provide to [the company], such as increasing sales or the company's value, are sufficient to justify their cost."[4]

Of course, the validity of this statement depends on the meaning of the word *cost*. If cost means *resources invested in obtaining the patent*, we would agree that it is important to rule out a few countries in which the investment is truly not justified by the value of the patent. If, for example, there is no possibility of enforcing a patent in a particular country, then the investment of acquiring a patent is not warranted. If there is no market in a country for a product, and the country has no relevant manufacturing capability or market for the product or services in question, then again the investment will not be justified by the return.

But ruling out countries in which the benefits of patenting clearly do not justify the resources invested in obtaining the patent does not, in the case of most innovations, reduce the total cost of filing patents in the remaining countries to an extent sufficient to satisfy budget constraints. The fact is that in many countries, the *potential benefits* of having a patent almost always justify the cost, if cost is narrowly defined as the resources invested in obtaining the patent. It may sound like a good deal to pay $10,000 for a Czechoslovakian patent and a chance to make an extra $1 million in profit. However, what if this choice forces the company to forgo spending the same $10,000 to obtain a U.S. or European patent on a next-generation platform idea? Or what if the $10,000 could be better invested in a critical proof-of-concept study?

One Texas chief executive told of her straightforward approach: "First you decide what patents you need, then you find the money to get them." Practically speaking, it is rare to have such access to capital, and if you don't, you will have to make some tough choices. In some cases, the $10,000 patent with the chance of making an extra $1 million may not be worth the *opportunity cost*. Most companies have limited resources to invest in protecting ideas. After all, they must use most of their resources to develop ideas into products, manufacture products, and take them to market. Companies seeking to develop an iProperty portfolio that includes a global patent portfolio must determine in which countries the potential benefits are likely to justify the resources invested in obtaining the patent. To meet budget constraints, companies usually must also identify a subset of these countries likely to maximize the return on the resource investment.

The opportunity cost is the most important cost to consider in the cost-benefit analysis that must be undertaken to determine how much to invest in global patent protection for a company's ideas. The best way to account for opportunity cost is to determine, in light of the company's technology and business strategies, what portion of a company's limited resources can be used to protect its ideas. Then divide this budget up among the ideas, investing a greater proportion of the iProperty budget and company resources to protect more valuable ideas and less to protect others. Thus, the opportunity cost is considered in the context of developing a budget that accounts for other investments being made by the company, such as those in research and development. Although this method does not specify how much of a company's budget should be allocated to investment in iProperty, there really is no rule of thumb for making this strategic decision. The value of iProperty relative to other investments differs for every company depending on the kind of technology it is developing and the kind of strategy it is using to deliver value to its customer.

Once the budget is established, informed decisions can be made by evaluating all of the iProperty opportunities relative to each other. The U.S. National Institutes of Health research grants system illustrates this process nicely by analogy. All applications for grants are first reviewed and either accepted or rejected for entry into the formal peer-review process. The accepted applications are then reviewed and given a numerical score and ranked ordered by that score. Reviewed grant applications so ranked are then funded in descending order until the total grant budget is reached (the funding line), after which none of the lower-ranked grants can be funded. Exceptions are made in this process (e.g., for first-time applicants or other special circumstances). In similar manner, the process for developing a global patenting strategy should be methodical but also flexible.

What Is the Patent Worth?

So far, we have been discussing the cost part of the cost-benefit analysis. Now we move on to consider the benefit portion. The value of a patent is the difference between the revenue that the company would generate with the patent and the revenue that it would generate without the patent. Or, as stated by Alexander Poltorak, chief executive of the intellectual property management firm, General Patent Corporation, "the incremental value of the enhanced cash flows resulting from the [patent] monopoly."[5] Of course, there are many problems in making this determination. For one thing, there is uncertainty as to the effectiveness of any patent. Even in developed countries with mature and operable patent systems, a patent can be invalidated during litigation, and a competitor may choose to initiate competitive activities that would infringe a patent based on its assessment that the patent would not withstand a litigated validity challenge. Furthermore, given the 20-year life span of a patent, coupled with the rapid and global pace of innovation and economic development, it can be daunting to predict, using classical discounted value analysis, whether an investment will deliver expected value in a developed country with a strong patent system; analysis of geographical regions that 20 years ago were not given even cursory consideration (e.g., India, China) is even more difficult.

Fortunately, when it comes to developing a patenting strategy, this kind of detailed assessment is not necessary. Instead, given an established budget for protecting ideas, companies should focus on ranking countries in which patenting is possible, based on a surrogate marker of potential value and other relevant factors. One such surrogate marker is Purchasing Power Parity adjusted Gross Domestic Product (PPP-GDP). PPP-GDP essentially compares countries' GDPs on a common scale of purchasing power, indicating how much purchasing power is produced by the country's economy. Other factors (e.g., strength of IP laws and enforcement measures) being equal, an economy with a greater PPP-GDP is likely to yield more value to the patent holder than an economy with less PPP-GDP. However, discussed in further detail later in this chapter, specific market figures or anticipated product sales are an even better measure.

Exhibit 6.3 illustrates the relationship among several countries with respect to cost of procuring and maintaining patent protection compared to the PPP-GDP of those countries. Relative to the other countries shown, the United States is clearly a good deal. The cost of obtaining protection is low and the PPP-GDP accessed is high. The Czech Republic is not such a good deal relative to Israel, Australia, and Canada, each of which accesses more PPP-GDP for less patent cost. When developing a global patenting strategy, it is helpful to prepare a chart like this one, comparing the cost of procuring and maintaining patent protection with the value of the market (or a surrogate that is likely to be proportional to the market's value) for your product in the target countries.

DEVELOPING A GLOBAL STRATEGY

Developing a global patenting strategy requires consideration of numerous complex issues. Thoroughly analyzing these issues each time a new idea is being considered for patent protection would be virtually impossible.

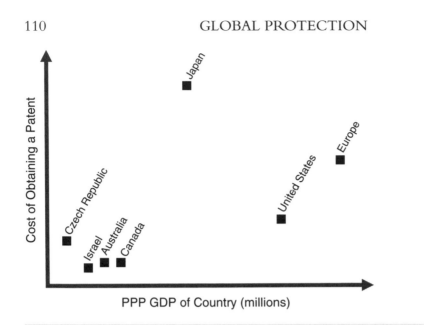

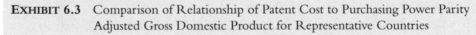

PPP GDP of Country (millions)

EXHIBIT 6.3   Comparison of Relationship of Patent Cost to Purchasing Power Parity
Adjusted Gross Domestic Product for Representative Countries

But this is exactly the approach that most companies take. In fact, not only do they attempt to make this analysis every time they have to make an international patenting decision, they often attempt to compact it into 15 or 20 minutes right before the deadline. The result, as you might expect, is that over a period of several years, the company develops an international patent portfolio with patent investments in countries where the investment is not justified and patents omitted in countries where protection would have provided significant value. To avoid mistakes, it pays to establish a global patenting strategy process that takes into account the numerous complexities and provides a simplified evaluation process that can be applied to the company's ideas well in advance of the moment when the patent counsel is clinging to your heels in the hallway pleading for a list of countries.

The patent prosecution process is deadline intensive. A few of the many important deadlines include those for:

- Deciding whether to file an international application under the PCT
- Deciding whether to file patent applications in countries that are not members of the PCT
- Filing national applications based on a PCT application
- Registering applications in European countries based on an EPO application

Once these deadlines have lapsed without filing the appropriate papers, the associated patent rights are permanently extinguished, nada, nil, gone forever. One of the most difficult aspects of implementing a working patent strategy is coming to grips with the timing of decisions. Decisions made under pressure at the last minute are likely to produce outcomes that are less desirable than decisions thoughtfully made well in advance of the deadline.

Patent firms typically use docketing systems to track filing deadlines. If your patent counsel is like most, he or she sits in the office with a comprehensive list of deadlines, identifies important deadlines, and sends out an endless series of discrete form letters notifying you of the deadlines and, of course, charging you for each letter. If you are like most clients, the letters wind up in that special patent attorney letter stack in the corner of your office. Essentially, you are paying the patent counsel to help clutter your office. In theory, this practice may protect the patent attorney from legal liability if you miss a deadline and lose important patent rights. But in reality, this process takes a useful, compiled set of information about deadlines and changes it into a less useful, distributed set of information. To make the information truly useful, you would have to recompile it into another list.

Why not skip this inefficient process and ask your patent counsel for a list of global patenting strategy decisions coming up in the next year? Then you can schedule a series of monthly meetings with appropriate decision makers to work through the costs and issues and ensure that these significant, expensive decisions are made well in advance of the deadlines to take full advantage of your patent strategy. The patent counsel may resist, but you are paying the bills. And, in the end, isn't the patent counsel more protected by communicating with you in a manner that makes it easier for you to meet deadlines and avoid losing patent rights?

Many companies recognize their need for a global patenting strategy only after the bills start pouring in. Preparing such a strategy requires an initial time commitment, as the team gathers the information and assembles appropriate decision makers to reflect on your capabilities, op-portunities, and values; consider the value of patent protection in various countries for your ideas; and make a plan that is in step with the timing of the patenting process. However, this initial time investment can pay big dividends as the company streamlines the decision-making process, eliminates last-minute decisions, reduces patent costs, and builds a strate-gically targeted patent portfolio with patent chips well placed on the worldwide patent playing board.

Evaluating Competitor Strategies

The geographical distribution of patents varies widely among industries and even among products within an industry. One way to get a feel for the countries in which patents are valued by a particular industry is to conduct a worldwide patent search on the key patents covering similar products of successful competitors. Exhibit 6.4 shows a quick view of patenting strategies for a group of competitor companies. The darker the shading, the more heavily the company files in that country. A similar chart could show geographic patent concentrations for various technology fields relevant to the company's business. These kinds of analyses provide a baseline for thinking about your own global patenting strategy. Of course, serious iProperty companies will want to think beyond the baseline to determine whether their competitors are all marching off the same cliff or whether there are opportunities that the competitor group is missing.

In addition to the industry-specific or product-specific analysis, factors such as patentability, patent strength, and market size vary from country

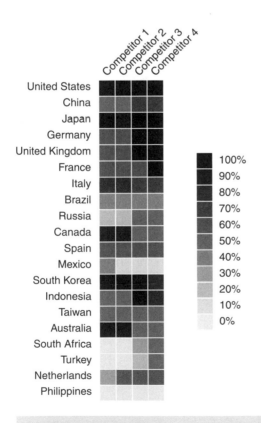

EXHIBIT 6.4   Quick View of Competitors' Global Filing Strategy

to country. Some countries, such as the United States, Japan, and those in Western Europe, have consistently strong patent protection and substantial markets. Other countries, such as India and China, have substantial markets but relatively weak patent protection. Still other countries have small markets and weak protection. To further complicate matters, this landscape can be expected to change often during the pendency of the application and/or during the 20-year term of the issued patent. These are difficult issues to wrestle with, but taking the time to work through a global patenting strategy is worth the investment. It may save the company from costly mistakes.

Evaluating the Existing Portfolio

For companies with an existing portfolio, of patents and patent applications a first step in implementing a global patenting strategy is to apply the strategy to the portfolio. What patent chips does the company own, and where are they placed on the worldwide playing board? Remember all those foreign agents that you hired? Does the global patenting strategy suggest the need to reduce or eliminate patent expenditures in certain countries so that the company can focus its resources on countries offering a better return or on other nonpatent investments, such as research and development, brainpower, or critical physical assets? Can any value be readily extracted by outlicensing or selling off portions of the existing portfolio? By jettisoning existing patent applications that are not justified, the company can free up funds to protect other ideas, invest in areas other than iProperty, and, for venture funded companies, survive to the next round of financing.

DECISION-MAKING PARADIGM

With these considerations in mind, we now outline a simple, rational, step-by-step approach for developing a foreign patenting strategy:

1. Assign a relative value to the idea.
2. Develop a Global Patent Strategy Matrix (see Chapter 7) based on comparative:
   a. Costs in each county
   b. Market potential in each country
   c. Enforcement risks in each country

3. Use the Global Patent Strategy Matrix to select a set of countries that is tailored to the current and expected characteristics and life cycle of the product being protected and that represents the highest value for the deployment of the resources invested.

4. Evaluate the selected countries to identify whether there are additional strategic considerations—ones that might suggest eliminating or adding specific countries to the list (e.g., the possibility of market growth beyond that used in step 3).

We focus on step 1 in the remainder of this chapter. In Chapter 7, we explore steps 2 to 4.

Assigning a Relative Value

Our decision-making paradigm starts with assigning a relative value to each idea that is being considered for protection. Assigning value requires examining each idea in light of a documented evaluation methodology with a consistent set of evaluation parameters. Chapter 11 discusses scoring of ideas. The evaluation parameters used to evaluate ideas for protection should be tailored to the company's business strategy. In an evaluation, each idea is scored according to the parameters. The company's ideas can then be sorted by the total evaluation score to place each idea at a relative position in a hierarchy of importance to the company's business strategy.

Having a *documented* methodology for evaluating ideas permits the company to regularly test and refine the assumptions of the evaluation methodology. The evaluation methodology itself should evolve as the company's strategic needs evolve. For example, if the company's strategy is revised to make aftermarket repair an important aspect of revenue-generating activities, then ideas related to the aftermarket repair service may become more valuable and warrant greater investment.

Can you rank order all of the patents in your portfolio from most important to least important?

Further, a documented and *routinely applied* methodology leads to consistent and efficient assessments of value, as opposed to an ad-hoc approach in which any particular decision maker may apply a different standard. Ideas can be evaluated periodically to determine whether factors have changed that would lead to a revised evaluation and thus to a change in the strategy for protecting the idea. For example, the company may find that an idea evaluated last year is technically difficult to enable. Reevaluation this year should lower the unworkable idea in the company's ranked list, possibly so low as to result in a discontinuation of all iProperty expenses related to it. New work may have demonstrated an inexpensive and easy way to enable an idea that was poorly enabled when it was evaluated last year. Reevaluation here may result in increased investment in the protection of the newly enabled idea.

Aligning Investment with Value

Rank ordering ideas is a useful practice whether the company is just starting up and proactively planning the development of a patent portfolio or whether it is reassessing the strategy for a new portfolio. Rank-ordered ideas can be grouped by score and targeted for different levels of investment, as shown in Exhibit 6.5. The chart illustrates a simple global patenting strategy in which ideas being protected are grouped into three categories: low value, moderate value, and high value. For example, the

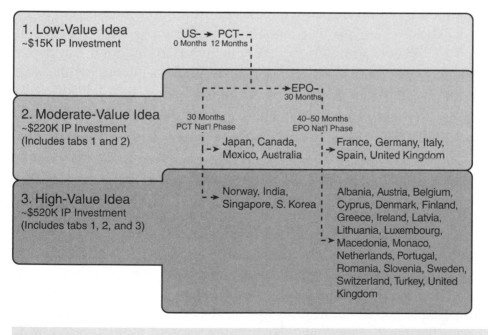

EXHIBIT 6.5 Sample Global Patent Strategy

company may rank order 100 ideas. Of these, it may decide that 35 ideas have scores that are high enough to warrant protection, 10 may be high-value, 20 may be moderate-value, and 5 may be low-value ideas that have a potential to move up in ranking depending on the outcome of additional work related to the ideas.

The dollar amounts shown are the potential cradle-to-grave costs for pursuing the strategy selected. It is important to keep the numbers in front of the decision makers so that they understand what they are committing to when they assign an idea to a level of protection; however, in some cases, something less than cradle-to-grave costs will suffice. For example, the amount that matters most to a startup company that plans to sell within three years is the amount required to support the patent portfolio for three years.

The countries listed are for a sample global patenting strategy, in which a patent application protecting the idea is filed in all countries listed, depending on the value of the idea. High-value ideas are filed in the countries listed in tabs 1, 2, and 3. Moderate-value ideas are filed in the countries listed in tabs 1 and 2. Low-value ideas are filed in the countries listed in tab 1.

Note that for low-value ideas, a provisional patent application and a PCT patent application are filed. Neither of these patent applications actually yields a patent. In both cases, regular national patent applications must be filed based on the earlier applications in order for a patent to be granted. The net result is that investment in the provisional application and the PCT application keep the company's options open to protect the idea in most countries of the world. However, a low-value idea will not receive additional investment in obtaining a patent beyond this initial investment unless it is reevaluated and moves up in priority to moderate value or high value.

Timing and Reevaluation

As we discuss further in Chapter 12, most of the world's patent systems operate in a first-to-file manner, meaning that if two companies file patent applications to protect the same invention, the company that was first to file its patent application has priority over the other company. Because of this need to rush patent applications to the patent office, ideas often must be protected in patent applications before they can be fully evaluated for commercial value. For example, the products a patent protects often are at an early stage of conception when a patent application is filed. And while the company may know how to implement an idea, the implementation may be too expensive to be commercially feasible, and it may be months or years before the company knows whether it is possible to meet the cost constraints needed to achieve a price that the market can bear. Fortunately, the world's patent system is timed so that the investment required to protect an idea in multiple countries is spread out over a number of years. This flexibility relieves some of the pressure, but it does not make the process painless.

As an example, consider the simple filing strategy illustrated in Exhibit 6.5. International protection can start with an inexpensive national application, represented here from the U.S. perspective as a provisional patent application filed in the United States at 0 months (the "priority date"). The provisional patent application secures a filing date and gives the applicant one year to further develop or test the idea being protected. If the research relating to the idea is moving at a fast pace, it is useful during this one-year period to file multiple provisional patent applications, each adding and protecting new details about the idea.

At 12 months from the priority date, the applicant can file an international patent application under the Patent Cooperation Treaty based on the provisional patent application filed at month 0 (or multiple provisional applications filed at months 0, 4, 8, etc.), which secures protection in most of the world's countries until 30 months from the priority date.

At month 30, the international application must enter PCT National Phase, or all rights will be lost. According to the patent strategy represented in our chart, entering PCT National Phase means that applications covering moderate-value ideas must be filed in Japan, Canada, Mexico, Australia, and the EPO, and applications covering high-value ideas must also be filed in Norway, India, Singapore, and South Korea.

The European patent application will keep rights in European countries active until time to enter European National Phase, which typically occurs at about 40 to 50 months from the priority date. For our sample strategy, this means entering France, Germany, Italy, and the United Kingdom, and further, for a high-value idea, entering the more complete list of European countries shown in tab 3.

If delaying expenses is an important goal, various countries have additional mechanisms for effecting further delays. Some countries, for example, do not begin the expensive examination process until the applicant requests examination.

As a result of the timing requirements just described, reevaluation of the idea being protected makes sense at several points in the process. For example, the idea can be reevaluated just prior to:

- The 12-month deadline for entering the PCT process
- The 30-month deadline for entering the PCT National Phase
- The 40- to 50-month deadline for entering the European National Phase

At each reevaluation, the goal is to provide the best assessment of the value of the idea and to avoid the twin mistakes of overinvesting and underinvesting. The reevaluation may result in abandonment of the patent application with no further expense or a change in the planned filing tactics and adjustment of the required investment.

MAXIMIZING GLOBAL PORTFOLIO VALUE

In the global economy, companies that compete based on their ability to conceive and implement novel ideas can protect and sustain the advantages conferred by those ideas in countries around the world using effective global patenting strategies. Companies that fail to consider international patent protection risk missing opportunities to protect markets and/or generate outlicensing revenues. But patenting around the globe can be expensive, and companies that are not prepared risk an unpleasant surprise when invoices start rolling in. Those that want to maximize the value of their portfolios must pay attention to the value of each idea being protected and ensure that the investment in each idea is proportional to its value. The value of patent protection must be assessed in each country, and investments must be made to maximize the value of the global portfolio. All these decisions require a well-conceived, documented global patenting strategy that is in place well in advance of the actual decision. In addition, the global patenting strategy must be revised periodically to ensure that it continues to support the changing business needs of the company. Companies that take the time to invest in such a strategy can avoid costly mistakes and unexpected expenses while maximizing the return on the investment in the patent portfolio.

NOTES

1. General Accounting Office, "International Trade: Experts' Advice for Small Businesses Seeking Foreign Patents," GAO-03-910, June 26, 2003; see also General Accounting Office, "International Trade: Federal Action Needed to Help Small Businesses Address Foreign Patent Challenges," GAO-02-789, July 17, 2002.

2. Global IP Estimator™, produced by Global IP Net (Kihei, Hawaii); data used with permission of Global IP Net.

3. The Patent Cooperation Treaty (PCT) is administered by the World Intellectual Property Organization, a specialized agency of the United Nations. The PCT was concluded in 1970, amended in 1979, and modified in 1984 and 2001. The PCT facilitates pursuit of patent protection for an invention simultaneously in each of a large number of member countries by filing an "international" patent application, commonly referred to as a PCT patent application. The PCT process is divided into two phases, the International Phase and the National Phase. During the International Phase, the PCT patent application is examined by an examining authority at an international level. During the National Phase, the application is further examined at a national level in light of the results of the International Phase examination. Patents coming out of the PCT process are granted only at a national level. There is no international patent.

   The European Patent Office was founded to support innovation, competitiveness, and economic growth for the benefit of the citizens of Europe. The office provides a uniform examination of European patent applications for 37 European countries. It was established in 1973 by the member states of the European Patent Convention, which came into force in 1977. For more information about the EPO, see the office's Web site at www.epo.org/about-us.html.

4. General Accounting Office, "International Trade: Experts' Advice for Small Businesses Seeking Foreign Patents," GAO-03-910, June 26, 2003; see also General Accounting Office, "International Trade: Federal Action Needed to Help Small Businesses Address Foreign Patent Challenges," GAO-02-789, July 17, 2002, 2.

5. Alexander Poltorak, "On Patent Trolls and Other Myths," in *Making Innovation Pay: People Who Turn IP into Shareholder Value,* ed. Bruce Berman (Hoboken, NJ: John Wiley & Sons, Inc., 2006), 60.

~ 7 ~

Global Matrix

Maximizing Return on the iProperty Investment

The Global Patent Strategy Matrix is a simple tool for helping companies to maximize the effectiveness of their investment in a global patent portfolio. The matrix is based on the assumption, as discussed in more detail in Chapter 6, that the primary issue in patent investments is not whether the patent investment justifies the expense of patenting, for it almost always does in isolation. Instead, the issue is how a company balancing out its investments in personnel, research and development, facilities, and the like against its investment in iProperty can invest a limited patent budget in a manner that maximizes return on investment. To identify the set of countries representing the best investment candidates, we use three key inputs for each country under consideration:

1. **Patent cost.** The cost of obtaining a patent
2. **Market protected.** The value of the potential market being protected
3. **Enforcement probability.** The probability that the patent will be effectively enforced

DEVELOPING A GLOBAL PATENT
STRATEGY MATRIX

These inputs can be used to create a Global Patent Strategy Matrix, as shown in Exhibit 7.1. In the matrix, the *y*-axis separates countries by the market protection value, which is equal to patent cost per dollar of

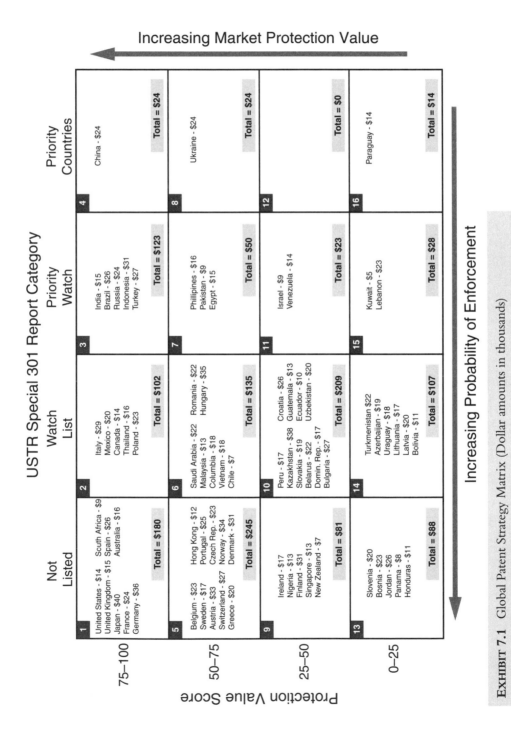

Increasing Market Protection Value

USTR Special 301 Report Category

Protection Value Score

	Not Listed	Watch List	Priority Watch	Priority Countries
75–100	**1** United States - $14, South Africa - $9, United Kingdom - $15, Spain - $26, Japan - $40, Australia - $16, France - $24, Germany - $36 — Total = $180	**2** Italy - $29, Mexico - $20, Canada - $14, Thailand - $16, Poland - $23 — Total = $102	**3** India - $15, Brazil - $26, Russia - $24, Indonesia - $31, Turkey - $27 — Total = $123	**4** China - $24 — Total = $24
50–75	**5** Belgium - $23, Hong Kong - $12, Sweden - $17, Portugal - $25, Austria - $33, Czech Rep. - $23, Switzerland - $27, Norway - $34, Greece - $20, Denmark - $31 — Total = $245	**6** Saudi Arabia - $22, Romania - $22, Malaysia - $13, Hungary - $35, Columbia - $18, Vietnam - $18, Chile - $7 — Total = $135	**7** Phillipines - $16, Pakistan - $9, Egypt - $15 — Total = $50	**8** Ukraine - $24 — Total = $24
25–50	**9** Ireland - $17, Nigeria - $13, Finland - $31, Singapore - $13, New Zealand - $7 — Total = $81	**10** Peru - $17, Croatia - $26, Kazakhstan - $38, Guatemala - $13, Slovakia - $19, Ecuador - $10, Belarus - $22, Uzbekistan - $20, Domin. Rep. - $17, Bulgaria - $27 — Total = $209	**11** Israel - $9, Venezuela - $14 — Total = $23	**12** Total = $0
0–25	**13** Slovenia - $20, Bosnia - $23, Jordan - $26, Panama - $8, Honduras - $11 — Total = $88	**14** Turkmenistan $22, Azerbaijan - $19, Uraguay - $18, Lithuania - $17, Latvia - $20, Bolivia - $11 — Total = $107	**15** Kuwait - $5, Lebanon - $23 — Total = $28	**16** Paraguay - $14 — Total = $14

Increasing Probability of Enforcement

EXHIBIT 7.1 Global Patent Strategy Matrix (Dollar amounts in thousands)

market protected. The expected amount of purchasing power accessed per dollar invested increases with the market protection value. The *x*-axis separates countries by enforcement probability. The probability of successful enforcement increases from right to left. Thus, the top-left cell of the matrix includes countries having the highest market protection value and the highest enforcement probability (i.e., the best and most reliable places to invest in patent protection). The bottom-right cell includes the countries having the lowest market protection value and the lowest enforcement probability (i.e., the worst and least reliable investments).

As we will discuss, the Global Patent Strategy Matrix is a flexible tool that can be adjusted to fit any company's strategy. Next we explain how to prepare a matrix.

Evaluating the Patent Cost

The first parameter considered in the preparation of a Global Patent Strategy Matrix is patent cost. One of the most intractable problems of patent strategy planning relates to budgeting for patent costs. Patent budgets are highly unpredictable, in part because of the unpredictable pace of innovation. Patent applications are also filed in multiple countries, each with its own price structure, examination procedures, and timelines. Some costs, such as the maintenance fees charged by patent offices, are fixed in each country based on a routine schedule and can be readily predicted. Other costs vary predictably; for example, filing fees and grant fees often vary in each country based on the number of pages, claims, and/or drawings in the patent application. Still other costs vary unpredictably (or at least relatively unpredictably) from the perspective of both timing and costs.

An example of a cost that varies unpredictably is the cost incurred when a patent examiner reviews a case and sends out an official action to which the applicant must respond. Official actions typically occur one to three times for each patent application pending in each country. The cost for responding varies depending on the number and complexity of issues raised by the examiner. The timing of official actions and response preparation varies from months to years based on the backlog of each specific patent office as a whole, the backlog of the particular technology group reviewing the application, the idiosyncrasies of the particular examiner who happens to be assigned to the case, and, in some countries, the timing of the request for examination. The cost and timing of preparing a response depends on, for example, the caseload, billing rate and efficiency of the foreign patent agent handling the case and the applicant's local legal counsel, as well as the responsiveness of managers, scientists, and employees involved in helping to formulate responses to the examiner.

Despite the various contingencies, a reasonable degree of patent budget forecasting and planning is possible and necessary. Global IP Net, a company based in Honolulu, has tackled the challenge most effectively. Global IP Net maintains an up-to-date database of cost estimates from patent agents and offices and compiles this information into a software program called Global IP Estimator that enables relatively accurate predictions of patent costs around the world. Global IP Estimator was used for the estimates presented in this book.

When analyzing patent cost as an input to the Global Patent Strategy Matrix, costs can include anything from initial filing costs only to total costs for a set period of years or total cradle-to-grave costs for the entire 20-year patent term. The GAO Report introduced in Chapter 6 emphasizes the need for companies to consider cradle-to-grave costs in their foreign filing predictions. This is good advice, particularly for established companies that plan to maintain patents for the entire *relevant* patent term. The relevant patent term will vary by product life cycle. Thus, for a product with a long development period or product life cycle, such as a novel pharmaceutical drug, the relevant costs may include the entire 20-year, cradle-to grave costs. The matrix in Exhibit 7.1 shows these patent costs.

In some cases, however, it may make sense to develop a matrix using less than the complete cradle-to-grave costs. For a product with a shorter life cycle, the full cradle-to-grave costs may include only those costs needed to keep the patent in force during the life of the product, after which the patents may be abandoned. Similarly, a startup company whose strategy is to build a valuable patent portfolio and sell the company in three to five years may wish to include the portion of the cradle-to-grave costs necessary to support the company through its exit. It may also be useful to operate on a shorter timeline, preparing, for example, a one-to three-year matrix to evaluate the initial phases of the patent investment. Then, three years out, the company can prepare another matrix for the three- to six-year costs for a second evaluation of the budget from that point forward. In the second evaluation, the matrix can be used to evaluate which countries will be cut from the list as the budget timeline progresses. Successful execution of such a phased approach depends on a formal, disciplined, and recurring review of a company's iProperty portfolio by an effective iProperty team.

Appraising the Market Protected

The second parameter to consider in the development of a Global Patent Strategy Matrix is the "market protected," which is used in calculating the protection value score. The market protected parameter is a relative measure for each country under consideration of the value of the relevant market that would be protected by a patent. The values for various countries need not be exact; they need only to be accurately ranked relative to one another. For example, in the sample matrix, we used the PPP-GDP as a surrogate for actual market numbers, based on the assumption that the PPP-GDP would be roughly proportional to product sales in each country. In many cases this assumption may not hold true, but it is useful here to illustrate the matrix approach. We used cradle-to-grave patent costs for our patent cost value divided by PPP-GDP as our market protected value in order to yield the market protection value score that is roughly relative to value of each dollar invested in patent protection in a particular country. The market protection value is used to sort countries in the matrix based on how good the patent deal is in that country; the deals get better as one moves up the matrix.

The approach used for the sample matrix does not take into consideration industries and markets of specific countries, factors that could significantly shift a country's assessed market. In actual practice, the accuracy of the relative value estimate and the reliability of the market protection value score depend greatly on the relative accuracy of the data used to provide the market protected value. A company patenting a new electrical saw for home use could, for example, learn something about markets being protected by comparing countries using PPP-GDP. A more precise evaluation would be based on the amount each country spends on electrical tools for home use, and a still more precise evaluation would be based on the amount each country spends on electrical saws for home use. The most precise evaluation of all would require an accurate prediction in each target country of the difference between expected product revenues with and without the patent in that country.

The amount of purchasing power protected per dollar invested in patenting varies dramatically from country to country. Consider, for example, the evaluation of a patent for validation in Europe following prosecution of a European patent application in the European Patent Office. Patent validation requires that documentation, including translations where appropriate, be filed in each European country before the stated deadline in order to ensure protection in individual European

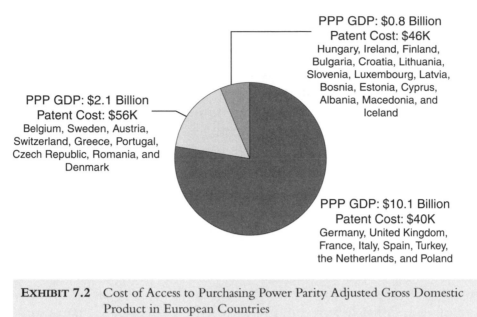

PPP GDP: $0.8 Billion
Patent Cost: $46K
Hungary, Ireland, Finland,
Bulgaria, Croatia, Lithuania,
Slovenia, Luxembourg, Latvia,
Bosnia, Estonia, Cyprus,
Albania, Macedonia, and
Iceland

PPP GDP: $2.1 Billion
Patent Cost: $56K
Belgium, Sweden, Austria,
Switzerland, Greece, Portugal,
Czech Republic, Romania, and
Denmark

PPP GDP: $10.1 Billion
Patent Cost: $40K
Germany, United Kingdom,
France, Italy, Spain, Turkey,
the Netherlands, and Poland

EXHIBIT 7.2   Cost of Access to Purchasing Power Parity Adjusted Gross Domestic
Product in European Countries

countries. Sorting the European countries by a market protection value
score equal to the cost of validating a European patent in that country
divided by PPP-GDP reveals a wide disparity in the cost of protecting
each country's PPP-GDP.

For example, using Global IP Estimator, we estimated that the cost
of validating a 75-page English-language patent application in all available European countries is about $154,000. Initiating our investment in
the countries with the highest market protection value, then moving to
the countries with the smallest market protection value, we found that
protection of the first $10.1 billion PPP-GDP in Europe is estimated to
cost about $40,000 (see Exhibit 7.2). Protection of the next $2.1 billion
PPP-GDP is estimated to cost $56,000. Protection of the final $0.8 billion PPP-GDP is estimated to cost about $46,000. Roughly speaking, the
first third of the potential investment protects a little less than two-thirds
of European GDP, while the last one-third of the potential investment
protects only 6 percent of European GDP.

Assessing the Enforcement Probability

The y-axis of the Global Patent Strategy Matrix separates countries based
on the relative probability that a patent can be enforced there. Again,
developing a measure of enforcement probability is a difficult prospect,

but we can obtain some assistance using the Special 301 Report.[1] Published annually by the U.S. Trade Representative, this report is based on extensive information gathering and analysis by the Trade Representative and information reported by industry. It provides a relatively detailed examination of the adequacy and effectiveness of iProperty protection in 90 countries and categorizes countries based on the adequacy of their iProperty protection, enforcement, and market access for persons relying on such protection. While the purpose of the report is to pressure other countries to live up to their international iProperty obligations, it also serves as a useful source for identifying potential iProperty issues (e.g., cost and risk/benefit) and opportunities for companies developing global business and iProperty strategies.

The 2007 report identified 43 countries with significant problems and placed each in one of four categories:

1. **Section 306 monitoring.** Countries with specific problems raised in earlier reports that resulted in bilateral agreements with the United States that addressed the problems
2. **Priority foreign countries.** Countries pursuing the most onerous or egregious policies that have the greatest adverse impact on U.S. right holders or products
3. **Priority watch list.** Countries that do not provide an adequate level of iProperty rights protection or enforcement or market access for persons relying on iProperty protection
4. **Watch list.** Countries meriting bilateral attention to address the underlying IProperty rights problems

The matrix requires an assessment of enforcement probability, and the sample provided in Exhibit 7.1 uses the Special 301 Report to separate countries into four groups in order of decreasing probability of effective enforcement:

1. **Not listed.** Countries that are not listed in the Special 301 Report are presumed to have the highest probability of effective patent enforcement.
2. **Watch list.** Presumed to have a lower probability of effective patent enforcement than countries in the not-listed category.

3. **Priority watch.** Presumed to have a lower probability of effective patent enforcement than countries in the watch list category.

4. **Priority countries.** Presumed to have the lowest probability of effective patent enforcement.

There are pros and cons to using the Section 301 Report as the basis of the matrix. First and foremost, the report is not intended for this purpose. Its purpose is to pressure foreign nations into adhering to international intellectual property standards. The decision to pressure or not to pressure involves many political and practical considerations in addition to the probability of enforcement. For example, the report does not mention Panama. Is this lack of mention due to Panama's excellent track record on iProperty enforcement? Or could it be that Panama's economy is too small to justify inclusion in the report or that Panama is not a signatory to the relevant treaties? Nevertheless, the report compiles a significant amount of information that would be extremely costly for a company to obtain independently, and it is a good place to start assessing enforcement predictability for many countries. Adjustments based on additional intelligence relating to specific countries of interest can improve matrix accuracy and value.

TAILORING PATENTING STRATEGY TO PRODUCT STRATEGY

Countries in the sample matrix in Exhibit 7.1 are listed with their total cradle-to-grave patent cost and are ordered from top to bottom (both on the matrix as a whole and within each cell) in order of decreasing market protection value and left to right in order of decreasing enforcement probability. According to the cradle-to-grave cost/PPP-GDP analysis, the United States represents the best value in terms of PPP-GDP protected in exchange for payment of the required patenting costs, followed by the United Kingdom, Japan, France, and so on.

The matrix is useful for selecting a set of countries for protection given a set budget. For example, if the cradle-to-grave patent budget for a specific project is $180,000, the best patent strategy according to the matrix would include the countries listed in cell 1. The matrix can be used to implement various strategy approaches, depending on the attributes of the product or technology being protected. Exhibit 7.3 illustrates three potential strategy approaches using the matrix:

Protection-Focused Strategy

A

1	2	3	4
1	2	3	4
1	2	3	4
1	2	3	4

Market-Focused Strategy

B

1	1	1	1
2	2	2	2
3	3	3	3
4	4	4	4

Protection/Market-Balanced Strategy

C

1	1	2	3
1	1	2	3
2	2	4	4
3	3	4	4

EXHIBIT 7.3 Tailoring the Global Filing Strategy

1. **Protection-focused strategy.** Appropriate to maximize enforceability (e.g., for a product with a short life cycle where anticipated improvements in enforcement are too far out to matter)

2. **Market-focused strategy.** Assumes improving protection in emerging countries over a 20-year period and is appropriate for a product with a long life cycle to protect maximum market size for each investment dollar

3. **Balanced strategy.** Focuses on countries where the strongest protection coincides with the greatest market value protected for each investment dollar

In each case, patent applications protecting specific ideas would be filed in an increasing number of countries based on the value of the ideas, starting with lowest-value ideas, which would be filed only in Tier 1 cells, and moving to higher-value ideas, which would be filed also in Tiers 2, 3, and 4. Filing in all tiers would represent a substantially complete filing strategy and would be warranted only for ideas with the highest possible value.

Protection-focused Strategy

For an idea with a *short product life cycle*, a protection-focused strategy may be most appropriate. The goal of this strategy is to maximize the probability of enforcement by focusing first on countries on the cells in the far left column of the matrix in which the probability of enforcement is relatively more predictable. Thus, for example, with a cradle-to-grave patent budget of $500,000, the best protection-oriented approach according to Exhibits 7.1 and 7.3A might be to file in the countries in cells 1 and 5 in Exhibit 7.1, plus Ireland from cell 9, representing a total cradle-to-grave cost estimate of $442,000.

Market-focused Strategy

Improving quality of enforcement in markets such as India and China also means that, in the long run, the asserting of patent rights is more likely to succeed. For products with a *lengthy product life cycle* approaching or exceeding the 20-year patent term, a prudent strategy may be to focus on maximizing the market size protected per dollar invested in patent protection rather than on the current enforcement probability. As illustrated in Exhibit 7.3B, this strategy involves filing in countries along the top row of the matrix. Thus, for example, with a cradle-to-grave patent budget of $500,000, the best market-driven approach according to Exhibits 7.1 and 7.3B might be to file in the countries in cells 1, 2, 3, and 4 in Exhibit 7.1, plus Sweden from cell 5, representing a total cradle-to-grave cost estimate of $442,000.

Balanced Strategy

In some cases it may be desirable to employ a strategy that balances enforcement predictability with market access. A strategy representing this approach is illustrated in Exhibit 7.3C. With a cradle-to-grave patent budget of $500,000, the balanced approach according to Exhibits 7.1 and 7.3C would be to file in the countries in cells 1, 2, and 5 in Exhibit 7.1, omitting Denmark or Poland, and representing a total cradle-to-grave cost estimate of just under $500,000.

CONDUCTING A REALITY CHECK

Even after a strategy is selected based on the considerations just discussed, the selected countries must be constantly subjected to reality checks. The decision makers must determine whether any country that is included should be excluded and, more important, whether any country that was excluded should be included, based on current business knowledge, competitors, political factors, economic trends, and company goals. For example, maybe Panama does not appear on the final list, but if you plan to build a manufacturing plant there, then you will want to give serious consideration to filing in Panama. Companies should consider, for example, where they will manufacture, distribute, and sell their products and where existing or future competitors are likely to arise as challengers.

With regard to these issues, it is possible to prepare a second matrix that sorts countries based, for example, on potential manufacturing threats that would be eliminated rather than on markets that would be protected. Protecting manufacturing hot spots is essential in the global economy in which information can be transmitted rapidly around the globe and manufacturing plants producing copies of a patented product can be set up quickly in distant countries lacking adequate patent protections.

Companies also should consider cross-border trafficking in places like Europe where consumers can readily cross borders to purchase goods in nearby countries. If, for example, the matrix suggests filing in Germany, Italy, and France, but not Switzerland, consideration should be given to patenting in Switzerland to reduce the risk that consumers will cross the border into Switzerland to purchase a cheap generic version of the product where there is no patent protection.

MASTERING THE MATRIX

Very little information is available to help companies implement sensible processes and tools for evaluating various patenting strategies. Companies can, however, improve their chances of success by implementing a rational decision-making process. By assigning relative values to markets and patent enforcement risk and taking into account the cost of patent protection in target countries, companies can identify countries representing the best patenting value, and they can use this information to focus a limited budget on countries that provide the most valuable protection. The matrix may also serve as a valuable tool for tailoring the global patent strategy to the characteristics and life cycle of the product being protected. Reality checks are essential for fine-tuning the strategy based on current, real-world factors, such as cross-border trafficking or shifts in geographical manufacturing and distribution capabilities. Developing a rational global patenting strategy involves predicting the future, but it does not require a crystal ball. The matrix approach described in this chapter may help to clear away some of the ambiguity and guide companies to select a strategy that will maximize the strategic value of the resulting portfolio.

NOTES

1. U.S. Trade Representative, "Special 301 Review, 2007," www.ustr.gov/Document_Library/Reports_Publications/2007/2007_Special_301_Review/Section_Index.html. Note that the matrix shown in Exhibit 7.1 was prepared using the 2006 Special 301 Review.

Part Three

iProperty Tactics for Maximum Impact

~ 8 ~

iProperty Culture

Creating a Culture that Values iProperty

iProperty is above all things about people. It is about ideas that are created by people. It is about strategies devised and executed by people. Intellectual assets begin their lives embodied in networks of neurons in the minds of people. They are by their nature intangible and ethereal. They can be misplaced or lost. They can be forgotten. An employee can quit and take them to another company or simply focus his or her energies on solving a different problem. Intellectual assets are also in many cases technologically complex, and they exist tenuously in the midst of rapidly changing market and business conditions.

Successful development and implementation of processes to solidify and protect ideas in the face of technical and business challenges is daunting enough. But in our experience, the most significant obstacle to the success or failure of corporate iProperty initiatives is neither technical nor business related; it is cultural. And if building a culture in which people offer up their ideas and invest themselves in processes and strategies to protect them were not already a sufficiently challenging problem, in the global economy, the creation of iProperty is now increasingly the product of multiple people, from different companies (subsidiaries, partners, suppliers, and customers), in multiple countries, and of varied cultural backgrounds.

Who at your company is responsible for developing an iProperty culture?

135

CULTURE MATTERS

Corporate culture, the norms of behavior and shared values in an organization, manifests itself in all corporate activities. How employees interact with one another, how they view themselves individually and as an organization, and even how the company is physically and organizationally structured are all functions of corporate culture. Given that corporate culture so profoundly shapes an organization, it is understandable that rapid evolution of iProperty management practices often requires sweeping cultural change. Overlooking this fact may seriously impede an otherwise flawlessly designed corporate iProperty program.

In his book, *Leading Change*,[1] Harvard Business School professor, John Kotter, lays out an eight-stage change process that is readily adapted to meet the needs of the iProperty community across geographical and cultural boundaries. These stages include:

1. Establish a sense of urgency.
2. Create the guiding coalition.
3. Develop a vision and strategy.
4. Communicate the vision and strategy.
5. Empower broad-based action.
6. Generate short-term wins.
7. Consolidate gains and produce more change.
8. Anchor new approaches.

The underlying principle of these eight stages is that in order to create lasting cultural change, individual companies and partnerships of global companies must first successfully alter people's behavior in a manner that benefits the group and that a link must be established between the group benefit and the new behavior. In this chapter, we review each of Kotter's eight stages, exploring their applicability to the implementation of an iProperty management program.

Stage 1: Establish a Sense of Urgency

Corporations have long considered management of iProperty assets as a necessary evil. In particular, the amassing of patent portfolios that are largely product-focused and defensive in nature has been viewed as an expensive insurance policy that takes years to develop and has only long-term relevance to the company's business goals. While this antiquated notion is fading, for many executive teams, the issue of iProperty management is still "important but not urgent."

One approach to this apathy is to "create a crisis." This does not mean fabricating a crisis where one does not exist. Instead, it means obtaining the data, performing an analysis, and preparing a reasoned argument demonstrating to management the clear need for immediate action. Among other things, achieving this wakeup call in the iProperty arena may involve:

- Mapping the company's patent portfolio against its product set and identifying the holes and vulnerabilities in portfolio protection
- Mapping the company's patent portfolio in comparison to the portfolio of a potential merger or acquisition partner showing the leverage/enhanced value that an enhanced iProperty portfolio would add to the deal
- Presenting the business deals that have not succeeded for your company because of iProperty issues

Stage 2: Creating the Guiding Coalition

As mentioned in previous chapters, it is still rare to find an executive team that can explain in detail how the company's iProperty strategy supports its business goals. More often than not, iProperty portfolios are driven by the technical staff in a bottom-up approach or, worse yet, by an outside patent counsel without any significant insight into the company's business strategy.

Stage 2 of Kotter's process is about ensuring an appropriate level of involvement among top management in the development and execution of iProperty strategies that can be communicated to the company as a whole. iProperty programs must be supported at the highest possible levels of the company. There are a number of reasons why management support is critical, but two key reasons are:

1. Without a mandate from the top, the iProperty team rarely has the clout to bring about the necessary changes or acquire the needed resources to execute even the most modest of iProperty strategies successfully.

2. Without the direct involvement of top executives, the chances of implementing an iProperty strategy that comports with the business strategy are slim.

Mark Haller and Edward Gold of PricewaterhouseCoopers lament that iProperty cultural issues are rarely considered in the context of due diligence for business transactions. According to Haller and Gold:

> With as much as 70% or more of the value of major corporations now represented by intangible assets, has the process for conducting due diligence in business acquisitions changed? "Not enough" is the answer, and the negative results can be significant.[2]

The result can be increased risk and failure to reap the potential benefits of the acquired portfolio. Haller and Gold suggest careful investigation of the iProperty culture of the target company and asking whether

> the [intellectual property] culture of the combined firm [is] able to support the target's product and services at the level required to ensure their continued success after they are integrated into our company.[3]

Answering this question involves evaluating the management cultures of the two companies and, where there are differences, evaluating whether positive cultural changes in the target are possible. Haller and Gold contend that the magnitude of the disparity in cultures correlates with investment required for cultural change.

With support and guidance from the top, the company can assemble a competent core iProperty team. This topic is discussed in more detail in Chapter 9; suffice it to summarize here that the iProperty team should include executive-level representatives from various disciplines, such as business development, marketing, research, product development, manufacturing, and legal. The participation of these individuals as the guiding force to create, administer, and ensure progress as measured against the iProperty strategic vision for the company must be an explicit part of their job descriptions and performance goals. The iProperty team must be made up of powerful, credible individuals who are respected for their industry expertise and leadership qualities. A cross-border, cross-company, and/or multipartner project must receive special attention with respect to the composition of the team, its proper size, and the processes of operating team activities.

Stage 3: Developing a Vision/Strategy

Most company execs and techies alike do not understand the strategic uses of iProperty beyond freedom of action and/or licensing for revenue. The challenge is to create a culture that appreciates the iProperty possibilities. Creating an iProperty-savvy culture involves, among other things:

- Educating personnel at all levels of the company about the benefits of iProperty (e.g., in business negotiations with suppliers, customers, and strategic business partners)
- Ensuring that the iProperty vision, as developed and communicated, has business relevance (e.g., defense, cost, profit, business leverage, etc.)
- Linking the iProperty vision to the need for changes to the iProperty process
- Driving the process deep into the organization with a disciplined program of constant education, monitoring, and feedback for course correction

The last two points are of critical importance. For instance, if the intent is to develop an iProperty strategy that is more tightly coupled with business goals, it must be clear that an existing ad-hoc and bottom-up approach to development and protection of intellectual assets will not suffice. A proactive, top-down approach to managing iProperty is the most suitable means to accomplish such an iProperty vision.

Stage 4: Communicating the Vision/Strategy

As mentioned earlier, the ideas protected by an iProperty program are by their nature abstract and intangible. Unfortunately, if an iProperty vision and accompanying strategy is not easy to explain, does not have clearly defined goals and deliverables, and/or its progress cannot be monitored and measured, it will be difficult to garner employee support. We recommend the creation of a graphical framework for communicating the iProperty vision. As discussed in Chapter 5, visual communication of data is much more efficient than the typical patent table. Simple visual representations can present large amounts of data in understandable ways.

While a principal partner at ipCapital Group (ipCG), an iProperty consulting firm in Burlington, Vermont, co-author Thomas Hunt and

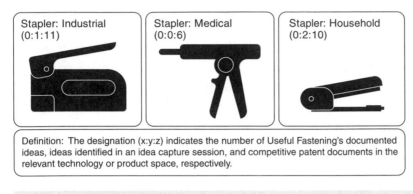

EXHIBIT 8.1   Sample Product Map iProperty Landscape

his colleagues often developed such visualization frameworks for client companies. Examples of such frameworks, known at ipCG as ipLandscape® graphics, are illustrated in Exhibits 8.1, 8.2 and 8.3. As shown, these graphical representations may, for example, take the form of a simple product map, a strategic business framework such as a value chain, or a manufacturing process flow. The visualization framework of each company, business unit, and/or product group may be represented by a unique graphic as needed to fully illustrate the complexity of the strategic framework. Whatever the end result, the graphic should include enough low-level detail to define the company's technology and product spaces accurately and include sufficient high-level concepts to communicate the business relationships among the company, its suppliers, partners, customers, and competitors.

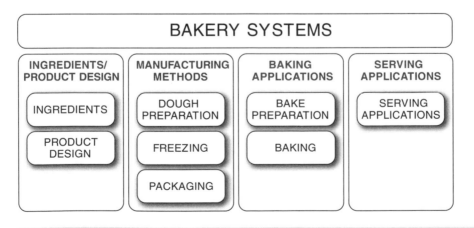

EXHIBIT 8.2   Sample Process Flow iProperty Landscape

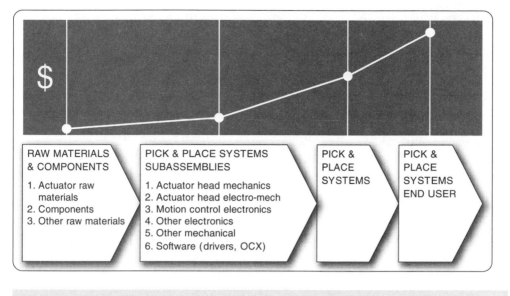

EXHIBIT 8.3 Sample Value Chain iProperty Landscape

Stage 5: Empowering Broad-based Action

Broad-based action requires participation from, and communication among, multiple groups to accomplish the goal of developing strategic iProperty practices. Broad-based action also implies that the broadest community, the community of employees within a company or a group of partnered companies, must be specifically targeted for involvement in the effort. There are several barriers to making broad-based action a reality. These barriers relate to issues of organization, education, and execution. To effect change, these barriers must be removed.

Organizational Barriers

Traditionally, intellectual property has been thought of as a legal function. The science and technology sectors produced the inventions, but the execution of all follow-on iProperty activities was carried out by an in-house patent attorney group or an outside law firm, often under the auspices of the corporate counsel's office. While the legal component is clearly vital, an iProperty organization that reports through legal is often more focused on eliminating risks than exploiting opportunities. Moreover, this organizational structure ignores the multidisciplinary nature of the iProperty function, leaving the decision makers in a legal silo that is separated from marketing, business development, strategy, and other important functions. Marcus Reitzig of Copenhagen Business School has suggested a need to "lead intellectual property rights out of their shadowy existence in the patent and legal departments and enable companies to tap into their strategic value."[4]

One way to overcome this counterproductive isolation is to create an organizational structure in which the iProperty legal group reports directly to a business chief of iProperty. A benchmarking study conducted by Thomas Hunt while at ipCapital Group revealed that companies that successfully implement strategic iProperty programs often move away from an iProperty organization that reports to legal. Their view of iProperty changes from iProperty as a legal function to iProperty as a business function with legal aspects. In most cases, the successful iProperty group is led by a nonattorney, reports to the chief financial or chief executive officer, and has a separate budget. Those involved in this kind of arrangement often report that it promotes a more cross-functional and broader-based iProperty organization.

Educational Barriers

Overcoming resistance to change requires all interested parties to understand the value of the iProperty program to them and to the company. Companies that want to implement a successful change in an iProperty program must work hard to educate executives, managers, and employees at all levels. Eli Lilly, for example, created a web-based inventor education module with a test that is required for all inventors. Companies wishing to overcome iProperty educational barriers must identify the specific deficiencies in knowledge that need to be remedied, and must also identify specific messages for remedying those deficiencies and media/forums in which those messages will be communicated.

Execution Barriers

Although active participation from the company's entire employee community is important, it is unrealistic to expect that the employees themselves will be skilled in the idea identification, capture, evaluation, documentation, and other steps required to implement an effective iProperty pipeline. Companies can overcome this execution barrier by identifying bottlenecks in the program and developing in-house capabilities to overcome them, using the program in a disciplined, supportive manner for all employees.

For example, when IBM (perhaps the ultimate iProperty company) was instituting its iProperty process in the mid-1990s, the company trained a team of IP Black Belts to identify, capture, and document ideas. Instead of relying on the 3,000 engineers working in the microelectronics division to perform these functions, the Black Belts worked with technical project teams proactively to identify potentially valuable ideas and write invention disclosures. These Black Belts produced more consistent documentation, got faster results, and made more efficient use of technical employees' time, leaving them to do what they did best: invent!

Stage 6: Generating Short-term Wins

Developing a comprehensive iProperty program can be a massive undertaking, particularly for large companies. It is foolhardy to think that such a program can be conceived and implemented in its entirety without first successfully demonstrating the utility of the process steps in a smaller and more focused environment. One solution to this problem is to build a pilot program. A well-designed, successfully executed test case will help to build support for the larger program.

If possible, start with a promising project that has (1) an eager and supportive project team with a reasonable awareness of the iProperty process, and (2) the prospect for near-term benefit, such as licensing revenue and/or leverage in an important business deal. Resist the urge to pick a rescue case, meaning a project in which individuals are challenged to prove the process by turning it around. The rescue case approach is usually a recipe for disaster. Finally, look for a modest return in order to ensure early success.

Stage 7: Consolidating Gains and Producing More Change

The business of changing the iProperty culture within a corporation can be exhausting. iProperty fatigue is not uncommon. When fatigue sets in, progress slows and may even reverse unless there is a conscious effort to maintain program momentum. With the success of a recently executed pilot program firmly in hand, it is only natural to want to take a breath and bask in that success. Go ahead and celebrate, but also use the energy of the moment to tell the success story to a wider audience. Communicate the success to everyone who will listen, pointing out as clearly as possible the direct correlation between the changes to the iProperty process and the benefits received.

Stage 8: Anchoring New Approaches

For cultural change to take place, companies must establish a clear connection between the new behavior and the benefits realized. Due to the intangible nature of ideas and iProperty, this link can be difficult for employees to see. Therefore, it is vital to communicate clearly the link between change and success, between the new iProperty effort and the successful attainment of goals. For example, companies can communicate on a company-wide basis the impact that the strategic iProperty practice has had on licensing revenue or business leverage.

Companies also can publicly reward those individuals who participate successfully in the effort. Simple recognition (and giving a physical commemorative item), cash incentives, and/or bonuses and promotions can all stimulate support for the program, especially when the recognition is made as public as possible.

Internal promotion using, for example, the company's intranet, innovation contests, and even external advertising can assist management with the effort to communicate the company's strategy.[5] Hewlett Packard famously changed its logo to include the word *invent* in an effort to reflect and maintain a culture of innovation. The internal promotion effort at HP starts at the very beginning of the employee interaction with communications to potential employees. According to the hiring section of the company's Web site:

> At HP, we believe in the power of ideas. From cutting edge personal digital equipment to the most powerful IT solutions, we use ideas to put technology to work for everyone. And we believe that ideas thrive best in a teamwork culture. That is why everyone at every level in every function is encouraged to have original ideas, to express them and to share them. We believe anything can be achieved if you really believe in it, and we will invest in your ideas to change lives and working practices. . . .Each individual is valued for the unique skills, experiences and perspective they bring. That's how we work at HP. And it's how ideas—and people—grow.[6]

VALUING AN iPROPERTY CULTURE

Companies that thrive on innovation require cultures that understand and value iProperty. iProperty is like a booster on the innovation rocket. It creates competitive thrust that makes the innovation rocket go farther in its attempt to pierce the market with a competitive advantage. In an iProperty culture, everyone from the engineering bench to the boardroom should be making decisions designed to create maximum thrust on the iProperty booster. But cultural change does not happen automatically. Nor does it happen rapidly. Creating an iProperty culture requires a significant and sustained effort. Success requires engaged and persistent champions in top management as well as a deep understanding of the company's culture, stakeholders, and politics. Key stakeholders must be tied into the process from the beginning. The globalization of businesses fosters innovation by many measures but also presents new and numerous complications to executing an effective iProperty program within and among companies. Achievements and successes must be demonstrated and communicated widely to the organization, and successes must be linked directly with the new initiatives in iProperty programs. For companies that develop an iProperty culture, the reward is reduced risks and sustained competitive advantage as employees work together, whether in a single location or from locations around the globe, to protect their companies' valuable intangible assets.

NOTES

1. John Kotter, *Leading Change* (Boston: Harvard Business School Press, 1996).
2. Mark Haller and Edward Gold, "Avoiding Transaction Peril: Value-Based Due Diligence," www.buildingipvalue.com, 2004.
3. Ibid.
4. Markus Reitzeig, "Strategic Management of Intellectual Property" *MIT Sloan Management Review* (Spring 2004), 35.
5. Ibid.
6. Hewlitt-Packard, Inc. corporate Web site, "Working at HP," http://h10055.www1.hp.com/jobsathp/content/informations/workingathp.asp?Lang=ENen (accessed June 25, 2007).

~ 9 ~

iProperty Team

Building a Team for Strategy Execution

An iProperty portfolio is essentially the sum of a series of decisions: whether to use intellectual property strategically, what strategies to use, what processes to implement, what ideas to protect, how to protect them, how much to spend, what countries to protect in, and when to stop worrying about iProperty and conclude that enough is enough. These decisions are all made by people with imperfect information. A team of business, legal, and technical iProperty gurus is the best way we know to minimize the risks of such decisions. Most companies make iProperty decisions without any guiding strategy, much less a fully functioning, radically creative iProperty team. Yet, just as disruptive new product innovations usually are conceived in an environment in which innovators are empowered to think outside the box, radical new iProperty strategies usually originate from an iProperty team that has the blessing of senior management to discard the worn-out mantras and reinvent the way the company uses iProperty to its benefit. While some short-term iProperty successes may be possible in the absence of a functional iProperty team, *none of the strategies or tactics described in this book can succeed in maximizing value for the long term without a functioning iProperty team.*

We recently spoke with patent counsel of a major biotechnology company who told us that iProperty decisions in his company are made by a committee consisting of the inventor who originated the idea and the company's patent counsel.[1] A technology transfer director at a major university told us that a faculty committee of technical experts makes iProperty decisions for novel ideas originating from university researchers. Both of these institutions are making iProperty decisions with less than sufficient attention. In the biotechnology company, there is no one to provide a business perspective. Even worse, in the university example, a decision about major iProperty investments is made by a group of tech-savvy academics without consulting either legal counsel or a business expert.

Whatever informal process is used, it is typically done at the last minute, just before legal rights are about to expire. Sometimes the evaluators unknowingly consider an idea even after the rights have been extinguished, for example, due to a publication of the idea or an offer for sale of a product embodying the idea, both of which can, under some circumstances, bar an applicant from obtaining a patent. Depending on the decision makers involved, the process may be repeated in various forms for each new innovation. The decisions being made are not meaningfully connected to the business strategy or the budgeting process. The result is a portfolio that protects a relatively random set of innovations using a relatively random set of strategies, and it is anybody's guess as to whether it actually supports the company's business objectives.

AMBIGUOUS THREATS

Even with perfect information about the present state of intellectual property laws and conditions around the world, iProperty decisions still would be difficult to make. For example, in a rapidly evolving technology space, a company might ask: "If we file our patent application now, it will publish in 18 months. But other companies are starting to be interested in our space. Should we file the patent application now and risk the damage that an early publication will reveal critical information to our competitors, or should we wait to file the patent application and risk the possibility that another company will file before us?" Or consider this one: "Our product will not reach the market in China in five years. We're not convinced that we could enforce a patent in China today. But should we file one anyway based on the expectation that enforcement opportunities in China will continue to improve?"

Underlying these questions are ambiguous threats to the company's success in a variety of endeavors. If the early patent publication starts a competitor quickly moving down a parallel technology path, it can wipe out a critical first-mover advantage. If China's patent enforcement record continues to improve, lack of a patent in China could permit the avoidable production of inexpensive copycat products that could be sold throughout China, Southeast Asia, and beyond. Many decision makers overlook important questions like these altogether, or they assume they know the answer based on "something somebody said at a meeting a few months ago."

As pointed out in Chapter 3, the goal of any strategy process is to "precipitate as well as make strategic decisions."[2] Achieving this goal is particularly difficult if the company is trudging forward on autopilot without stopping to consider its iProperty strategy. And further, where threats are ambiguous, as is frequently the case in the iProperty arena, it is "frighteningly easy to underestimate ambiguous warning signs."[3] This underestimation can lead to a failure to respond to critical danger signals.

MENTAL MODELS FOR iPROPERTY DECISIONS

Like all decisions, decisions about iProperty are made in the context of the decision maker's mental models. A mental model is an intellectual facsimile of the world in which we play out mental scenarios to ascertain the potential consequences of a variety of potential choices. In his book, *The Fifth Discipline*, Peter Senge points out that the mental models we use "determine not only how we make sense of the world, but how we take action."[4] We use our imaginations along with our rational abilities to conceive of potential scenarios, play them out, and assess what the future might hold for each scenario, and we make our decisions in light of this assessment. Senge points out that mental models influence what we do because they affect what we see. Inaccurate or warped mental models lead to ineffective decisions.

Simple mental models are adequate for many decisions about which the outcome is readily predictable (if I do not fill my car with gas, it will not run). However, complex mental models are required for making decisions with many variables, such as decisions about iProperty. In his book, *The Wisdom of Crowds*, James Surowiecki observes that "cognitive diversity is essential to good decision making . . . it expands the group's set of possible solutions and allows the group to conceptualize problems in novel ways."[5] Frans Johansson has coined the term *Medici effect* to express how bringing together different disciplines and cultures can lead to an explosion of new ideas.[6] Some traditional thinkers in the intellectual property arena feel it is odd that the field is always in need of new ideas. The field may seem fairly settled, but it is routinely challenged by new technologies, business strategies, and changing economic realities.

Companies had to think outside the box to build business models around open-source strategies, and open source is just the beginning of a new era of truly creative iProperty strategies. Companies willing to accept the challenges inherent in bringing together a diverse group of decision makers, often across companies and countries; to think, question, and debate the use of iProperty can create an explosion of ideas that yields new and more effective approaches to protecting innovative products and services.

iProperty decisions include complex considerations in the fields of technology, law, and business. At a minimum, all three fields should be represented on the iProperty team. The technical experts can explain technical dimensions of the company's products and technologies, and the state of the art in which the company operates. The legal experts can educate the group on changes taking place in the legal environments of relevant countries, guide selection of appropriate forms of protection, assess issues of patentability, and explain relevant procedures for obtaining protection. Finally, the business experts can evaluate the strategic importance of the ideas being considered for protection, assess probable market value and strategies for delivering the product or service to consumers, and determine whether the protections afforded by various forms of iProperty are sufficiently supportive of the business strategy to justify the investment.

Exhibit 9.1 illustrates the concept of a collective iProperty mental model in action. The decision-making process, which includes assessment of input information and a collective judgment leading to a decision, occurs in the context of the collective mental model created by aggregating the individual mental models of the business, legal, and technical team members. The members of the iProperty team use some input information, such as the iProperty strategy, to create a more robust and predictive collective mental model. They process other input information, such as information about ideas being analyzed, and make collective judgments using the enhanced mental model.

The mental models of those individuals who make a company's iProperty decisions determine the company's actions and ultimately the success or failure of an iProperty program. Companies can use the mental model concept to improve their iProperty decision-making process in several ways:[7]

- Enrich the iProperty mental model to create a more comprehensive view of the relevant issues
- Enhance the quality of input information

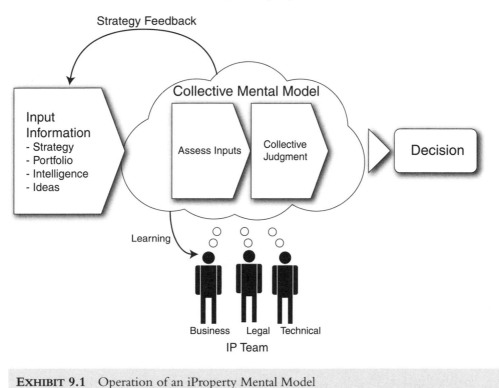

EXHIBIT 9.1 Operation of an iProperty Mental Model

- Systematize and streamline the analysis of input information and the assessment of options

The result of these improvements will be better decisions and the selection and development of a more powerful, and therefore more valuable, iProperty portfolio.

Enriching the Mental Model

Companies often make decisions about iProperty in an ad hoc manner. An idea is mentioned to a supervisor, who may dismiss it out of hand. If the supervisor views the idea as important, he or she may mention it at a meeting or start an e-mail discussion in which the idea is bounced from person to person in a chain of e-mails, each recipient making a personal, subjective decision about the idea based on parameters that he or she believes are important and forwarding the e-mail to the next decision maker.

When the analysis leading to an iProperty decision occurs in a series of individual encounters, rather than a collaborative meeting, an important opportunity for a synergistic meeting of intelligent minds is lost.

Companies can improve their iProperty decisions simply by bringing the right decision makers together in the same room to create a composite mental model that is much more complex than the sum of the group members' individual mental models. Each team member can challenge the assumptions of the other members, and together the team can consider a more diverse set of potential sources of risk.

Of course, as with any decision-making group, the iProperty team must be a functional team that avoids the common perils of group decision making. A bully leader, for example, can make all decisions for the group and effectively eliminate the advantages the group is intended to confer. Another peril is groupthink. Symptoms include "an illusion of invulnerability, a willingness to rationalize away possible counterarguments to the group's position, and a conviction that dissent is not useful."[8] Groupthink is more likely in groups that lack diversity, so simply including the disciplinary diversity required for an iProperty team helps to avoid the problem. Each discipline finds itself answering outside-the-box questions of other group members. However, the more cohesive the group becomes, the more susceptible it is to groupthink.

Groupthink is a truly pernicious enemy of effective group decisions. Information that challenges the group's conventions is excluded or rationalized away.[9] Members have the satisfaction of having their beliefs confirmed and reinforced by the group. They walk away from group interactions with even greater conviction of the accuracy of their positions. Of course, maintaining complete diversity in a group would mean that the members are new every time, which would eliminate some of the advantages of having a well-trained group. An intermediate approach is to include in the group an extended set of individuals who rotate through meetings on a regular basis. Sometimes, the addition of a neutral person can provide a helpful outside perspective.

An effective group regularly evaluates the changing business, technical, and legal context in which decisions are made and regularly challenges the strategy that guides the decisions. In the end, it makes more effective decisions in view of its collective view of the world. Building a successful multidisciplinary group for iProperty decisions requires an investment of time. It is much more time consuming than just bouncing e-mails around to make a decision. However, in the long run, getting the legal, business, and technical members on the same page regarding the iProperty strategy actually saves time and money. Preparation of the relevant documentation is faster. The company can rule out unnecessary investments and potentially avoid spending hundreds of thousands of dollars building an iProperty portfolio that does not support its business strategy. Most important, the resulting iProperty portfolio is more valuable because it does more of what it is intended to do.

Enhancing the Inputs

Inputs into the decision-making process serve two purposes: They (1) inform and shape the mental model, and (2) provide information required to make specific decisions. Much of the effort needed to inform and shape the mental model is described in Chapter 3, where we discuss the internal and external factors required for the development of an iProperty strategy. Internal factors include the business strategy, the company's existing iProperty portfolio, and the company's innovative capabilities. External factors include intelligence about the iProperty of competitors, freedom-to-operate analyses, and information about the legal and cultural environments of relevant countries. An iProperty team that is not informed about these issues will not make effective iProperty decisions.

The second kind of information is input required to make specific decisions. For example, the focal point of the many decisions made by an iProperty team is whether, when, how, and how much to invest in protecting each specific idea. In the iProperty pipeline (see Chapters 10 and 11), this step acts as a filter, stopping the progress of ideas that lack sufficient value to justify the cost of their protection. It also acts as a valve, directing each idea that is selected for protection down a path that leads to maximum protection, depending on its individual characteristics. This decision, made many times over as each new idea enters the pipeline, determines the structure of a company's iProperty portfolio.

In the absence of a documented iProperty strategy and without an informed iProperty team, managers typically make such decisions in an unstructured manner, sometimes in consultation with patent counsel. But they almost always make the decision without systematic evaluation of the idea in relation to other ideas or in light of the company's strategic needs. Decisions to protect ideas that do not support the company's business strategy or protect ideas in countries where the investment is not justified can result in significant wasted resources. Can you imagine an operating manager supporting a product in the market with revenues less than its cost-of goods? Decisions not to protect an innovation that would support the company's strategy or to forgo protection in certain countries will diminish the value of the company's iProperty portfolio. Decisions to protect innovations using inappropriate forms of iProperty—for example, patenting an invention that would have been more appropriately protected as a trade secret—can lead to a mistaken belief that the innovations are protected when really they are at risk.

Systematizing the Analysis

A documented methodology for evaluating ideas permits the members of the iProperty team to conduct meetings and analyze ideas systematically and efficiently. Assumptions of the evaluation methodology can be regularly tested and refined. Further, the evaluation methodology itself can evolve with the company's strategic needs. Changes in strategy can be reflected in changes to the evaluation methodology so that the output of the methodology supports the revised strategy. Efficient assessments of value also promote quicker protection, which, in a world in which the speed of innovation continues to increase, is a significant competitive advantage over the slow-moving elephants of the business world.

One step to consider when systematizing the evaluation of ideas for iProperty protection is drafting a patent claim or at least an outline of a claim that precisely states the probable scope of any anticipated patent. The role of the business expert in the decision-making process includes assessing the probable value of patenting the idea as compared to other forms of protection, such as trade secrets or publications. Since the claims will determine how broad the patent will be, it is difficult to imagine how this evaluation of value can be done effectively in the absence of a claim. By drafting a claim and exposing it to the scrutiny of the business and technical team members, potential prior art, scope, and language problems can be brought to light, and the claim can be revised as needed. Only after the team has prepared a claim that is potentially valid can the business team member assess the potential value of patenting the innovation. Moreover, when the legal member prepares the patent application, he or she will have gained important knowledge about the business needs and technical background needed to draft a patent application with claims that will not only withstand prosecution in the world's patent offices, but also have significant business value.

Another important step in the systematic analysis of information is assessing enablement. Enablement is a legal rule that requires the patent applicant to describe the idea in a manner that "enables" an ordinarily skilled scientist in a relevant field to make and use the idea. The enablement requirement impacts whether ideas are patentable, and if so, how broad the patent claims can be. As an example, testing an anticancer agent on a single type of cancer may enable narrow claims covering use of the agent for treating only that type of cancer. However, successfully testing the agent on a wide variety of cancer types might enable a broad claim to the treatment of cancers generally or to the treatment of specific classes of cancers. When an enablement assessment is made as a part of the review process, the patent counsel can recommend experiments that would help the company to achieve broader patent protection; the technical expert can assess the feasibility, timing, and cost of such experiments; and the business expert can assess the value of the potential increase in patent scope.

Another approach to systematizing the review process is to implement a review board process. For example, in one approach, each member of the review board has a vote, and a unanimous decision is required for the determination of next steps for any idea. The review board may involve a live meeting at which ideas are evaluated or, with well-trained iProperty team members, the evaluation can be done electronically, as described in Chapter 11. In any event, the review process should be relatively transparent to the innovators who are submitting ideas to ensure that the process is open and inclusive. A fairly administered process will promote and inspire confidence in the process among the company's innovators, encouraging them to trust that their ideas will be evaluated fairly.

BIASED MENTAL MODELS CAUSE INEFFECTIVE DECISIONS

Companies also can enrich their iProperty mental models and make more effective decisions by exposing and replacing inaccurate tacit mental models. Tacit mental models are assumptions about which the participants are unaware or that go unchallenged. Would-be decision makers are barraged with inaccurate messages about intellectual property. Many such messages are internalized and become tacit mental models. Often, when speaking with executives about managing iProperty, their eyes glaze over and a smug look of "I know all about this" comes over their faces. Usually the smug look is followed by a completely unsupported and erroneous belief that is so lacking in factual details that it is difficult or even impossible to refute.

Misconceptions about iProperty are epidemic. The problem is sufficiently severe that, at the risk of seeming to digress, we will take a moment to discuss a few of the more common handicapping misconceptions in some detail. A whole world of urban legends and business folklore surrounds iProperty topics. The media create and repeat these misconceptions, and even in the academic literature numerous mistakes lead to misunderstandings about iProperty topics. Others grow out of misinterpreted business experiences. The CEO whose company failed and whose patents did not save the day thinks patents are worthless. The fact that his or her particular patents were poorly crafted or lacking in novelty is lost to the self-interested historian. The misconceptions are repeated until they sound like obvious truths to those who hold them.

Other tacit assumptions grow out of changes in circumstances. At the end of his or her career in a Fortune 500 company, an executive takes on a leadership role in a startup company. The executive does not realize that the small company must use iProperty in a strategically different manner from the large company. Expensive decisions result in the filing of patent applications in a large set of countries and unexpectedly large legal fees, and patent applications must be abandoned because they cannot be supported. A significant investment goes up in smoke. After this debacle, the executive refuses to consider filing patent applications outside a few of the highest-value countries.

Overzealous Advocacy

Often extreme opinions about iProperty matters grow out of legitimate and important debates in which one or both sides warp the facts to support the desired conclusion. Patents, in particular, are a hotly debated form of iProperty. They are viewed as everything from the protectors of small entrepreneurs against corporate giants to weapons wielded by the corporate giants to maintain their preeminence. They are bludgeoning clubs of patent trolls used to bring hardworking manufacturers to their knees, and they are worthless pieces of paper that any smart engineer or scientist can bypass. They are responsible for depriving AIDS patients of their medicines in Africa and for overpriced drugs for seniors in the United States, forcing them to fill their prescriptions in Canada, and without patents, no new drug would ever be developed.

Each of these opinions relates to important and sensitive issues. Yet people are prone to make quick emotional judgments about the problems and required solutions rather than reasoning through the complex policy issues involved. As economist Henry Hazlitt observed about a similarly misunderstood field, economics, self-interested groups make convincing cases about the policies that benefit them the most. They hire the best minds to make the most persuasive arguments and present a case that "will finally either convince the general public that its case is sound, or so befuddle it that clear thinking on the subject becomes next to impossible."[10]

Hazlitt also astutely observed that people have a tendency to focus on the immediate effects of an economic policy on a particular group, without looking beyond to the wider consequences of the policy.[11] For example, seniors who want cheaper drugs often fail to consider what a price cap on drugs would do to the potential for developing revolutionary improvements in healthcare for future generations. Critics of patents typically assume that they benefit only the companies that own them; for example, patents enable drug companies to get rich by overcharging. As Franklin Pierce Law Center professor Thomas Field Jr. has observed, when "most people think about patents and other forms of intellectual property at all, they tend to be aware that the owners of such intellectual property may have the legal capacity to limit market entry—without fully appreciating the extent to which products or processes that can be easily copied by others might otherwise be unavailable."[12] The desired drugs and other useful and important products probably would not exist without patents or some other form of incentive for investors to undertake the overwhelmingly expensive and risky research required to discover and develop the new products and take them to market. There may be ways to get less expensive drugs for seniors without killing the goose that laid the golden egg, but in the cacophony of extreme positions, few voices providing balanced solutions are loud enough to be heard.

Biased Subcultures

Many of the public messages about iProperty are themes for subcultures that grow up around common biases. For example, many in the software community love the idea of open source and hate the idea of patenting software algorithms for business methods. This much is understandable, but the bias against software patents often leads to irrational conclusions. For instance, some people simply assume that business method patents are impossible to defend. The U.S. Supreme Court disagrees:

> We take this opportunity to lay this ill-conceived exception to rest. . . .Since the 1952 Patent Act, business methods have been, and should have been, subject to the same legal requirements for patentability as applied to any other process or method.[13]

Even when business leaders understand that business methods are patentable, some refuse to consider patenting them out of a belief that they are either immoral or bad policy. They may be bad policy, but that does not mean that businesses that use them have to use them in an immoral manner. It is one thing to use a patent to stop academic research;[14] it is another to use a patent to protect a small company from a predatory software giant. Even worse, the bias against software patents often leads software companies into an irrational sense of security about infringing the software patents of others. This bias can have bitter results when the software company is sued for infringement.

In another example, people tell us all the time that universities cannot be sued for patent infringement. A common rationale is that the researchers are working on grants that are funded by government agencies. The reality is that universities are commonly named in patent infringement suits. When Duke University tried avoid liability for infringement of a patent for electron laser equipment, the Court of Appeals for the Federal Circuit said that "so long as the act is in furtherance of the alleged infringer's [Duke's] legitimate business and is not solely for amusement, to satisfy idle curiosity, or for strictly philosophical inquiry, the act does not qualify for the very narrow and strictly limited experimental use defense."[15] In other words, university researchers are not immune to patent infringement.

Patents as Economic Monopolies

Even the professional and academic business literature is littered with misunderstandings about the nature, scope, and operation of intellectual property laws. Frequent mistakes in the economic literature prompted one law professor, Edmund Kitch, to write an article titled "Elementary and Persistent Errors in the Economic Analysis of Intellectual Property."[16] Among the errors discussed is the common assumption that patents are economic monopolies.

The assumption is that a patent will give its owner monopoly power in the market, enabling the patent holder to prevent competition and charge monopoly prices. However, patents rarely if ever confer such extensive rights. According to Kitch, a patent is a monopoly "only if the claims cover all of the relevant market, i.e., there is no alternative way for competitors to provide the same economic functionality to their customers without infringing the claims." So the issue boils down to "economic functionality." Patents rarely cover all ways to deliver a particular economic functionality. For example, in the drug industry, it is common to patent the chemical structure of a drug. While the drug may be useful to treat a specific disease, it is rare that a specific disease is treatable by only a single drug. The "Zantacs" of the world are quickly followed by the "Pepsid ACs." And often the Pepsid ACs are better. When other drugs are available for treating a certain disease, no economic monopoly exists.

Patents and Freedom of Action

An equally persistent error is the belief that if a company owns a patent, the company can make, use, or sell its patented idea without fear of infringing the patents of others. For example, even the highly reputed Delphion.com patent search Web site defines a patent as "[a] document issued by the Patent office that purports to give an inventor the exclusive right to make, use and sell an invention as specified in the claims of that patent."[17] In fact, patents confer no such right. Instead, they confer the right to *prevent others* from making, using, and selling the invention covered by the claims of the patent. As correctly defined in the U.S. Patent & Trademark Office's glossary, the right conferred by a patent is the right to *exclude*:

> a property right granted by the Government of the United States of America to an inventor "to *exclude* others from making, using, offering for sale, or selling the invention throughout the United States or importing the invention into the United States" for a limited time in exchange for public disclosure of the invention when the patent is granted.[18]

The power behind the right to exclude is the right of the patent owner to walk into a federal court and sue the infringer for an injunction to stop the infringement and/or for compensation for economic damage caused by the infringer.

This subtle distinction may seem like splitting hairs, but it has an important implication: The right to prevent others from doing something does not necessarily entail the right to do the thing oneself. Just because you have a patent protecting an idea does not mean that you actually can make, use, or sell a product or service embodying the idea. A simple example is a patented drug formulation. Let us say that after extensive studies and tests using a variety of formulations, your company finds that combining Drug X with ingredients A and B in a tablet facilitates getting the drug into a patient's system more quickly. Your patent on the formulation permits you to go to court to stop others from using this approach, but if another company owns the patent for Drug X, until that patent expires you will have no right to use your own formulation without permission from the patent's owner. Because of this distinction, we would add to Professor Kitch's rule that a patent gives monopoly power only if (1) the claims cover all of the relevant market, and (2) the claims are not blocked the claims of another patent.

Underestimating Patent Strength

Another common error is underestimation of the protection against competition that a patent can confer. Some business leaders assume that patents grant monopoly powers, as discussed above. Others assume that any patent can be engineered around and thus no patent has any significant value. Although this may be true in many cases, especially when only a single patent is involved, smart companies employ entire fleets of carefully crafted patents with claims that cover important functional aspects of their products or processes. They also identify gaps in their own patents and fill in their portfolios with patents that block those gaps. A sophisticated portfolio is likely to present an infringer with an impossible or cost-prohibitive set of constraints to work around. When the patent system is working well and when patent owners are using the system effectively, patents grant enough power to enable their owners to recoup their investment in and profit from developing products that may easily be copied by others. The head of a major nutrition firm once asked one of us: "Why should we spend the money on a patent? With a little work, any patent can be engineered around." Tell that to the companies that routinely pay IBM more than $1 billion each year to license its iProperty.

Enforcing Patents in Developing Economies

One of the most persistent iProperty fallacies is the blanket belief that patenting in developing countries is an essentially worthless endeavor. We hear this sentiment almost on a daily basis. Yet even though there are significant challenges to enforcing patent and other iProperty rights in these countries, "the times they are a'changing," and companies that fail to recognize the new opportunities will be at a disadvantage in the future compared to competitors with more foresight.

As discussed in Chapter 2, the number of patent applications filed in China and India is dramatically increasing, suggesting that at least a substantial subset of companies envisions the opportunities. With every day that passes, these countries become more and more integrated into the world economy. Over a billion new consumers in these countries are expected to enter the marketplace in the next decade.[19] As stated in a recent article in *The Economist*, annual growth in developing countries has been increasing at a rate of 7 percent, well above the rate of developing countries. The article states:

> [The] increased vitality in emerging economies is raising global growth, not substituting for output elsewhere. . . . They will thus help to lift growth in world GDP just when the rich world's graying populations would otherwise cause it to slow. Developed countries will do better from being part of this fast-growing world than from trying to cling on to a bigger share of a slow-growing one.[20]

It is difficult to imagine how executives and managers could, with virtually no serious consideration, just brush off the idea of investing in iProperty protections in rapidly growing countries such as India, China, Singapore, Mexico, Brazil, and many others. But these kinds of decisions are made every day in hallways and at water coolers.

Solving Complex Problems

Other tacit mental models relate more to beliefs about what can be accomplished in the area of iProperty. John Cronin, managing director of ipCapital Group, points out that when faced with uncertainty, the most common response is to do nothing. We have seen this again and again in the iProperty domain. A software client working on complex imaging algorithms once invited one of us to help identify ideas for protection and develop a strategy for protecting those ideas. We spent a full day with the client discussing developments in every area of its technology *except* the area where the most ideas resided. When we tried to steer the discussion into this highly productive area, the scientists repeatedly steered us away: "You really don't want to go in that direction, it is too complex, and there must be hundreds of innovations." The team could not solve the problem because they held onto and vigorously defended a tacit mental model that said "the problem is too big. It can't be solved." The company later sold for a fraction of what it would have been worth had it done a better job of capturing and documenting even a subset of its most critical innovations.

In a similar vein, a former chief patent counsel from a Fortune 500 firm recently told one of us that during his tenure, the company never figured out how to decide when to abandon patents in its massive portfolio, resulting in millions of dollars in unnecessary expenses (maintenance fees and annuities paid to the world's patent offices) keeping the patents alive when they were not being used. This is clearly a solvable problem. We wonder what assumptions blocked the company from identifying and implementing a solution. As an aside, we note that maintenance fees and annuities are big business. One company, Computer Patent Annuities, handles annuities for 2 million cases each year for more than 40,000 companies.[21]

Challenging Biases

The biases and untested assumptions described here are just some of the tacit mental models that plague iProperty decision makers. Companies with a commitment to and a relentless focus on using iProperty to establish and defend their competitive advantages cannot afford to be waylaid by untested assumptions like these. They must be willing to confront and deal with tacit mental models that adversely impact their ability to envision the future and make the best possible strategic decisions. Given the complexity of these issues and many others that we have not discussed, we advocate a multidisciplinary, strategy-guided but open-minded set of really smart people for making iProperty decisions.

MASTERING THE DECISION-MAKING PROCESS

Given the significant expense required to build an iProperty portfolio and the portfolio's potential contribution to shareholder value, it is surprising that companies often invest so little brainpower in making the decisions that determine the composition of their portfolios. Decision makers are confronted with a variety of misconceptions in the popular and academic business literature, misconceptions that often originate and are repeated over cocktails at business dinners on a daily basis. These misconceptions infect the mental models used by attorneys, managers, and employees to make iProperty decisions and adversely affect the quality of their decisions. Overcoming misconceptions and creatively using iProperty to maximize enterprise value is a multidisciplinary challenge that requires input from intelligent and creative technical, business, *and* legal experts. Any effort at making iProperty decisions that includes less than the full complement of expertise is omitting a field of knowledge that is critical for effective decisions.

Forward-thinking iProperty companies pay careful attention to *how* they make iProperty decisions. They place the decisions in the hands of a well-qualified iProperty team that is empowered to act in light of a real understanding of the business strategy, the strengths and weaknesses of the idea in question, and the current state of intellectual property laws and policies in relevant countries. Collaborative evaluation creates a more complex, composite mental model that can be used to assess a greater variety of opportunities and risks. Challenging tacit assumptions can enhance the effectiveness of the group's mental model. Moreover, supplying the iProperty team with more reliable inputs and a systematic process for analyzing these inputs improves the efficiency of the team and the quality of its analysis. By filtering each idea through a predetermined strategy, the team can ensure consistency of decisions and the development of an iProperty portfolio in which each unit of iProperty has a strategic reason for existing. Better iProperty decisions translate into reduced waste, in terms of time and money, and increase the value of a company's iProperty portfolio.

NOTES

1. This story was first published in William Barrett, "Quantity In, Quality Out: Maximizing the Value of Your Intellectual Property Pipeline," *BioProcess International* (February 2003), 20.

2. David Aaker, *Developing Business Strategies*, 5th edition (New York: John Wiley & Sons, Inc., 1998).

3. Michael Roberto, Richard Bohmer, and Amy Edmondson, "Facing Ambiguous Threats," *Harvard Business Review OnPoint Article* (November 2006), 1.

4. Peter Senge, *The Fifth Discipline: The Art & Practice of the Learning Organization* (New York: Currency Doubleday, 1990), 175.

5. James Surowiecki, *The Wisdom of Crowds: Why the Many Are Smarter than the Few and How Collective Wisdom Shapes Business, Economies, Societies and Nations* (New York: Doubleday, 2004), 36.

6. Frans Johannson, *The Medici Effect: What Elephants and Epidemics Can Teach Us about Innovation* (Boston: Harvard Business School Press, 2006), 2–3.

7. William Barrett, "Stopping the Bouncing Disclosure: Making Better IP Decisions to Build a Stronger IP Portfolio," *Current Drug Discovery* (August 2002), 37-39.

8. James Suroweiki, 37.

9. Ibid.

10. Henry Hazlitt, *Economics in One Lesson* (Norwalk, CT: Arlington House, 1979), 15.

11. Ibid., 16.

12. Thomas Field Jr., "Pharmaceuticals and Intellectual Property: Meeting Needs throughout the World," *Pierce Law Faculty Scholarship Series*, Paper 28, January 1, 1990, http://lsr.nellco.org/piercelaw/facseries/papers/28.

13. *State St. Bank & Trust Co. v. Signature Fin. Group,* 149 F.3d 1368, 1375 (Fed. Cir. 1998).

14. We are not expressing an opinion here about the morality of enforcing patents against academic research. Much academic research is done with the aim of generating patents

and creating spin-out companies, which amounts to competitive commercial activity. We do think, however, that a carefully crafted research exception to patent infringement for academics would be a good thing.

15. *Madey v. Duke Univ.*, 64 USPQ 2d (BNA) 1737 (Fed. Cir. 2002) (citations omitted).

16. Edmund Kitch, "Elementary and Persistent Errors in the Economic Analysis of Intellectual Property," *Vanderbilt Law Review* 53, no. 6 (2000), 1727.

17. Delphion, Inc., "Glossary of Patent Terms," www.delphion.com/help/glossary.

18. U.S. Patent & Trademark Office, "Glossary," www.uspto.gov/main/glossary/index.html, emphasis added.

19. Ibid.

20. "The New Titans," *The Economist* (September 16, 2006), 4.

21. Computer Patent Annuities, "About CPA," corporate Web site, http://www.cpaglobal.com/about_cpa (accessed September 9, 2007).

~ 10 ~

iProperty Pipeline

Part I: Amassing a Wellspring of Ideas

Ideas start with and are shaped by the inventors' own personal history and the environment in which those ideas are conceived. A particular kind of education, a mood that permeates the company's culture, what the inventor ate for breakfast, the personality of a supervisor—all these things and many more influence the kinds of ideas that form in the minds of a company's inventors. An idea begins like a newly formed seed. It germinates and grows to its full potential only with the right kind of cultivation. Often potentially valuable ideas are not recognized as significant and are not cultivated. Left in an inventor's mind, an idea that is not cultivated may be washed away or may simply languish. Who has not woken in the night with an exciting idea only to find that the idea is gone by morning, cleared away with the mental rubbish as a simple function of sleep?

If the idea is recognized in some manner—offered up in a meeting, e-mailed to a colleague or supervisor—the risk remains that it will be lost in a flood of communications, never entered into a process in which it can be managed and cultivated. Once identified as an important idea, it will compete with other important ideas for survival and investment in the form of time and resources needed to develop and protect the idea. In the absence of an iProperty strategy rogue ideas will fight their way through the system, using forceful personalities and powerful people. Quiet gems from less aggressive inventors will languish without being heard. The ideas that survive will find themselves in a misaligned iProperty portfolio that protects ideas having little value, fails to protect ideas having great value, and protects even the great ideas poorly. And, as observed by Daniel McCurdy, chief executive of ThinkFire, an intellectual consulting firm, "Failure of senior management to identify and fully deploy their companies' innovations, and to link them masterfully to the firm's strategy and business plans, will not go unnoticed by competitors or shareholders."[1]

In this and the next chapter, we introduce the concept of an iProperty pipeline. It is a pipeline that starts inside the minds of inventors and ends with a valuable portfolio of iProperty for the enterprise. The pipeline development process is divided into stages and describes criteria for moving from one stage to the next, specific outputs required at each stage, and people responsible for the stages. In this chapter, we focus on the early stages of the iProperty pipeline, which deal with the ideation (creation) and capture of ideas. In Chapter 11, we discuss the later stages of the pipeline, which deal with the development of an iProperty portfolio from the evaluation of captured ideas to the formation and maintenance of the portfolio. Insightful innovator companies pay careful attention to their iProperty pipelines from beginning to end.

INTRODUCING THE iPROPERTY PIPELINE

The early stages of the pipeline begin tenuously as tens, hundreds, or thousands of idea streams flow from the minds of the company's inventors. The creation of these streams must be fostered, and the streams must be identified and strategically channeled and supplemented through the pipeline with other information from inventors, business teams, and legal teams. The goal is to ensure that the pipeline's output is tied directly to business objectives.

Of course, a truly effective link to the business strategy is not possible in the absence of a documented iProperty strategy, as discussed in Chapter 3. The iProperty strategy connects the iProperty pipeline to the business strategy; it ensures that decisions made about the pipeline reflect business strategy needs and that the pipeline will yield a portfolio that actually supports the business strategy.

Coupled with an effective iProperty strategy, a well-designed iProperty pipeline process can ensure maximum return on the time and resources invested in protecting the company's ideas. Implementing a successful iProperty pipeline process is no easy task. Among other things, it requires companies to ensure that the busy people, often scattered at distant locations all around the globe, who are working tirelessly to add value to the company and to protect the company's ideas are actually tied into the company's business objectives so that the output of this often-frenetic process will be aligned with those business objectives. Doing this may seem simple and obvious, but it is rarely attempted and it is almost never accomplished. What is required here is virtually flawless execution of iProperty management to ensure alignment of iProperty with the company's strategic objectives.

Leaky Pipelines

Every company has an intellectual property pipeline. Planned or not, the pipeline evolves. Like the formation of the Grand Canyon, channels are carved where the ideas flow most frequently. One employee thinks everything he or she does is brilliant and consistently brings his or her ideas to the attention of management. Another thinks nothing he or she does has value and never makes waves about the need to protect any idea. One manager believes in the value of patents and trade secrets and seeks out ideas that need protecting. Another is cynical about the value of iProperty, believes that any patent can be invented around, and rarely allots any time to the protection of trade secrets.

Pipelines that evolve in such an environment are leaky, inconsistent, and ineffective. The responsibility for each step in the pipeline process is not allocated to specific individuals or teams. Decisions are made in an ad-hoc manner by whoever happens to be involved. There is no formal way to tie evaluations of ideas and iProperty investment decisions to strategic business objectives. The overall process is passive and relies on ideas to bubble up from inventors and managers.

Like an oil or water pipeline, an iProperty pipeline must be built well *and* it must be maintained well. Maintenance requires consistent review of the iProperty pipeline and its contents in light of strategic objectives within the current and projected business environment. In the words of the classic navy commander, "You get what you *inspect*, not what you *expect*." In our experience, the concept that many executives have of their iProperty portfolios is based much more on their expectations than on actual inspection.

Integrated Pipelines

Together, Exhibit 10.1 and Exhibit 11.1 in Chapter 11 illustrate an integrated iProperty pipeline. This pipeline focuses first on the context in

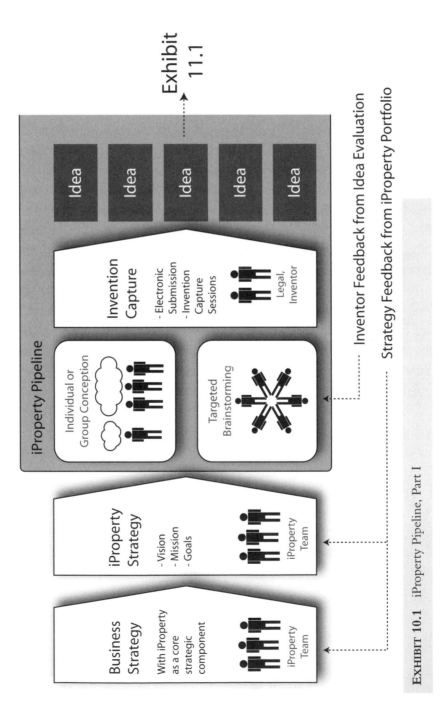

Exhibit 11.1

EXHIBIT 10.1   iProperty Pipeline, Part I

which ideas are conceived by individuals or groups. It sets up the business strategy as the driving force and the iProperty strategy as the means for connecting the business strategy to the pipeline. It includes the inventive efforts of individual inventors working independently and/or group ideation or brainstorming techniques to fill the pipeline with relevant ideas. Ideas are captured using electronic idea submission and "in-the-trenches," organized idea capture sessions. Then, as discussed more fully in Chapter 11, captured ideas can be evaluated based on a standard set of evaluation parameters and assigned a disposition. Ideas that warrant further protection are the immediate subject of standard inventor interviews to gather additional information. Output from formal inventor interviews is provided to skilled technical writers who write formal disclosure documents. These disclosure documents serve as input for the preparation of legal documents by legal counsel, and the output is a strategically targeted portfolio of iProperty.

A TRICKLE OF NEW IDEAS

The mind of a person is at once a boundless and tenuous beginning for a company's most valuable asset. Companies would do well to remember that the human brains of individuals are exactly where ideas do begin— people who have dreams and aspirations, random and structured ideas, families, problems, and needs. The first step in creating and harnessing a flood of valuable ideas is to assemble a group of capable people and place them in an environment in which their creativity can flourish. The next step is providing them with the support and information needed to channel that creativity in the company's desired strategic direction.

Providing a Creative Environment

Because companies competing for supremacy in the global economy live or die based on the ideas of their employees, they would do well to give serious consideration to establishing a creative work environment. Many hardcore engineers and scientists cringe when we start this kind of discussion. In fact, many principles of management were formulated at the peak of industrialization, when managers feared disorder and chaos as the most serious threats to a healthy organization. These days, creative organizations view lack of flexibility and suffocating control with equal trepidation.[2]

Google is one example of a company that strives to provide a flexible, creative environment for its employees. Its founders have emphasized to shareholders that Google is not a conventional company and does not intend to become one. Google values its employees, affectionately called Googlers, and seeks to provide them with an environment in which they can thrive. Among other things, Google has provided its employees free meals, doctors, and even washing machines on site. Google's creativity vision is a big one:

> Talented people are attracted to Google because we empower them to change the world; Google has large computational resources and distribution that enables individuals to make a difference. Our main benefit is a workplace with important projects, where employees can contribute and grow. We are focused on providing an environment where talented, hard working people are rewarded for their contributions to Google and for making the world a better place.[3]

Ideas are conceived in minds, and for minds; having a creativity-fostering environment matters. Google gets it. Lots of companies do not.

Different Employees Create Different Challenges

As described by Tom Kelly of the innovation consulting firm IDEO, innovation requires visualization of concepts that are new to the world, and useful innovation requires visualization of such new concepts in the context of prospective customers who will make use of them.[4] Innovations may result from a novel mental combination or creation of inventive elements: "What if we put a firefly gene in a tobacco plant?" Innovations may be sparked by an unexpected discovery: "We were treating this guy's blood pressure with a medication later known as Viagra, and well . . . the rest is history."

Innovating comes naturally to some people. Sparks are constantly flying, and the flow of new ideas seems never-ending. For these natural innovators, the challenge is twofold: (1) channeling their innovative minds to the right problems, and (2) managing the resulting flow of ideas to support business objectives. Without such guidance, highly innovative employees can remain unfocused and fail to solve key problems blocking the path to market. From an iProperty perspective, innovation without strategy can produce a portfolio that does not support the business strategy, one that is characterized by the personal interests of innovators rather than the company's strategy. This can be particularly distracting in an early-stage company, full of idealists, academicians, and idea-generators without bounds.

Moreover, the speed with which high-yield innovators create and discard ideas can lead to lost opportunities. They are quick to fly on to the next idea, leaving a string of homeless ideas in their wake. Failure to identify and promptly evaluate these valuable ideas can result in missed opportunities. If the innovator regularly submits ideas for evaluation, lack of a system that ensures that the ideas receive proper attention creates a demoralizing dam that blocks the creative employee's willingness to expend the time and effort to disclose ideas for evaluation.

For other employees, conception of new ideas is not a natural skill, but it can be learned. One way to teach innovation skills is active, communal brainstorming or ideation sessions. Experienced inventors are grouped with less experienced inventors so that the neophytes can learn by observation. It is surprising to us that in today's economy, where the need for innovation is paramount, so few companies have concerted efforts to help their employees master innovation. The result is a reprehensible under-utilization of brainpower assets.

FROM MIND TO IDEA

One of the most important idea-generating tools is group ideation or brainstorming. Yet, as observed by IDEO's Tom Kelly, while many companies think they are good at brainstorming, few truly master this important technique:

> Many businesspeople treat brainstorming as a check box, a threshold variable, like "Can you ride a bicycle?" or "Do you know how to tie your shoes?" They overlook the possibility that brainstorming can be a skill, an art, more like playing the piano than tying your shoes. You're always learning and can get continuously better. You can become a brainstorming virtuoso.[5]

Excelling at brainstorming is not easy. Exceptional brainstorming requires group members to put aside the regular inhibitions used to screen unusual or even absurd ideas. Brainstorming works best when the group achieves a playfulness that is not normally present in serious work situations. Members must also forgo judging ideas during brainstorming.

This last requirement may be the most difficult. Scientists and engineers endure years of training designed to help them evaluate and critique ideas. In a recent brainstorming session we observed participants so intent on judging ideas that instead of using critical language, they excessively praised outlandish ideas in a way that effectively served the same function as criticizing the ideas. Many are simply cynical about the value of a playful activity like brainstorming and scornful of the social sciences that support its utility. The use of facilitators, with few or no ties to the participants or even to the subject matter, can be remarkably helpful in orchestrating such sessions.

Fortunately, as we have noted, brainstorming and other ideation skills can be learned. John Cronin, managing director of ipCapital Group and prolific inventor, often tells the story that when he was at IBM, he kept a chart on the back of his door with goals for the number of inventions he would generate that year. Attaining these goals required that he practice a set of repeatable invention creation techniques to stimulate and direct his efforts.

When Cronin is inventing, he uses a creativity technique that involves associating dramatically different things. For example, when looking for a solution to a problem on a semiconductor chip, he may pull out a toy spider and ask, "What attributes about this spider could help me solve the problem?" This is a technique that Cronin teaches to others in facilitated invention sessions. He explains the technique in this way:

> The theory of how this is done relies on two well-known processes that come together in a unique way. The first is "associative thinking," which uses creativity tools to generate associations to find the "seeds" of an idea. The second is "continuous improvement thinking," which takes the seed of an idea to improve it through multiple rounds of critical and engineering thinking, to get the idea to a workable invention that is "bought" by the team.[6]

While working for IBM, Cronin practiced his technique during his drive home from work with a goal of conceiving of a new invention every day. He was eventually named as an inventor on over 100 IBM patents and produced hundreds of technical publications.

Successful iProperty companies do not just sit back and hope that employees will conceive of ideas, they proactively learn how to be better inventors. Further, as Rich West, chief executive of Advanced Liquid Logic, Inc., likes to emphasize, ideas must come from all levels of the company: "Executives must contribute to the idea flow, support a creative process, and allocate money and time where it is needed to support the process."[7]

Waiting for Ideas to Surface

Generating ideas is the critical first step in the iProperty pipeline, but even if great ideas are as numerous as seagulls on the Jersey shore, they cannot be evaluated unless they are recognized and captured. On a recent trip to San Diego, Bill Barrett took some time out for a whale-watching expedition.[8] Whale watching is a mostly passive endeavor. The passengers sit back, relax, and enjoy the ride, until a whale actually surfaces. Then what started as a group of leisurely passengers turns into a highly energized mob, as the watchers rush from their seats and pile up at the edge of the boat, cameras flashing. For many companies, protecting innovation is a lot like whale watching. Managers and patent attorneys passively sit back and wait for a valuable idea to show up. They go into action only when idea happens to make its way above the surface and is big enough to be noticed.

The problem with this approach is that, when an idea is stored in the neurons of an employee, it is at great risk. The employee could move to another company and take the idea with him or her. The employee could put the idea aside due to other pressing concerns and eventually even forget about it. The employee could be too shy or embarrassed to bring up the idea, or he or she could keep the idea a secret out of fear that it will be misused or even stolen. One scientist we know spent a significant amount of time conceiving of ideas for his next company, hedging the risk that his present company might fail. It did fail. Needless to say, his approach was not a helpful way to make the company succeed.

In the typical approach, as employees conceive of and enable their inventive concepts, they document the ideas in laboratory notebooks, in word processing files and spreadsheets, or on the ubiquitous bar napkin. When potential ideas are distributed everywhere, they are invisible to management and cannot be managed. We refer to this documentation as "alpha docs." The content and nature of a company's alpha docs has a dramatic influence on the quality of its iProperty decision-making processes. Yet in most companies, there is no consistency to how alpha docs are created or what happens to them afterward.

We wonder as well why so many companies continue to use paper notebooks, when electronic notebooks are available. One researcher describes the old-fashioned method in this way:

> In the not so distant past, I can remember when getting my laboratory notebook witnessed was a big chore. I recorded data and entered them into a data file using Microsoft Excel, Lotus 1-2-3, or Fox Pro; generated graphs and tables; pasted them into my lab notebook; signed and dated the results; and then went about the task of asking my colleagues to witness my data. Of course, none of this occurred in a reasonable or logical time frame. In fact, days became weeks before the data were properly signed. By the end of the year, the lab notebook swelled to twice its original size. It became incredibly cumbersome and heavy.

At the company where I worked, there were at least 200 employees, most of whom followed these notebook practices. This must have been a nightmare for archivists, not to mention the frustration it could cause the intellectual property staff.[9]

A set of paper laboratory notebooks must be manually mined for ideas. The hurdle is so large that most companies never get around to mining ideas. So the lab notebooks turn out to be a dead end for many potentially valuable ideas. Moreover, paper lab notebooks are subject to destruction by flood or fire, loss or theft, so they need to be scanned in and backed up offsite. But most companies never get around to this step, either. Even when they do, there is always a substantial lag time during which the newest notebooks have not been copied and are at risk. Further, due to the time-consuming nature of entering ideas in a laboratory notebook, many ideas never get written down. These problems result in lost opportunities.

Capturing Those Pesky Ideas

While an idea in the mind of an employee may technically be a candidate for the iProperty portfolio, it is essentially impossible to evaluate and protect it until it is captured. Further, while the creation of alpha docs is a critical skill, alpha docs remain distributed throughout an organization, and in most cases they also are essentially unavailable for evaluation. Lab notebook entries of different employees may be located in different places; they are commonly supplemented by information in word processing files, databases, printouts from laboratory equipment, Post-It® notes, and employees' minds. Key information about a single idea also may be distributed throughout one or more lab notebooks, separated by pages of irrelevant material. It is difficult for anyone other that the notebook's owner to find and aggregate the relevant information. And if the employee is not well trained to recognize important ideas, he or she may not recognize or document certain valuable ideas.

Ideas simply cannot be managed until they are captured. By "capture" we mean getting ideas out of the minds of employees, alpha docs, and other sources and into a format where they can be readily reviewed and managed. The essential elements of the idea must be recorded in a database along with basic information sufficient to permit evaluation. This information must be entered into a process (the iProperty pipeline process) that ensures that the evaluation will occur in a strategically effective manner.

As already suggested, the typical iProperty development process results in the loss of large numbers of valuable ideas. In our experience, the largest loss occurs at the conception and alpha docs stages. At the conception stage, researchers informally screen and discard innovations for a variety of reasons: The innovation is outside the direction of the investigator's core research; it does not involve fundamental science and is thus not suitable for publication; the investigator does not believe that the innovation has commercial value; and the like. At the alpha docs step, ideas are documented in their bare essentials but are not entered into a system that facilitates their evaluation and management. The simple step of erasing a whiteboard may send a potentially valuable idea into oblivion.

What ideas were lost the last time you erased a whiteboard?

To avoid this invisible loss of potentially valuable iProperty, we follow one simple rule: *Capture first, evaluate later.* A variety of capture techniques are available, but most can be grouped into two categories: (1) training and providing incentives for employees to submit their own ideas, and (2) sending a trained facilitator into the trenches with employees to identify and document potentially valuable ideas so that employees do not have to.

Incentivizing Disclosure

Getting employees to submit their own ideas is often like pulling teeth. Many scientists and engineers simply hate to write. Most are so busy designing and experimenting that they do not have time to put together documentation, so without prioritization of tasks from management, the documentation will never get done.

To make matters worse, the amount of information required on the typical invention disclosure form is often overkill for the decision that needs to be made. At the capture stage, the amount of information needed should be no more than what is required to determine whether the idea is worth the effort required to document it in further detail.

At Advanced Liquid Logic (ALL), Inc., where Bill is vice president of intellectual property, the company achieves idea capture using a simple, one-page, electronic idea submission form. As an incentive to complete the form, the names of everyone who submitted ideas during the month are placed in a hat at the regular Friday employee lunch. The employee whose name is drawn receives a gift certificate, which the company buys using points from its credit card. ALL employees have made a game out of seeing who can submit the most ideas and win the drawing. During meetings when someone mentions a potentially useful idea, the company culture encourages others to point them out for submission. Further, as discussed in more detail in Chapter 11, when an idea is evaluated, the employee receives feedback on the evaluation and the disposition of the idea, so no submitted ideas are lost in the system.

> Why not add an interactive voice response or web-based system with which employees can phone in or log on to answer a series of simple questions to capture their inventive ideas for consideration any hour of the day or night?

Getting in the Trenches

Forward-thinking iProperty companies incentivize employee-initiated idea capture, but even with the best incentives, they do not wait passively for ideas to land on the desks of the appropriate managers. These companies use processes for getting into the trenches with the employees to dig up new ideas. In the absence of a proactive idea capture process, the flow of the iProperty pipeline is proportional to the ability of employees and managers to recognize potentially patentable and valuable innovations.

In the Research Triangle Park facility of Ericsson, one of the patent attorneys schedules regular meetings in which patent counsel from various firms meet with groups of Ericsson engineers. Several groups assemble to discuss their work with patent counsel and identify ideas for protection. The ideas are evaluated during the day, and the patent counsels leave with a list of ideas for patenting. The patent counsels contribute their time without charge because they understand that the sessions will generate significant paid work as they prepare and prosecute patent applications to protect the ideas identified.

John Cronin has developed an invention capture process that he refers to as an ipScan® process. The process involves a facilitator meeting with a group of innovators and walking them through a structured interview process to capture ideas in ipCapital Group's inventions database. Cronin emphasizes that regular identification of intellectual property

is essential because key personnel may leave your company, many inventors believe their own work is unoriginal and disregard valuable ideas, and a documented invention inventory allows executives to monitor progress and make IP decisions that are aligned with their business goals.[10]

All three of this volume's authors have participated in ipScan sessions, and we can confirm that in addition to being effective, the process is a lot of fun. Participants typically finish the session more energized than ever about their ideas.

Capture Facilitates Evaluation

Ideas submitted by employees and ideas proactively captured fatten the iProperty pipeline and facilitate strategy-guided evaluation of the ideas. In short, captured ideas can be managed. In managing captured ideas, we find it particularly useful to populate a database with the ideas and to assign each idea a set of evaluation parameters. We discuss evaluation parameters later.

An idea capture session can provide a diagnostic for how well the company is managing its iProperty pipeline.[11] Each idea is characterized by three parameters: business priority, idea development phase, and documentation status. To assign business priority, score the idea based on how well it will help the company to accomplish its business objectives. Assign an idea development phase based on how well the employee can describe the basic technical details of how the subject of the idea is made and used. For idea documentation status, simply indicate the highest level of documentation: for example, no documentation, alpha docs, formal documentation in an invention disclosure document, or legal documentation (i.e., a provisional or full patent application).

Of the ideas in the high-priority category, how many are fully explained? Of those fully explained, high-priority ideas, how many are formally or legally documented? The percentage of fully explained ideas that are formally and/or legally documented provides a very basic indicator of how well a company is managing the early stages of its iProperty pipeline. The lower the percentage, the greater the probability that high-priority ideas may be slipping through the cracks.

What percentage of the ideas are early-stage ideas versus well-developed ideas? Early-stage ideas are the raw material supplying the iProperty pipeline. Companies whose products are becoming commoditized often have few early-stage ideas. To compete in the global knowledge economy, such companies must focus on ideation to enhance the number of early-stage ideas. Other companies have a large number of early-stage ideas and only a few well-developed ideas. This situation is common in entrepreneurial and startup companies. Success for such companies requires an investment in the development of these early-stage ideas.

A UNIVERSITY PERSPECTIVE

At a recent conference breakout session led by Marshall Phelps, deputy general counsel for intellectual property at Microsoft, he pointed out that despite the incredible inventive potential of universities, few make the most of their resources. Phelps argued that universities should break down the individual silos and, for example, that engineering and business schools should collaborate on the creation and protection of ideas.[12] Universities certainly do not suffer from a shortage of ideas. They publish many more ideas than they protect, and most of their publishing is done with no consideration as to whether publication will provide the best outcome for the university or even whether publication is the best way to ensure that the idea will benefit the public. Many published ideas cannot be developed because they cannot be protected in a manner that justifies the development cost.

University technology transfer offices (TTOs) are assigned the mission of facilitating the transfer of new ideas into the public sector, where they can be developed for the benefit of the public and generate cash for the university. In recent years, some technology transfer functions have become increasingly sophisticated, closing high-profile, multimillion-dollar deals and creating hundreds of spin-out companies. Patents facilitate the creation of spin-outs by helping to ensure that those who invest in the development of such technology will be sheltered from easy competition that could prevent them from obtaining sufficient return to justify the investment.

Yet the vast majority of university-originated ideas are never patented or otherwise protected due to inadequate processes, funding, and management. Most of these ideas are eventually published, with the consequent loss of patent rights. Since patenting is often a prerequisite to the successful development of technology, the low number of innovations actually patented suggests:

- Many potentially valuable ideas are not developed for the good of the public because they are not patented.

- Universities are not achieving the highest potential licensing revenue.

- The investments that universities are making may not be in the most promising technologies.
- The total investment by most universities in technology transfer is greatly inadequate to even partially capitalize on their investment, and that of taxpayers, by means of grants and awards.

In the typical technology transfer process, a university invests in the patent applications and offers those potential patents to companies for licensing with the hope that a successful license will result in reimbursement for the original investment plus some profit. The resource constraints inherent in this model result in diminished size and diversity of the university's iProperty portfolio. This difficulty can be remedied at least partially by focusing on idea capture and using captured ideas to facilitate investor participation earlier in the iProperty pipeline.

The addition of a capture step opens the door to partner funding of the iProperty development process. Advantages include:

- Selection of the best ideas for protection
- Facilitation of early evaluation by potential commercial partners
- Freeing up university funds for investment in other ideas

University researchers constantly conceive, informally screen, and develop or discard ideas, often with little or no input from outside their labs. Of the ideas that are formally documented and communicated to the TTO, financial constraints require the TTO to select only the best candidates, or "home runs," for legal documentation and patent prosecution. As a result, the university patent portfolio is dramatically smaller than the inventive output of the institution would suggest and terribly disproportionate to the investment in research.

As in the company setting, in the absence of a proactive idea capture program, the large leap from the laboratory notebook to the typical invention disclosure document required by the TTO introduces a significant barrier to the disclosure of new ideas before they are published. This problem is exacerbated by the publish-or-perish tradition of academic researchers. Undisclosed ideas remain invisible to the TTO, and eventual publication or other public disclosure by frustrated researchers renders them unpatentable.

Rather than requiring a detailed invention disclosure document as an initial disclosure, the idea capture step requires only a brief abstract of the idea. If the form is longer than one page, it is probably too long. As an alternative to a written document, the abstract can be obtained from a verbal interview, further reducing the researcher's initial disclosure burden. The verbal interview could be accomplished using a junior TTO staffer or an idea hot line that automates the interview process. The succinct idea capture process also lowers the TTO's per-idea review burden, allowing the TTO to manage a larger number of ideas. The capture step aggregates ideas from the alpha docs in a centralized database where they can be managed.

By lowering the initial documentation bar and centralizing ideas in a database, the capture step ensures that virtually all potentially patentable ideas are captured in a form that permits them to be reviewed by the TTO. Although the TTO will almost certainly decide not to pursue some of the ideas, the capture process ensures that the TTO has the opportunity to consider the ideas prior to discarding them. In this way, the capture step helps to stop the invisible leakage of potentially valuable ideas. Once captured, the university can assemble an IP team to view all potential ideas together, reviewing them from a technical, legal, and business perspective, so that the most promising ideas can be selected for investment in the patent process.

In some cases, the university may wish to permit a partner to fund an idea capture session. The partner may be:

- A company interested in a first look at new technology coming out of a particular laboratory
- A potential licensee who wants to establish the full potential of the scope of licensed technology prior to licensing
- An existing licensee who is interested in determining the extent of potential iProperty that has been developed since the execution of the license for a potential follow-on license

The partner can pay for the idea capture session and may also pay the university for the right to a first look at the technology. The first look may involve brief descriptions of the ideas that mask technical details and may require a confidential disclosure agreement to prevent the company from misappropriating the information. If the company is interested in learning more, it may fund the drafting of a more detailed disclosure document. This funding will reduce the financial burden on the university by permitting the company to pay a third party to interview the researcher, write the disclosures, and file the disclosures as provisional patent applications prior to disclosure to the company.

If the company decides that it is not interested in documenting ideas identified by the idea capture session, the university can offer the ideas to other companies for review. If the ideas ultimately are licensed, the university may reimburse the company for the cost of preparing the idea disclosures. The results of the process may vary from direct licensing of captured ideas to corporate investment in the further development of captured ideas.

PRIMING THE PIPELINE

The first and most important determinant of the output of an iProperty pipeline is the input. Companies cannot create masterful iProperty portfolios without first creating masterful ideas. Companies that seek to master their iProperty pipelines must start by focusing on the creation of ideas. Once conceived, ideas must be identified and documented in a manner that permits their evaluation. This documentation step is a major bottleneck for most companies. Idea capture, including proactive facilitated idea capture sessions, can open the bottleneck and improve the flow of new ideas into the pipeline by simplifying the process of disclosure for the innovators. Once captured, ideas can be managed and shepherded through the iProperty pipeline. The next chapter discusses the evaluation of ideas in the pipeline and the steps from evaluation to the assembly of an iProperty portfolio that provides maximum support for the company's business strategy.

NOTES

1. Daniel McCurdy, "Seeing Through the Illusion of Exclusion," in *Making Innovation Pay: People Who Turn IP into Shareholder Value,* ed. Bruce Berman (Hoboken, NJ: John Wiley & Sons, Inc., 2006), 39.

2. Howard Davis and Richard Scase, *Managing Creativity: The Dynamics of Work and Organization* (Philadelphia: Brunner-Routledge, 2001), 1.

3. Google, Inc., corporate Web site, "An Owner's Manual for Google's Shareholders," http://investor.google.com/ipo_letter.html.

4. Tom Kelly with Jonathan Littman, *The Art of Innovation* (New York: Doubleday, 2001), 7.

5. Ibid., 55.

6. ipCapital Group, Inc., "IOD," corporate Web site, www.ipcg.com/thoughtleadership/IOD.htm.

7. Rich West, e-mail conversation with the author, June 15, 2007.

8. William Barrett, "Diving for Inventions: A Proactive Capture Process," *Current Drug Discovery* (May 2002): 45–46.

9. Marc Fitzgerald, "The Evolving, Fully Loaded, Electronic Laboratory Notebook," *Chemical Innovation* 30, no. 1 (January 2000), 2–3.

10. ipCapital Group, Inc., corporate Web site, "Understand the Value of Your IP and Identify and Visualize Your Assets," www.ipcg.com/whatyoucando/1-Identify.htm.

11. William Barrett, note 8.

12. Anna Skibinsky, "Experts Call for Revamping of US Patent System," *The Epoch Time* (April 30, 2007).

~ 11 ~

iProperty Pipeline

Part II: Producing a Strategically Targeted Portfolio

The iProperty pipeline exists in context, a business environment, and thrives or falls short based on the set of practices, processes, and disciplines established by an enterprise. The context includes the culture in which inventors invent and the information content that shapes their thoughts and attitudes about the kinds of ideas that the company considers valuable. The context influences the problems innovators solve and the tools they use to solve them. Within the context, ideas are formed, and each step in the iProperty pipeline enhances, fails to enhance, or detracts from the value of the company's ideas by creating, selecting, and further solidifying the body of ideas that will be protected at an increasing level of detail, enablement, and degree of legal protection. If the context is shaped by a strategy, the iProperty pipeline culminates in the creation of a strategic portfolio of legally protected intangible assets that render the business strategy more effective than it would be without the iProperty assets. If the context is not guided by a strategy, the result is the investment in a relatively haphazard collection of legally protected intangible assets and a hope that at least some of them will support the company's business.

The development of an iProperty portfolio starts, as described in Chapter 10 (see Exhibit 10.1), with the business strategy and iProperty strategy. The strategic concepts embodied in these documents condition the minds of the company's inventors and influence the output of individual and group ideation efforts. Ideas are captured and fed into a database with key information about those ideas for analysis. But this is only the beginning. As illustrated in Exhibit 11.1, once populated with captured

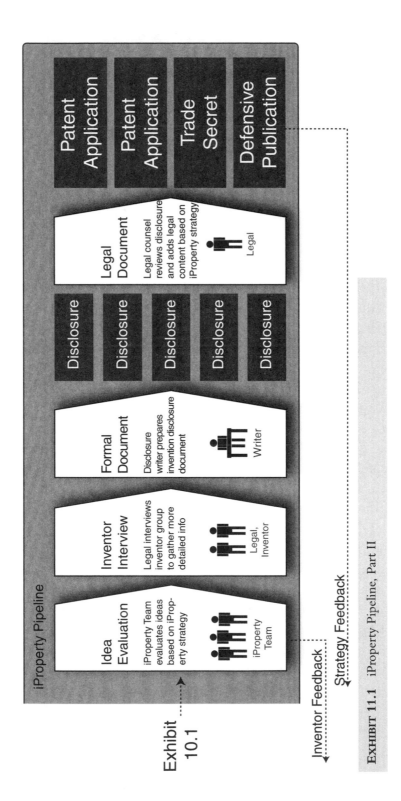

EXHIBIT 11.1   iProperty Pipeline, Part II

ideas, an iProperty pipeline that is effective needs processes for strategically evaluating ideas and selecting appropriate forms of protection and geographical regions for protection. The pipeline also needs processes for documenting ideas with increasing levels of sophistication in a manner targeted to ensure that they achieve a specific purpose, for example, as trade secret documentation, a patent application, or a defensive publication (see Chapter 12). It is this strategy-guided process that yields a strategy–aligned portfolio.

Poor evaluation and decision making can result in inadvertent loss of iProperty and/or wasted resources invested in the acquisition of iProperty that does not justify the opportunity cost of its acquisition. For example, a poorly thought-out (or nonexistent) evaluation process can result in (1) the failure to file patent applications in countries in which a patent portfolio would be expected, at the very least, to inhibit competition, or (2) wasting resources on patent applications in countries in which the investment is not warranted. Trade secrets frequently are overlooked altogether. The failure to protect an idea is often the worst mistake, since this has a direct impact on the company's ability to sustain its competitive advantage in localities around the world. A related issue is filing in the right countries but failing to execute business strategies that take advantage of the portfolio. Consistent investment in protection that is not justified can result in mounting portfolio costs (sure to be felt even by the largest companies) and little or negative returns on investment (most certainly to be noticed). With the proper foundational components in place, the steps of the integrated iProperty pipeline can be executed as a refined iProperty-generating engine that carefully crafts a targeted iProperty portfolio.

Do you have a process for systematically evaluating ideas in light of your strategy and determining where and how to protect them?

EVALUATING IDEAS FOR PROTECTION

Because ideas in alpha docs, the initial idea records, cannot be managed well, and because the jump from alpha docs to a detailed invention disclosure is a large hurdle, ideas can become stuck in lab notebooks and other documents, where they remain virtually invisible to management. We discussed in Chapter 10 that an integrated iProperty pipeline can help solve this problem by providing an intermediate capture-development step between alpha docs and formal documentation. Capture involves the documentation of a brief description of the idea along with other pertinent facts required to evaluate it, such as evidence that it will work, technical and/or business advantages conferred by the idea, and problems that are solved by the idea.

Once captured, ideas must be evaluated here is the typical approach: George comes up with an idea and mentions it to his boss at the water cooler. His boss, Mary, informally screens the idea, using her own standards and context—something about inventions that a professor mentioned to her once while she was in grad school. She may or may not discuss the idea with anyone else; at best, she may bounce the idea around with a few of her colleagues. If Mary's own standards happen to be well aligned with the company's strategic needs, and if she happens to have a good understanding of the technology and the legal standards for protection, she may make the best decision for the company. Or, if she is just plain lucky, she may also do so. Who wants to depend on that?

But the reality is that unless Mary is an individual with exceptional foresight and one of her passions just happens to be iProperty, the odds are against making the best decision in this unusually complex field. There is no documented iProperty strategy to guide her determination. If she happens to be biased against the usefulness of iProperty, she will be a dam blocking the protection of potentially valuable ideas. If she happens to have a superficial perspective on iProperty, she may protect the ideas that her employees think are important just to make them like her. If she is difficult to approach, forceful innovators may work the system to get their ideas pursued, while more timid innovators may see their ideas languish despite their potentially significant value.

Strategically Guided Decisions

As discussed in Chapter 9, iProperty portfolio decisions are best made in a structured process by a multidisciplinary team guided by an iProperty strategy. When a single person makes an iProperty portfolio decision or when an idea is simply bounced from person to person without the benefit of a strategic discussion and consensus decision in light of the relevant technical, business, and legal facts, the resulting portfolio is bound to be technically weak and misaligned relative to the company's business objectives. In contrast, as illustrated in Exhibit 11.2, in an iProperty company, the business strategy drives the iProperty strategy that guides idea evaluation by the iProperty team. This process takes the turbulent flood of ideas entering the iProperty pipeline and shapes it into a strategically focused portfolio.

The iProperty team's strategic context includes the iProperty vision, portfolio, intelligence, and the global patent strategy matrix. The iProperty vision must be kept in front of the iProperty team at all times so that all decisions made will be in line with the vision and the current environment in which the vision is being expressed. The iProperty team also must have deep knowledge of the company's existing iProperty portfolio. For example, what if the idea being evaluated has already been patented? An iProperty team without this knowledge might mistakenly invest in an attempt to protect the same idea again. The team must also be aware of the company's iProperty intelligence. Is the idea new, or has it already been published or patented by someone else? What is the nearest technically similar idea that is known to the public? What kinds of strategies have competitors used to protect ideas like this one? Finally, the Global Patent Strategy Matrix is an iProperty strategy input to the idea evaluation process. Discussed in detail in Chapter 7, the Global Patent Strategy Matrix provides a way to select target countries for a global patenting strategy.

Creating a Strategy Grid

An important goal of the decision-making process is to assign each idea a relative value, illustrated in Exhibit 11.2 as low, medium, and high value, and to distinguish among different categories of ideas, illustrated as idea categories A, B, C, and D. The iProperty team assigns the value in light of the idea's relationship to the business strategy. High-value ideas are those that are core to the business strategy (i.e., those that provide the most support for the business strategy). Low-value ideas are those that provide least support for the business strategy. The categories are tailored to the kinds of ideas the company generates. Ideas in similar categories get similar treatment under the iProperty strategy. For example, for a pharmaceutical company, categories might be drug molecules, drug formulations, synthesis methods, treatment methods, biological assays, and so on. For a medical device company, the categories might be systems, devices, manufacturing methods, treatment methods, and business methods. For a consumer products company, the categories might be different types of products.

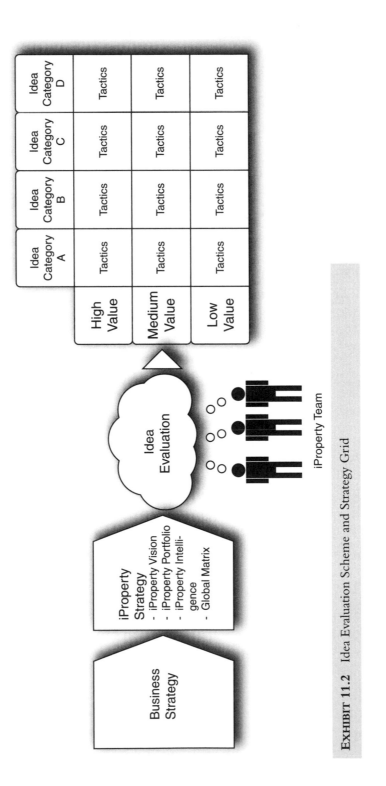

Exhibit 11.2 Idea Evaluation Scheme and Strategy Grid

Companies often rate ideas as high value even when they do not support the business strategy. After all, commercially important ideas may be outlicensed to generate revenue, even when they are not core to the development of specific products or services. The assessment of commercial value may be correct. The company may have a valuable technology but may not have resources to develop it. In such cases, outlicensing the technology to a third party may be the best choice. The mistake here is the common belief that licensing of iProperty can be consistently successful, even if licensing itself is not part of the business strategy. In many cases, the best solution is not to exclude commercially valuable iProperty from protection but to include, outlicensing as a core business strategy and to allocate sufficient resources to monetize such noncore iProperty.

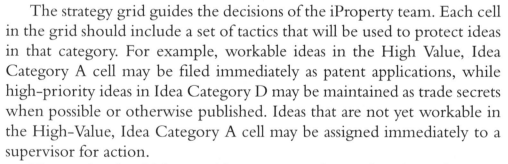

Are your iProperty portfolio decisions guided by a comprehensive iProperty strategy?

The strategy grid guides the decisions of the iProperty team. Each cell in the grid should include a set of tactics that will be used to protect ideas in that category. For example, workable ideas in the High Value, Idea Category A cell may be filed immediately as patent applications, while high-priority ideas in Idea Category D may be maintained as trade secrets when possible or otherwise published. Ideas that are not yet workable in the High-Value, Idea Category A cell may be assigned immediately to a supervisor for action.

The tactics should be specific. For example, High-Value, Idea Category A ideas may be filed as patent applications within one month of evaluation, to include a U.S. utility application, a Patent Cooperation Treaty (PCT) application, a European application, and a Canadian application. In contrast, Low-Value, Idea Category A ideas may be filed as provisional patent applications and reevaluated prior to the deadline for filing the provisional patent application as a utility patent application, PCT patent application, and/or in one or more foreign countries. Similarly, patent applications covering High-Value, Idea Category A ideas may be pursued rapidly even though doing so will increase near-term costs for protecting these ideas, whereas Medium-Value, Idea Category A ideas may be pursued in the same set of countries as High-Value, Idea Category A ideas, but the cases may be pursued as slowly as possible, taking advantage of opportunities to delay expenses wherever possible.

The iProperty strategy grid assists the iProperty team to assign strategic options to specific categories and priorities of ideas without having to reinvent the wheel for every idea. Of course, as we have discussed elsewhere, no written strategy should replace good judgment. Once a strategy is formulated, there should always be a moment for a reality check during which the strategy may be adjusted as needed.

MANAGING INFORMATION FLOW

Once a decision is made about the disposition of an idea, the remaining steps of the iProperty pipeline are about execution. In particular, the documented information about the idea must be enhanced. More detailed technical, business, and legal information must be added to the documentation. And companies that are serious about execution must employ processes for creating this high-quality end product quickly and efficiently. Furthermore, the outcome must be fed back to the innovators who started it to give them confidence in the process and keep them motivated and contributing. This last action is one that is more often than not ignored, yielding distrust and tension, and diminishing healthy iProperty culture.

Formalizing the Information Content

Once the iProperty team makes a decision to proceed with protecting an idea, the idea must be formally documented. Recall that, for the sake of efficiency, the idea capture process involves documentation of only a minimal amount of information. Formal documentation provides an avenue for fleshing out the details of the idea, its inventors, and pertinent dates in an invention disclosure document. This document is prepared for use in the manner prescribed by the iProperty team; for example, it may be provided to patent counsel for incorporation into a patent application, maintained in a set of documented trade secrets, or published as a defensive publication.

Companies could educate employees to prepare high-quality invention disclosures with a consistently formatted set of detailed business and technical content. However, even when fully trained, the average scientist has little interest in writing invention disclosures. He or she is rarely motivated to do the writing required to produce high-quality documentation. Many scientists and engineers actually detest the task. Even those who like to write find it difficult to set aside the time required to prepare detailed formal documentation. In the absence of a standardized process, the quality of invention disclosures in an organization varies widely, and many invention disclosures lack key details needed by the patent counsel and management to understand and evaluate the idea being described, leading to even more frustration and wasted resources. Where the invention disclosures are intended to provide input into the patenting process, incomplete invention disclosures increase the time and effort required for the patent counsel to prepare patent applications and thereby increase the total expense of each patent application, potentially reducing the total number of patents that the company can afford to pursue.

Even if employees are trained and motivated to produce well-written invention disclosures in a timely way, this is a less-than-effective use of their time. The company should want to keep its innovators busy creating and refining new ideas. Innovating is presumably the most critical aspect of their jobs in today's global innovation competition. As an alternative, we believe that companies should relieve their employees of this burden altogether while improving their documentation dramatically by establishing a process that places the responsibility for documenting ideas in the hands of a trained interviewer and technical writer.

In our experience, a structured interview (sometimes called an oral invention disclosure) combined with documentation by a technical writer (see Exhibit 11.1) provides an efficient approach to gathering information from an inventor. In the interview, a trained facilitator, such as a patent counsel, meets with inventors to discuss an invention in a structured manner designed to quickly elicit the facts that are needed for documenting the invention. Most ideas can be documented in an interview of no more than an hour. During the process, the interview can be recorded, preliminary drawings can be made, and important laboratory notebook entries and other sources of data can be identified. These records can be provided to a trained technical writer for formal documentation.

A useful format divides the interview into two parts. The first part is a free-thinking process during which the interview group works through the idea together, paying attention to the current state of the art, the problems solved by the idea, degree of enablement, technical features, and various alternative constructions and ways that others might engineer around the ideas. Participants may make sketches during this portion of the interview, ideally using permanent colored pens to maximize the details being communicated and create a permanent record.

The second half of the interview is a performance. Everyone knows his or her role and the information that needs to be conveyed. A digital tape recorder and/or video camera is turned on, and the group walks through a structured interview process, explaining the background and general concept of the idea and describing each of the drawings that were sketched during the first half of the interview. During videotaping, it is helpful to focus the camera on the drawings to capture speakers' interactions with them. All evaluation of the fitness of the idea should be done during the first part of the interview so the recording does not contain material that could be picked apart by an unscrupulous litigator at a later date.

The output of this process is a set of drawings and an oral disclosure that can be provided to a technical writer for documentation. Advanced Liquid Logic, Inc. (ALL) uses this process, and as soon as the interview is complete, the drawings and recording are uploaded to an InfoStrength® portal, where these materials are time and date stamped to establish an "at least as early as" date for the idea being documented. ALL is located in Research Triangle Park in North Carolina, but its network of disclosure writers is distributed around the country. For example, writer Tom Bachelder lives in Albany, New York. He can download the interview materials, and with 8 or 10 hours of work, produce an invention disclosure document according to ALL specifications, complete with patent-style numbered drawings, and upload it to the InfoStrength portal.

Using this approach, the ALL team can schedule multiple inventor interviews in a single day and assign the technical writing in parallel to multiple specialized technical writers whose billable hour rates are typically less than one-third of the billable hour rates for experienced patent counsel. Within one week, all of the invention disclosure documents are done and ready for next steps. Where the idea is intended to be protected in a patent application, the invention disclosure can be downloaded from the InfoStrength portal by in-house or outside patent counsel and used as the basis for preparation of a patent application. Usually only minor changes are required, and the patent counsel converts the disclosure document into a provisional patent application and files it within a few hours. The process saves considerable resources by placing the technical writing task in the hands of trained technical writers rather than expensive patent counsel.

Legalizing the Information Content

Ideas that are selected for patenting typically are conveyed to patent counsel for legal documentation. Because every patent application is part technical writing and part legalese, the patent counsel's highest value added to the application is the incorporation of the required legalese, including the preparation of a detailed set of patent claims. The practice in many organizations of handing off photocopies of lab notebooks and other rough documents to patent counsel without a formal invention disclosure forces the patent counsel to fill the role of technical writer at patent counsel hourly rates. Companies that take this route can expect to pay the maximum amount of legal fees for the preparation of patent applications.

Further, dumping disclosure materials on the patent counsel without any strategic guidance can result in many poorly used, expensive hours as the patent counsel prepares patent applications or advances them in ways that are not in line with the company's business strategy. Legal fees can be minimized by ensuring that the patent counsel is up to speed about the strategic reason for obtaining the patent. Of course, there is no better way to do this than to include the patent counsel in the regularly meeting iProperty team.

Many companies that are reluctant to pay their outside patent counsel to participate in a one-hour meeting would cringe if they could see the long-term cost of not keeping the counsel in the strategic loop from the beginning. At best, uninformed counsel spends a multitude of billable hours researching publicly available information on the Internet, trying to understand the company's needs and strategy. At worst, the uninformed patent counsel prepares the patent application without any consideration of strategy at all. In either case, the consequences can be severe. Generally speaking, once a patent application has been filed, it cannot be changed. Strategic options that are left out of the application at filing generally cannot be added in later. Filing a patent application is like launching a rescue boat. Once launched, there is no opportunity to add anything new. Arrival at the scene of the crash is not the time to start developing a strategy about what to bring. Likewise, many a patent counsel has spent countless hours mourning a critical missing detail—even a single word!—that was left out of a patent application.

> If you opened your patent counsel's file for one of your important patent applications, would you find a concise description of the strategic reasons your company chose to invest in that application?

Once the patent application is filed, it enters a period referred to as "patent prosecution." Patent prosecution is essentially a negotiation with the relevant patent office in the country where the application was filed over whether claims will issue in the application, and if so, how broad the claims will be. "Claims" are concise statements at the end of a patent that describe the limits of protection provided by the patent. Patent applicants usually request very broad claims, and as claims are amended during prosecution, the claims are narrowed. The resulting scope of protection may look quite different from the original set of claims. Unfortunately, managers and employees often view the patent prosecution stage as the domain of the patent counsel. However, if not carefully reviewed, amendments to claims made during prosecution may introduce technical inaccuracies or unnecessary restrictions that diminish the value of the resulting patent to the company, perhaps by failing to protect a product or making the claims easy to engineer around. What is worse is that these deficiencies may not be noticed until it is too late to repair them.

In order to be protected effectively in a patent, an idea must, among other things, be novel—it must be new to the world. By definition, the innovator who creates a novel idea knows more about that idea than any other person. Consequently, the innovator should be intimately involved in the prosecution of the patent application. However, the reality is often quite different. Many innovators are turned off by the legalese of patent applications, particularly patent claims, and fail to read them carefully, with predictable consequences.

Business decision makers also often fail to understand their patent applications. This failure is sometimes attributable to lack of creative communication skills by patent counsel, who cannot comprehend that busy executives do not have time to read patent applications. The common attitude is much like that of a patent counsel who drafted a complex legal opinion about a competitor's patent for a former company. When the patent attorney was asked to include an executive summary on the opinion for the company's chief executive officer (CEO), he refused, saying that including an executive summary would discourage the CEO from reading the entire opinion. For busy executives, time is the scarcest resource. iProperty companies must select patent counsel who know how to communicate strategic information to executive decision makers clearly, concisely, and at the right time to facilitate effective decisions.

Feedback Loops

The output of the iProperty pipeline is a portfolio of legally protected units of intellectual property, including a patent portfolio of patents and patent applications, a portfolio of documented and protected trade secrets, and in many cases, a portfolio of defensive publications. One of the most important facets of the enhanced iProperty pipeline is *feedback*. Feedback loops supply information about the portfolio to those responsible for the pipeline's strategic direction and to those responsible for generating the innovations that supply the pipeline. These feedback loops are illustrated in Exhibits 10.1 and 11.1. Feedback takes place during execution of the iProperty strategy to build the iProperty portfolio by keeping business decision makers informed about the progress, setbacks, and the resulting strengths and weaknesses of the portfolio.

Of course, success requires that the business leaders make the time to listen. As discussed earlier, this iProperty portfolio is likely to be one of your company's most valuable assets, if not the most valuable asset. Executives should know at least as much about the iProperty portfolio as they know about other assets of similar value. Decision makers must understand how the company is performing against its iProperty and business strategies and where additional investment or management attention is required.

Feedback to your innovators is also critical. Feedback reveals strategic weaknesses and prompts innovators to identify potential improvements. For example, companies using patents to protect their ideas must review the scope of the resulting patent claims with innovators to consider how the claims may be invented around. By "invented around," we mean how a product or process might be redesigned to avoid infringing the claims of the company's patents. If your company is making a healthy profit from its innovations or heading toward a lucrative market, you can bet that competitors will seek to invent around your patents' claims.

Ironically, just as all the children in Garrison Keillor's fictional Lake Wobegon are above average, most innovators believe that they can engineer around the patents of others but that few others can engineer around their patents. If not checked, this bias can lead to a false sense of security. A competitor looking at a lucrative market that is blocked by a patent will pick a patent claim apart word for word to identify any weaknesses and loopholes that the original innovators never considered. For this reason, iProperty companies must learn to put themselves in the minds of their competitors to find the weaknesses themselves and plug the holes before their competitors have a chance to exploit them. It pays to invent around your own patents before your competitors do.

MANAGING THE PIPELINE

At ALL, Bill uses the OVO Incubator™ software system by OVO Innovation, Inc. to manage the early stages of the iProperty pipeline. Employees fill the pipeline by submitting a one-page electronic form, and the submission is entered into the system. Idea evaluation is divided into three parts, shown as screens in Exhibits 11.3, 11.4, and 11.5, which must be

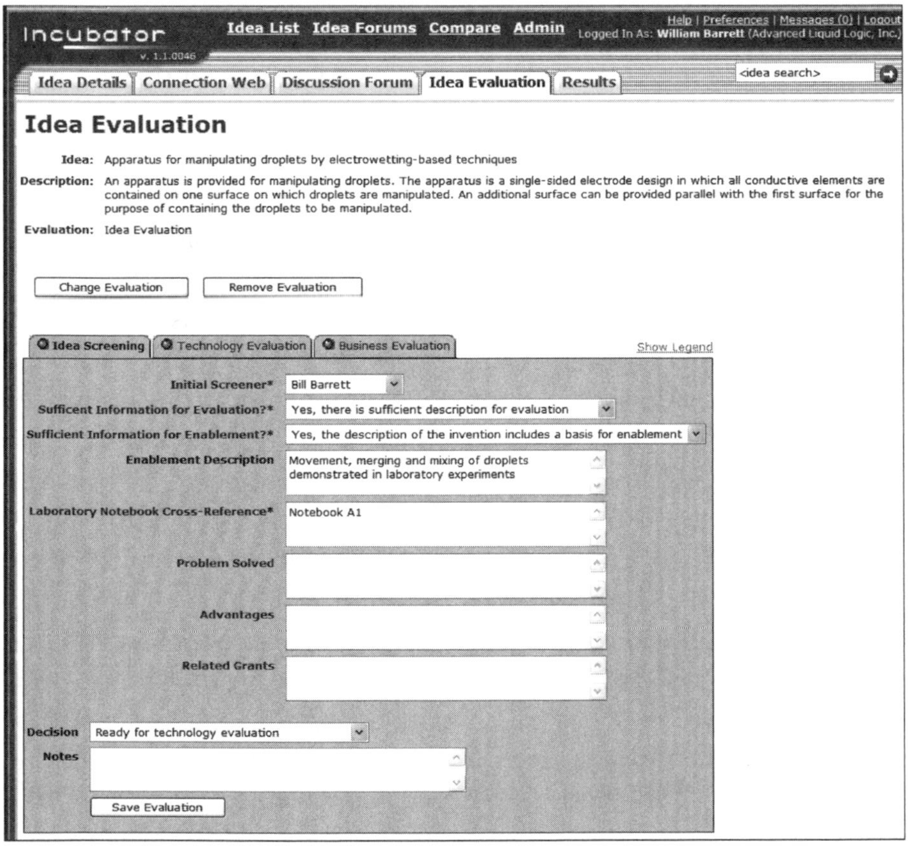

EXHIBIT 11.3 Screen Shot of Idea Screening Evaluation Tab from OVO Incubator
Source: Courtesy of OVO Innovation, Inc.

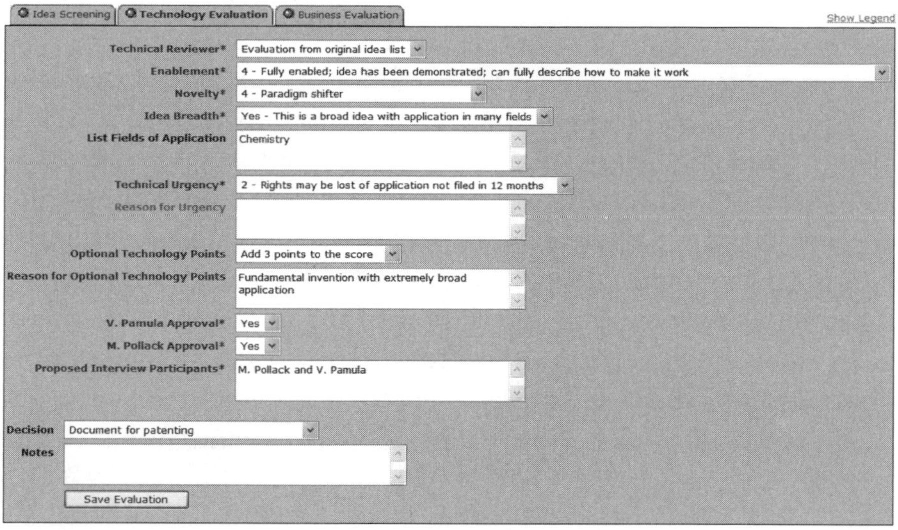

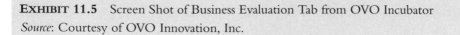

EXHIBIT 11.4 Screen Shot of Technology Evaluation Tab from OVO Incubator
Source: Courtesy of OVO Innovation, Inc.

completed sequentially:

1. **Idea screening.** Determines whether sufficient information has been provided to permit evaluation of the idea
2. **Technology evaluation.** Evaluates the idea based on a series of technology-oriented questions
3. **Business evaluation.** Evaluates the idea based on a series of business-oriented questions

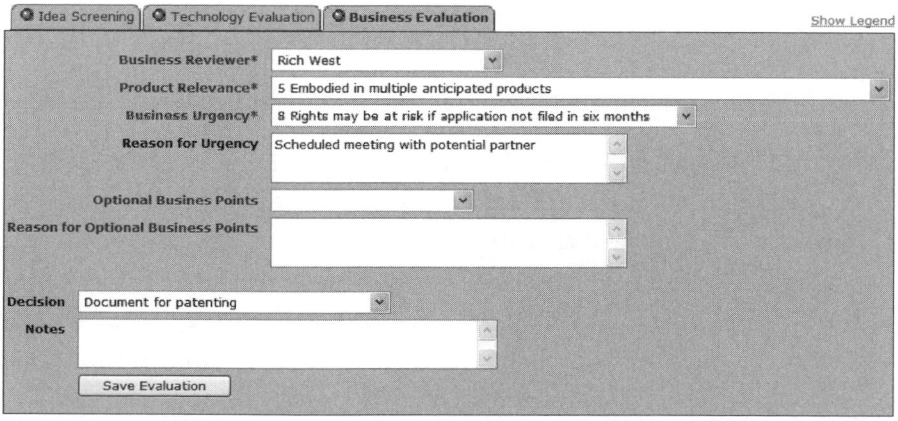

EXHIBIT 11.5 Screen Shot of Business Evaluation Tab from OVO Incubator
Source: Courtesy of OVO Innovation, Inc.

Idea Screening

The Idea Screening screen, shown in Exhibit 11.3, includes a series of questions designed to determine whether sufficient information has been provided to permit evaluation of the idea. A first yes/no parameter focuses on whether the idea submission form was filled out completely. A second asks whether sufficient information was provided on the idea submission form to provide a demonstration of enablement. The screening step also requires entry of a description of the basis for enablement. This description could be a brief reference to laboratory work done to demonstrate the validity of the concept or a statement that the inventor can prepare drawings illustrating the making and using of the idea.

How does your company regulate the flow of ideas in its iProperty pipeline?

The screening step also requires a cross-reference to a laboratory notebook. In addition to providing a record of the location of the idea in a properly documented laboratory notebook, the notebook cross-reference also serves as a reminder that the idea must be documented properly in a notebook. The idea cannot be entered into the OVO Incubator system if there is no laboratory notebook reference. Once the required screening steps are complete, the system permits the user to move to the technology evaluation screen shown in Exhibit 11.4.

Technology Evaluation

The Technology Evaluation screen shown in Exhibit 11.4 includes a series of questions designed to facilitate evaluation of technological aspects of the idea. Among other things, this step requires answers to questions that are used to assign a score indicative of the idea's value to the company. For example, the screen includes an evaluation of the degree of enablement of the idea, novelty of the idea, and assessment of factors relating to technical urgency. A wide variety of parameters may be used, depending on the company's iProperty strategy, but most companies can evaluate ideas using a carefully selected subset of parameters, for example: Each answer should be associated with a score, which is not shown.

Enablement

The Idea Screening tab provides an initial assessment that the idea has some degree of enablement. Here, the evaluator assesses and scores the degree of enablement. The question is, how much detailed information is available, e.g., from experiments or diagrams, that supports the operability of the idea? Examples of suitable answers are:

- Fully enabled, the idea has been empirically demonstrated and we can fully describe the best known means to make it work.
- The specific idea has not been demonstrated or has been demonstrated in a limited way, but most or all of the relevant experiments/observations have been made and there is little chance that it would not work.
- Some relevant experiments/observations have been made, but other key experiments remain to be done. There is a chance that the idea would not work or that a specific embodiment could not be described.
- There is some basis for the idea, but major key experiments pertaining to feasibility need to be done.

Novelty

This field evaluates the technical novelty of the idea. To what degree does the idea represent an advance over the current state of the art? Examples of suitable answers are:

- Paradigm shifter
- Breakthrough idea, a huge step forward
- Good solid innovation
- Incremental innovation

Idea Breadth

This simple yes/no parameter evaluates the idea based on the breadth of the idea. The parameter asks whether the idea is broadly applicable across many fields or a narrow idea with application in only a few fields. Examples of suitable answers are:

- Yes. This is a broad idea with application in many fields.
- No. This is an idea with a narrow scope of applicability.

Technical Urgency

This parameter assesses factors that would indicate a need to move quickly to protect the idea. In particular, the parameter focuses on factors that would be apparent from the research and development side of the business. Examples include previous or upcoming technical publications, technical discussions with suppliers, and shipment of proprietary materials to service providers. The numbers are scored high to ensure that truly urgent ideas move to the top of the list. Examples of suitable answers are:

- Rights may be lost if application not filed in 1 month.
- Rights may be lost if application not filed in 6 months.
- Rights may be lost if application not filed in 12 months.
- Idea can be maintained in secret for one year or longer.

If the answer to technical urgency suggests a heightened urgency, the user must include a reason why this is the case. It is important to include a reason so that when evaluating business urgency on the Business Evaluation screen, the business reviewer can be sure not to duplicate the urgency evaluation, which would give the idea an artificially high score.

Optional Technology Points

This parameter permits the technology reviewer to add points to an idea due to aspects of value not identified in the other technology parameters. If the technology evaluator adds any optional technology points, he or she must justify the addition with a notation in this field. This approach helps to identify any important parameters that have not been accounted for in the established evaluation process, so that the process can be modified accordingly.

Decision

The technology evaluation step concludes with a set of possible decisions. The decision is a recommendation by the technology reviewer regarding the proposed disposition of the innovation. Examples of suitable decisions are:

- Document for a patent application
- Document for trade secret protection
- Document for defensive publication

- Return to inventor for additional work
- Return to inventor for additional information
- Reevaluate in 6 months or 12 months
- Take no further action

Business Evaluation

Once the technical evaluation is complete, the system permits the business evaluator to conduct the business evaluation. This part of the process includes a series of questions designed to facilitate evaluation of business aspects of the idea. Among other things, the business evaluation includes questions about the relevance of the idea to anticipated or actual products and the business urgency of the idea.

One aspect of the business evaluation, the product relevance parameter, evaluates the idea based on whether it is relevant to a specific anticipated product in development or soon to be. Examples of suitable answers are:

- Embodied in multiple anticipated products
- Embodied in near-term product or the making/using of a near-term product
- Not embodied in an anticipated product but has high licensing potential in an adjacent field
- Probably relates to or embodied in a second-generation product
- Not in a product for the foreseeable future

Like technical urgency, a business urgency parameter permits identification of known or expected events that could result in loss of patent rights or otherwise heighten the urgency for protecting the invention. The system also provides for optional business points, like the optional technology points described above, and permits the business reviewer to enter a decision about the disposition of the idea.

The ultimate recommendation to management or decision (if the iProperty team is so empowered) is made by consensus. If the recommended decisions of the business and technology reviewer are the same, the consensus decision is entered and acted on appropriately. Where the decisions differ, the recommendation can be discussed and the differences resolved by the iProperty team.

Idea Ranking

The scores permit all ideas in the system to be ranked. Ideas receiving the highest score merit attention first, followed by ideas receiving lower scores. In essence, the process singles out the apparently most valuable, strategically targeted ideas for action. Ideas that require documentation can be scheduled for interviews, interview materials can be sent to technical writers, and invention disclosures can be sent to in-house or outside patent counsel for legal documentation. Similarly, high-scoring ideas that require additional experimental or design work can be assigned to managers for action. By proactively controlling the flow of ideas, the pipeline filters out the less valuable ideas and strategically produces an output iProperty portfolio that is aligned with the company's business strategy. The system operates in real time as a fast-moving iProperty-generating engine.

The factors that lead to an efficient and helpful ranking of ideas differ for each company. Examples of additional factors that may be included in an analysis include: the likelihood of successfully solving the problems needed to take the idea to the market; the market size of product or service opportunities; the intensity of competitive pressure that the idea is likely to face in the market; and outlicensing potential.

Feedback

The OVO Incubator system permits a variety of e-mail alerts to be set up, and e-mails are sent to idea originators and others to keep them posted on the outcome of the idea evaluation. If the recommendation requires the use of company resources to flesh out a design or test an idea to see if it works, the appropriate managers can be informed so that the necessary resource decisions can be made. This feedback helps innovators to understand that the system provides impartial and fair treatment for their ideas, and it helps them to recognize the kinds of inventions that are likely to make it through the pipeline successfully.

MAXIMIZING OUTPUT VALUE

Building an integrated and fully supported iProperty pipeline offers a number of important advantages to an enterprise. By standardizing the steps of iProperty development, companies can reduce wasted effort and streamline the process, thereby reducing the per-unit cost of developing iProperty. Companies can improve their iProperty portfolios both quantitatively and qualitatively, capture the maximum amount of potential iProperty, develop a portfolio that is aligned with specific business objectives, and eliminate iProperty that does not support revenue streams. Companies can increase the speed of iProperty development by directing employees to work on the most important problems and by moving quickly to protect important ideas when they are identified. Finally, companies can avoid costly strategic mistakes by keeping decision makers informed of the output of the iProperty pipeline and can close loopholes in their patent protection by carefully scrutinizing their own patent claims. Building an enhanced iProperty pipeline requires an effort similar to the effort required for the development of any core business process. A variety of software and other systems are emerging for managing the iProperty pipeline, and companies that are serious about the process would do well to deploy such systems. Companies that live and die in the global marketplace based on the quality of their ideas, increasingly the norm and not the exception, must pay careful attention to the development of an enhanced iProperty pipeline.

~ 12 ~

iProperty Options

Tactical Considerations for the Global Economy

Once a valuable idea has been identified, the fundamental choice from an iProperty perspective is what exactly to do with it. Aside from doing nothing, the basic options include maintaining the idea as a trade secret, patenting the idea, and publishing the idea as a defensive publication to block patents by others. For simplicity, we will ignore certain specialized forms of protection, such as copyrights for computer codes or semiconductor mask works. Further we want to be clear here that we are discussing making tactical decisions for specific individual ideas. An inventive concept may include numerous ideas, and a technology or product may involve hundreds or even thousands of individual ideas. A strategy for an inventive concept, technology, or product may involve patenting some ideas, maintaining others as trade secrets, and publishing others. Each individual idea should have a specific iProperty disposition.

When considering forms of protection for ideas, we like to think through the options in this order: trade secrets, patents, and defensive publications. The analysis begins by considering for each specific idea whether the idea is a good candidate for trade secret protection. When an idea is suitable for trade secret protection, the decision is a no-brainer. If the trade secret is maintained properly in secret, it can last forever. The problem, as we will discuss, is that many important ideas are not suitable for trade secret protection as a long term strategy, since they cannot be kept secret, for any number of reasons.

If the idea is not a good candidate for trade secret protection, the analysis proceeds to consideration of whether patenting is justified, giving consideration to a variety of factors, including cost. If the answer is yes, then the idea should be thoroughly documented and presented to a patent attorney or patent agent for preparation of a patent application. If the answer is no, the analysis should proceed to a consideration of whether the idea should be published. A defensive publication exposes the idea to the public and is thus "prior art," and as such prevents anyone else from patenting the idea. If you have managed to stay with us for the last 11 chapters, you will not be surprised to hear that we believe that decisions about forms of protection should be made in the context of a well-managed iProperty program and in light of a comprehensive iProperty strategy.

KEEPING SECRETS

Trade secrets are often seen as the ugly stepsister of patents. Or, as more eloquently stated by Bill Landes and Richard Posner in *The Economic Structure of Intellectual Property Law*:

> Judges and lawyers have sometimes reasoned that because trade secret law provides less protection to the inventor than patent law does, no rational person who makes a patentable invention would fail to seek a patent; and therefore trade secret law *must* protect a class of lesser inventions, as well as things like customer lists that are not inventions at all.[1]

Landes and Posner disagree with the line of reasoning that assigns trade secrets second-class status in the world of iProperty, and so do we. Further, we believe that trade secrets are, for reasons to be discussed further, in many ways a superior form of iProperty protection—at least for ideas that are good candidates for trade secret protection. Just ask Coca-Cola, a company that has effectively used trade secrets for decades. When deciding how to protect any novel idea, the first question to ask is whether the idea is a good candidate for trade secret protection.

Trade secrets protect against misappropriation of ideas that are kept secret and not against independent discovery or reverse engineering. Thus, if Company A decides to keep its new widget as a trade secret, and Company B independently invents the same widget, then Company A cannot use trade secret law to prevent Company B from making the widget. The same is true if Company B analyzes the widget and learns how to make it. What is potentially even more damaging is that Company B could patent the independently invented widget and enforce the patent against Company A.

Because of these risks, an idea is generally a good candidate for trade secret protection when (1) it is not patentable (e.g., a customer list or a secret that lacks the requisite novelty and nonobviousness to justify a patent), (2) the period of time during which there is market demand for the product is shorter than the time it takes to obtain a patent, or (3) when all of the following conditions are true:

- The idea embodies a high degree of complexity and novelty that would make rapid independent invention by a competitor unlikely.
- Novel aspects of the idea can be kept secret; that is, they are available in a form that prevents them from being quickly reverse engineered.
- The idea is so securely protected that it is not likely to walk out the door with a customer, supplier, or employee, purposely or not.

The classic example of a good candidate for trade secret protection is a breakthrough manufacturing process that cannot be deduced from the product manufactured. The *breakthrough* characteristic suggests a high degree of novelty that would be difficult for another company to duplicate independently for an economically significant period of time. The fact that it is a manufacturing process means that it can be hidden away in the "bowels" of the company, where it will be difficult to detect and where security protections are most effective. Access by employees and outsiders can be limited to a few key individuals, which minimizes the risk of transmission outside the company.

A discovery, for example, that a previously patented drug can be synthesized more efficiently using a highly unusual set of reagents and reaction conditions fits these requirements. Patenting such a process would require disclosure of the idea to the public, and the risk of being caught and sued for infringement might not be a sufficient deterrent to prevent others from using the patented process in the secrecy of their own factories. Nevertheless, such an idea should be maintained as a trade secret only if the company is committed to taking extraordinary security measures to maintain the secrecy of the idea.

Secrets Are Hard to Keep

Globalization affects the analysis of whether and when to use trade secrets, depending on specific business strategies. Companies making maximum use of the global economy by outsourcing or offshoring processes or innovation, may find that trade secrets are more difficult to protect when employees around the globe have access to them. In an interview for Thomas Friedman's book, *The World Is Flat*, Microsoft's chief technology officer, Craig Mundie, commented: "The world is decidedly not flat when it comes to uniform treatment of intellectual property." As summarized by Friedman, Mundie went on to explain:

> It is wonderful . . . to have a world where a single innovator can summon so many resources . . . assemble a team of partners from around the flat world, and make a real breakthrough with some product or service. But what does an innovative engineer do . . . "when someone else uses the same flat-world platform and tools to clone and distribute his wonderful new product?"[2]

In the flat world, trade secrets are difficult to protect. In a country in which laws protecting trade secrets are inadequate or poorly enforced, it is unlikely that a company can avoid trade secret losses under all but the most secretive conditions. The same global communications infrastructure that facilitates communicating with the plant in China also can make it easy for detailed process information or plans to be transmitted from that plant to a competitor anywhere in the world. Further, global improvements in technology capabilities often mean that competitors can rapidly duplicate the process and put competing products on the market.

Another issue weighing against trade secrets in many developing countries is extensive employee turnover. Employees may be lured away by competitors for a small increase in salary and take the company's trade secrets with them. Paul Beamish, Professor of International Business at Richard Ivey School of Business at the University of Western Ontario, points out that the turnover rate among Chinese workers is unusually high. Beamish suggests that a source of the problem is extremely low wages: "When you are making [less than $130 per month], a five-cent-an-hour raise is a significant increase."[3] When the turnover is among highly skilled workers, such as programmers and engineers, the trade secret losses can be enormous, especially when highly skilled workers are leaving to take their know-how to competitors. Companies that care about iProperty should account for the cost of labor churn when setting wages for workers in developing countries. In the long run, the amounts saved by paying a few cents less may not be worth the potential loss of valuable trade secrets, training, and know-how to competitors.

Secrets May Be the Only, and Best Option

For an idea that will not be part of an outsourcing or offshoring program, trade secrets may become even more important than ever in the flat world due to several factors. In exchange for granting 20 years of exclusive patent rights, the patent laws require the innovator to disclose to the world how to make and use the invention. Further, the best mode of operation, not some barely effective rudimentary method, must be included in the patent application, which publishes 18 months after the application (or its parent application) is filed in the patent office. In other words, the applicant has to publish the "special sauce" to the extent that it is known when the application is filed.

While the innovator's highly detailed patent disclosure is published and made available to the whole world, the patent rights are valid only within the countries in which the innovator chooses to invest in patent protection. In the flat world, the vast global distribution of innovation hot spots means that there is considerable risk that any valuable idea will be duplicated in regions where the company chooses to forgo patent protection (e.g., due to limited financial resources) or where there is no reliable patent protection. This risk means that where the three criteria mentioned earlier in the chapter—difficult to duplicate, capable of being protected, and security—are satisfied, the company may need to opt between an extensive foreign patenting strategy and trade secret protection as the best approach available for a specific idea.

A related risk of patent protection is that even where reasonably good patent protection is available, the patent disclosure may enable a competitor to engineer around the patent more quickly than the competitor would be able to obtain access to the trade secret.[4] In this case, patenting might protect the product but facilitate competition in the form of alternative products on the market sooner due to the information that competitors could glean from the company's patent disclosure. If the company is not inclined to invest heavily in identifying an extensive set of alternative approaches and patenting these approaches in a large set of countries, then a strategy in which more ideas are protected as trade secrets may be a reasonable option. Nevertheless, a better option would combine (1) a comprehensive patent strategy that protects a wide variety of alternatives to the technical approach employed in the company's product or service, with (2) a trade secret strategy for ideas that can effectively be maintained in secret for an economically sufficient period of time.

If there simply is no reliable government protection of any form of iProperty, secrecy, however leaky, may be not only the best strategic option but the only one.[5] In these cases, companies must work hard to secure trade secrets by strictly limiting access and by motivating key employees to stay with the company. If a company is conducting manufacturing operations in China, for example, it is important to limit the information provided to the factory to the minimum amount needed to accomplish the required task—keep the crown jewels out of China.[6]

Companies should also consider separating product development and manufacturing process steps across multiple sites within a country or among countries so that no one site has access to all the steps of the process. Militaries use this approach, called compartmentalization, to protect classified information. Only personnel with a need to know have access to a specific type or "compartment" of information. The most sensitive information may be classified as "your eyes only" and other highly defined, restricted distributions.

Other significant advantages to trade secret protection include the fact that it is inexpensive, it lasts indefinitely, and it can have a global reach. Landes and Posner observe that the cost of trade secret protection should be roughly proportional to the value of the trade secret, whereas patent costs are relatively fixed on a per-country basis for each idea regardless of its value.[7] Trade secret protection is potentially forever, while patents last only 20 years from the date the patent application is filed. Further, patents are territorial, whereas in some circumstances, trade secret laws can provide certain remedies regardless of the offender's location around the world.

For example, as pointed out by Professor Karl Jorda of Franklin Pierce Law Center, misappropriation of trade secrets from the United States even by a foreign company is actionable as a felony under the Industrial Espionage Act of 1996.[8] Moreover, Professor Jorda emphasizes that damages and injunctions awarded for trade secret misappropriation cases are not insignificant, referencing as examples:[9]

- A jury awarded two individuals $240 million in a suit against Walt Disney Co. for theft of trade secrets for a sports complex.
- Cargill, Inc., was required to pay Pioneer HiBred International $300 million for misappropriation of trade secrets relating to genetically engineered corn seeds.
- Pizza Hut was ordered to pay C&F Packaging $10.9 million for misappropriating trade secrets relating to packaging of pre-cooked sausage.

- A court ordered Barr Laboratories to stop using a secret manufacturing process for Premarin that was misappropriated from Wyeth.

In considering a strategy that combines trade secrets and patents, it is important not to stumble over the "best-mode" requirement. That is, companies often adopt a strategy of patenting a basic idea while retaining detailed information about some special, perhaps subtle aspect of it, such as a superior method for making it. However, as mentioned, U.S. patent law requires the patent application to describe the best mode for carrying out the idea subjectively known to the patent applicant at the time the application is filed.[10] The best mode requirement helps maintain the balance of the patent "deal" (discussed below) by ensuring that the public obtains a description of the applicant's best-known embodiment of the idea in exchange for surrendering temporary patent rights to the applicant. Failure to include the best mode can result in the invalidation of the resulting patent. Companies should thus never attempt to retain as a trade secret the best mode while actively seeking a patent on other, less effective modes.

On the other hand, Professor Jorda argues that companies should not overemphasize the impact of the best mode requirement.[11] Even when the best mode is adequately described in the patent application at the time it is filed, it is likely that in the months following the filing, the best mode will continue to evolve in significant ways that are difficult for competitors to replicate. Such evolutionary developments may make excellent trade secrets. Thus, in many circumstances, an opportunity exists to patent certain aspects of an idea while retaining other aspects as trade secrets without violating the best-mode requirement. However, decisions concerning such strategies should be made as part of a comprehensive strategy in consultation with a patent counsel who has been fully informed of all aspects of the idea.

Mastering Trade Secrets

Coca-Cola, or Coke, is perhaps the most famous user of trade secrets. In almost every presentation about trade secrets we have ever heard, the Coke formula has been used as the prime example. Ironically, while the soft-drink formula was probably an excellent candidate for trade secret protection when it was created, it is probably not the best trade secret today, given the ability of chemists to analyze and reproduce the contents of Coke. As iProperty, the Coke formula probably has far greater value in marketing the mystique of its long secrecy than in the intrinsic value of the formula.

Nevertheless, Coke continues to develop trade secrets of intrinsic value. Recently three people were arrested and charged with stealing confidential Coke documents and a product sample. An administrative assistant for a senior manager at Coke was seen on video surveillance stuffing documents and a product sample into bags. The group allegedly tried to sell the items to Pepsi. Pepsi tipped off Coke to the scheme, and the suspects were charged with wire fraud and unlawfully stealing and selling trade secrets.

There are some important lessons to be learned from the incident. One is that Pepsi, Coke's biggest competitor, tipped off Coke on the scheme. Pepsi's decision may have been the result of its high moral standards, but it certainly also had something to do with the criminal liability that could have resulted from its knowing participation. The Industrial Espionage Act makes it a crime for a company to knowingly participate in the theft or misappropriation of trade secrets.

Another lesson from the Coke case relates to the fact that it was Coke's own trusted employees who attempted to take the information to Pepsi. While people often think of industrial espionage as one company spying on another to gain access to confidential information, more often the problem comes from within. And a corollary lesson comes from the fact that Coke actually takes the steps needed to protect its trade secrets from employee theft, even going so far as to use video surveillance. Taking reasonable steps to ensure that trade secrets do not walk away with un-scrupulous employees is one of the requirements for calling something a trade secret. If it is not protected, it is not a trade secret. For example, the Industrial Espionage Act broadly defines what is considered a protected trade secret, but it only includes information that "the owner thereof has taken reasonable measures to keep such information secret."

Is your company serious about trade secrets? Does it have a trade secret policy? Can you specifically identify your most important trade secrets?

Video surveillance is not strictly required to maintain information as a trade secret, but many companies do very little to protect their confidential information. At a minimum,

- Trade secret documents should be marked as confidential.
- Access should be granted on a need-to-know basis.
- Employment agreements should include confidentiality obligations.
- A confidential information policy should be in place.
- Employees should be routinely reminded of this policy and their obligation to protect the company's confidential information.
- When employees leave, they should be reminded of their continual, general obligation not to divulge confidential information to others.
- Confidential information should not be shared with third parties without a Confidential Disclosure Agreement in place.

In addition to the IEA at the federal level, U.S. states also have a variety of trade secret laws, many of which are based on the Uniform Trade Secrets Act, which was prepared by the National Conference of Commissioners on Uniform State Laws. The Uniform Trade Secret Act establishes liability for misappropriation of trade secrets such as formulas, patterns, compilations, program devices, methods, techniques, or processes that are secret and that derive their economic value from their secrecy.

Importantly, for companies looking to outsource or offshore innovation, many of the countries in which labor costs are attractive do not have such laws. Even where they exist on the books, they may not be enforced. As a result, when working in such countries, companies should take exceptional measures to protect trade secrets.

Know Your Enemies

When employing a trade secret strategy, it pays to have a broad definition of who your enemies are. A mentality slightly bordering on paranoia is perfectly appropriate. It is also important not to underestimate the enemy. Just like most people see themselves as having above-average intelligence, most engineers and scientists think very highly of their own ability to pick up valuable information from a walk through a competitor's factory or a discussion with a scientist at a poster session, but they generally underestimate their competitors' ability to do the same.

In one example of an admirably creative method of protecting trade secrets, a large tire company installed a machine on its highly confidential factory floor. When the machine malfunctioned, the internal technicians called the company that made the machine and tried to work out a fix over the phone. When that failed, the tire company realized it had to bring an outside technician into its factory. When the technician arrived, and the door at the entrance was opened, all he saw was the inside of a giant flexible tubing, large enough for a person to walk through. The factory workers had set up the tubing from the door to the machine so that the technician could walk through the tubing, repair the machine, and go out again without ever seeing the layout of the factory.

Preemption Strategies

Some companies rely on trade secret protection during the product development process, knowing that when the product is launched, it will be copied. Harvard Business School professor Bharat Anand and University of Chile professor Alexander Galetovic refer to this strategy as *preemption,* a "nip-it-in-the-bud" strategy: "Preemption entails being first to the market so that you can capture profits of monopoly scale before reverse engineering, imitation or piracy eat into them."[12]

Long term, a successful preemption strategy involves staying at the top of the game, being the fastest to innovate and the fastest to get that innovation to market. Success relies on maintaining secrecy about the product until launch so that competitors will have to take time to copy the product and to manufacture and take their copies to the market. The better the prelaunch secrecy, the longer competitors will need to wait. In some cases, a preemption strategy may be the only choice. Anand and Galetovic point out that for computer chip maker Intel, patenting chips is enormously complex; new designs are likely to be out before the patents even issue, and patented designs are likely to be obsolete before the patents expire. Thus, a preemption strategy may be the best option for products with a short product life cycle. But don't think that Intel does not also use patents to protect its ideas. A search of the U.S. patent assignment database reveals no less than 18,000 patents and patent applications assigned to Intel!

In the new global economy, the preemption strategy is not right for everyone. Seychelle Environmental Technologies, Inc., a water filtration company, is known for avoiding the use of patents.[13] Preemption has worked well for Seychelle's founder. He sold two companies prior to Seychelle for nine-figure sums in 1973 and 1986. But that was then and this is now. We are skeptical of a pure preemption strategy in the global age for new companies that lack the massive brand recognition of Intel. Among other markets, Seychelle plans to sell its water filters in China and Singapore, where products can be reverse engineered, manufactured, and, in the absence of iProperty protection, sold and even imported back into the home country within a matter of months. This approach sounds to us like the Prussians in their final battle with Napoleon: They ignored changed conditions, with predictable results.

PATENT OPTIONS

The patent is the form of iProperty that managers most commonly associate with the protection of new ideas. Most companies jump right to the idea of a patent strategy, skipping the potential benefits of a strategy that includes trade secrets and/or defensive publications or a combination of all three. As discussed, we think companies should consider trade secrets before patents. However, in many cases, specific ideas are simply not good candidates for trade secret protection or the business environment is unsuitable for keeping secrets. Moreover, from a big-picture perspective, we agree with Professor Jorda that companies should not see trade secrets and patents as an "either/or" choice. When developing a strategy for a set of related ideas, some ideas can be protected by patents, while others can be protected as trade secrets. Appropriately balancing the benefits of the two forms of protection is, as stated by Professor Jorda, "a most important and practical, profitable and rational IP strategy."[14]

What Is a Patent?

To explain what a patent is, we must take a brief excursion into the political rationale for the patent system. A patent is fundamentally a legal deal between a patent applicant and the government. The deal requires the applicant to disclose the invention to the public. This is why patents include detailed descriptions of how the patented invention works. Even the word *patent* means "open," indicating that the ideas being protected are available to the public.

In exchange for this public disclosure of knowledge, the government grants the applicant temporary exclusive patent rights for his or her invention. The patent deal provides a benefit and a detriment for each party. The exclusive rights are a benefit to the patent owner, and a detriment to the public. The patent owner can often charge a higher price during some portion of the patent term, and the price differential (patented product compared to a hypothetical unpatented product) is borne by those who purchase the patented product. The requirement for a detailed disclosure is a benefit to the public and a detriment to the applicant. The public can get to work right away on understanding the invention and perhaps engineering around it. Further, as discussed in Chapter 5, the patent's disclosure can provide a rich source of competitive intelligence that may be used by a wise competitor to outcompete the patent owner. Patent laws are designed to maintain a balance between the benefits and detriments to the public and the applicant and to prevent the grant of a patent when this balance is not present.

The exclusive rights conferred by a patent are strictly limited to the novel and nonobvious aspects of the invention. The rights only permit the applicant to exclude the public from making, using, selling, and importing the invention. Some patent watchers are aghast when they read the titles of patent applications, assuming that the title accurately represents the extent of the rights granted by the patent. This is not the case at all. In order to understand the extent of the patent rights, you must look to the claims of the application, which include precise language circumscribing the extent of these rights. The claims are almost always much narrower than the title would lead you to expect.

For example, as mentioned in the introduction, as we are writing this book, there is an uproar in India over patents granted relating to yoga. U.S. Patent 6,640,359, for instance, is entitled "Yoga mat." You might expect that Dawnn Alane, who owns the patent, now has a monopoly on mats for yoga exercises. However, a quick look at the claims shows that Alane has exclusive patent rights for a very specific type of yoga mat, shown in Exhibit 12.1. In order to infringe this patent, one would have to make, use, or sell a yoga mat that, among other things, "includes two generally rectangular, parallel, narrow elongated straps." These straps must be "formed monolithically with the mat." An "end of each strap must be located at the end of the mat." Another end must have "a fastener attached thereto." The mat must also have "a shoulder length carry strap attached to the end of the mat between the two straps." And the mat must have a "means to removably attach the fastener ends of each strap to a coordinating fastener at the mat end of each strap, when the mat has been rolled up."

Any yoga mat that does not have *all* of these very specific characteristics will not infringe Alane's patent. For example, a mat lacking the shoulder-length carry strap would not infringe. If the shoulder-length carry strap were attached outside the two straps, the mat would not infringe. A wide

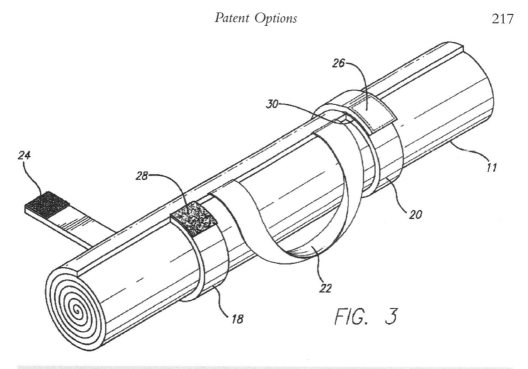

EXHIBIT 12.1   Yoga Mat from U.S. Patent 6,640,359

variety of yoga mats that do not infringe this patent can be envisioned by anyone with a slight dose of creativity. Whether or not you agree with the patent office that the characteristics of Alane's yoga mat are sufficiently novel to warrant the granting of a patent, it is clear that the patent is quite narrow and is nothing like a patent covering all yoga mats.

The requirement that a patent applicant must describe the idea in sufficient detail to enable it to be repeated (the "enablement requirement") helps to ensure that patents are not granted where the applicant has not truly disclosed the idea to the public. Similarly, the requirement that an idea must be novel and nonobvious helps to ensure that the patent office will grant patent rights only where the public does not already possess the details of the idea. The patent office may have failed the public in our yoga mat example.

When an applicant publishes an idea before filing a patent application, patent law may prevent the applicant from obtaining a patent because he or she already disclosed the idea to the public. Granting exclusive rights in this circumstance would actually take an idea away from the public that was already in its possession. There is currently an exception to this rule (only in the United States) that permits the applicant to file for a patent within one year after he or she publishes the applicant of the idea.

Patents and Innovation

It is perhaps easiest to understand the need for patents by considering problems that would occur in the absence of patent protections. Consider Suzie, a seller of farm goods, who wants to create an improved plow. Suzie stays up late at night for months studying the physics of plows and working on the new design. She orders expensive new materials and coatings to try on the plow as well as costly forging equipment for making experimental plows. She acquires land and pays a helper to test the plow designs. After a few years, Suzie finally completes the new design and offers it for sale in her farm goods store; her plow sales double. In the absence of any protection for her innovative plow, the owner of the competitive farm goods store next door buys one of her new plows, studies the improvements, and, within a few days, starts making and selling an identical plow. In essence, he reaps the benefits of Suzie's investment in time and resources.

Patent laws are a policy response to this type of market failure. In the absence of patent laws, Suzie might not have an incentive to invest the time and resources required to develop a new plow due to the likelihood that she would not be able to recoup her investment. Because of this risk, she and others like her might forgo investing in the development of new innovation. The new plow and many other innovative products would not be made. Moreover, the benefits to society from these innovations— improved crop production, new medicines for untreatable diseases, more efficient automobiles, and the like—also might be lost or at least delayed.

Can you defend your company's use of patents to your employees, shareholders and the public?

Although the complexities of the relationship between patent policies and innovation are still poorly understood, societies have nevertheless designed their patent laws with the goal of motivating investment in innovation. Patents permit patent owners to charge an increased price for goods embodying the patented ideas. Economists consider this increase in price to be a kind of "tax" that compensates innovators for the risk undertaken by investing resources in developing the new innovation. Helpfully, this targeted tax is paid only by consumers who actually benefit from the patented product.

A particularly important economic attribute of patents is that they facilitate the sale of ideas. Ideas are notoriously difficult to define and value. But the patent system has evolved to provide as much precision in the definition of ideas as human languages will permit. Ideas can thus be defined in patents, the patents become assets, and the patents can be sold or licensed in the marketplace, which sets the economic value, an arrangement that is much more effective than trying to sell unprotected and undefined ideas. One advantage of this attribute of patents is that rights to inventions can be transferred at any stage of the development process. For example, the transferability of patent rights permits flow of rights from nonprofits, such as universities, to small research and development (R&D) companies, to large corporations. The nonprofits create the new ideas, the R&D companies take on the initial burden of development, and the big corporations complete the development process and take the product to market. It should be noted that trade secrets are also a valuable part of a technology transaction, but due to the inherent ambiguity in defining trade secrets, we think an ideal transaction has patents at its core, surrounded by a "cloud" of trade secrets and know-how.

Remember Suzie? Her company can patent her invention and sell or license it to a large farming manufacturing company to bring in revenue. Based on the strength of her patents, she also can raise money from investors to support her endeavor. Even as a local business owner, patents global opportunities to her. For example, she can patent her invention in South America, license the idea to a South American company, and reap royalties and other payments from a market that would be difficult for her to serve from her current location.

Why Do Companies Patent?

We have already noted that patents confer an exclusionary right. This is the right to prevent others from doing something, not the right to do the thing oneself. Activities that can be prevented typically include making, using, selling, and importing the patented thing or using a patented process. Patent rights are territorial. A U.S. patent can be used only to exclude activities in the United States. Patent rights are also limited by the patent's claims. A thing that can be protected is a thing within the class of things described in the patent's claims. A process that can be protected is a process within the class of processes verbally circumscribed by the words of the patent's claims. U.S. law also prevents importation of things made abroad by processes patented in the United States, even if the thing itself is not patented in the United States.

It is useful to think of the right to exclude granted by a patent as a right to *attempt* to exclude with only a *probability* of success. A variety of factors impact that probability of success. Some countries are better at enforcing patents than others. Patents may be attacked during litigation and invalidated based on the argument that the patent office improperly granted the patent. Some patents are more vulnerable to this kind of attack than others. Patents on ideas with a low degree of novelty—the yoga mat patent, for example—are more vulnerable than patents covering highly novel ideas. Further, patents with narrow claims may be easy to engineer around. A company may believe that its competitors' product infringes its patent, but if infringement is not clear from the language of the patent's claims, a court may disagree.

Almost everyone who is involved in the development of a product has sat in a meeting to decide what to do about a competitive patent. In most such meetings, the goal is to avoid infringement. If the meeting occurs early enough in the product development process, the product design may be changed, thereby leaving the distinctiveness of the patented idea in the hands of the competitor. As described in Chapter 5, and illustrated in Exhibit 5.1, if the patent cannot be avoided, it may be studied to determine its validity. If a good case for invalidity can be made, the probability of the competitor's successful enforcement of the patent may be judged to be low. The product may then go forward as designed based on the assumption that the company can invalidate the patent if the competitor asserts it in a lawsuit. If the company is large enough, it may try to buy the competitor, or it may seek a license to the patented technology. Rarely does a group decide that a patent is valid and would be infringed by their product, but simply choose to ignore it. After all, who wants to risk a large investment in product development or manufacturing scale-up only to be shut down after launch by a patent infringement suit? The lesson is that patents have significant power to deter competitors from infringement, even if they are never enforced. This deterrent power is even greater when the company has a whole fleet of patents.

Similarly, we often hear the question, "If I don't have a war chest to support patent litigation, why should I invest in patents?" This question does not take into account the capacity of patents to deter without being enforced. Further, when the goal of a company is to sell itself or outlicense a product to a larger company that will take the product to market, the deterrent effect rests on the financial ability of the larger company that ends up with the patent rights, not the financial ability of the small company that creates the patent rights. In this case, the patents facilitate the sale or licensing of technology and also provide value to the large company in the form of a deterrent and, it is hoped, an enforceable right. The group of decision makers at the competitor's company may realize that the small company cannot afford to enforce the patent, but they also realize that the goal is to get the patent into the hands of a company that can. Further, some law firms will take exceptional patent cases on a contingency fee basis; that is, the law firm gets paid only if it wins the case.

When and What to Protect with Patents

Patent protection is especially preferred in these categories:

- Core or platform technologies with multiple applications
- Improvements to core technologies, where the core technology is not already protected by patent
- Improvements to patented ideas where the product has a long life cycle (e.g., a novel formulation for a blockbuster drug)

A platform technology with multiple commercial applications generally provides the foundation for broad patent protection. If the technology is truly a next-generation platform solution, it is likely to find its way into numerous applications. Having 20 years of protection on such a technology is a truly valuable thing to possess. As applications for the technology are developed and modified, improvement patents can be obtained. These improvement patents have a patent term that extends beyond the term of the original platform technology patents.

If an idea has potential long-term marketability, patenting incremental ideas embodied in products is thus advisable, even though an existing patent already protects the idea. In such circumstances, patenting incremental ideas can help to extend the life of the patent coverage for the product. In some industries and markets, this is a critical part of iProperty strategy. In pharmaceuticals, for example, the time from idea to market launch can be 10 or more years for a new drug molecule, leaving only 10 or fewer years left on the patent life before generic competition. Furthermore, the parallel R&D of competitors often produces "me-too" drugs that treat the same condition within a couple of years of the market launch of the first drug. This can erode sales dramatically for the first company to market. It is essential, therefore, for the company to continuously in-novate around the drug molecule to provide new, patentable products. Such incremental ideas typically include novel formulations, new meth-ods of administration, specialized drug delivery devices, improved dosage regimens, and dosage forms combining multiple active ingredients. This strategy effectively provides a greater return on the Company's investment for at least the original 20-year period.

Those critical of the pharmaceutical industry often refer to this practice as *evergreening*. For example, a new drug compound is discovered and patented by the "innovator company" with a patent term of 20 years. Ten years later, a new formulation is developed for the drug—for example, the formulation makes the drug orally available so that it can be swallowed rather than injected. The company developing this formulation can obtain a new patent that also lasts for 20 years, resulting in a 30-year period from the filing of the new drug patent to the expiration of the formulation patent. This is a fair outcome. It is a significant and novel contribution to society often requiring a multimillion-dollar investment to develop a way to make a drug orally available and save a patient population from having to take the drug by injection. The patent covering the drug itself will expire in 20 years, and generic companies can make inexpensive versions; after the expiration of the drug patent, they are prevented only from using the patented oral formulation. In addition, other companies that specialize in drug delivery can develop their own patented formulations using the off-patent drug to compete with the innovator company's new products. Again, fair outcomes.

The press often misrepresents the result of patenting such improve-ments, suggesting that patenting the improved formulation actually ex-tends the life of the original drug patent. This is a misconception. When drug companies and other companies get new patents, it is generally be-cause they have invested significant resources in R&D and have devised important novel improvements to the original technology. They are also, as pointed out above, at risk that other companies will develop competi-tive products based on the innovator's drug. It is only the improvements, not the original inventions, that are covered by the new patents with later expiration dates.

A related strategy involves patenting improvements to platform tech-nologies that are not protected by patent. Such improvements often form the basis for narrow but valuable patent protection. For example, consider the situation in which a cancer drug has been known for many years and is therefore not patentable. A company develops a way to deliver the drug, for example, by inhalation into the lungs, which improves the drug's efficacy for treating a certain type of lung cancer. This improvement opens the door to narrow patent protection for an inhalable formulation for the unpatentable drug itself.

Moreover, in some cases the incremental improvement actually may have broader application than previously thought. For example, the inhalable formulation for the cancer drug may be useful for many drugs having the same basic chemical characteristics. In this case, the formulation patent may itself be a platform patent with many opportunities for generating revenue outside the immediate sphere of interest. For example, the formulation can be licensed to another company for use with drugs for treating lung congestion.

Speed Matters

In the global innovation competition, innovation happens at an astonishing pace. Innovations must get to market fast, or the innovator will be trumped by a better version. The same is true with protecting innovation. The whole world, except the United States, uses a first-to-file system to determine who has the right to patent an idea. In other words, the first person (or company) to file the patent application wins against others who file later, even if the first filer was not the first to conceive of the idea. The United States has a system that gives priority to the first to conceive of the idea, so long as that person can show that he or she has been reasonably diligent in pursuing the idea. But, as previously noted, Congress is currently considering changing the system to a first-to-file system to align the U.S. practice with the rest of the world.

Is your company nimble when it comes to patenting? How long does it take you to file a provisional or full patent application once you recognize that an idea has strategic value?

Regardless of whether U.S. law changes, the world is a first-to-file world, and for companies that want to exploit their iProperty globally, speed matters. Gone are the days when a company could give an invention disclosure to outside counsel and be happy with a turnaround time of three months or more. Novel, enabled ideas must be protected quickly (within days or weeks at most) after their conception or someone else may file first. This risk is often difficult for those outside the patent field to believe. What are the chances that only a few days will matter? Every patent counsel can tell numerous stories of battling the patents and publications of others that came into play just days or weeks before their patent application was filed. Speed matters, and companies cannot afford bottlenecks in the process. As discussed in Chapter 11, a system that uses trained interviewers and disclosure writers can get an idea from the mind of an inventor into one of the world's patent offices as quickly as possible.

PROTECTING IDEAS BY GIVING THEM AWAY

Some ideas do not make good trade secrets and should be considered for patenting. However, often it is too expensive to patent every idea, especially when the company is supporting an international portfolio. In some cases, the best option may be to publish an idea in order to prevent others from patenting it. In general, publication should be considered when neither trade secret nor patent protection is justified based on the factors already described.

Publishing and Perishing

The word *publish* often brings fear into the heart of patent counsel, and rightly so. In many sectors, patents are the preeminent form of iProperty, a prerequisite to protecting some of the most valuable intellectual capital and a key to competitive survival. Ill-considered and untimely publications can be patent poison. A decision to publish is a decision to irreversibly surrender potential patent rights. This important decision should be made only in the context of a comprehensive iProperty strategy.

Like any poison, publishing also can be used as a weapon. In attempting to avoid damaging their own patent potential by poorly timed publications, companies and academic institutions should take care not to overlook the defensive use of publications. A successfully executed defensive publication strategy can help secure freedom to operate by preventing others from patenting in the technology space described in the publication; moreover, such a strategy can achieve this objective without the need for expensive patent applications.

The classic scenario for use of defensive publications involves incremental inventions that are (1) covered by existing patent claims and (2) not embodied in a product with potentially long-term marketability. In this case, the value of incremental additional patent protection for the idea, which is already protected by another patent, may not be sufficient to justify the opportunity cost of investing in a patent. The law of diminishing returns applies even to patents. The additional investment for each new patent is about the same as for the first patent, but at some point, the added protection is no longer justified. Consider the example of a novel gene. If a strong patent portfolio exists with claims broadly covering the gene and methods for making the gene product using any bacteria, a discovery that yet another bacteria species produces a proper gene product might be a good candidate for publication rather than patenting. This discovery could form the basis for a patent, but the patent would fall within the broad claims of the already existing portfolio of patents.

We like the publication strategy in narrow circumstances, but it should be considered with great care. A variety of factors could render publication an ineffective strategy. If the idea is not covered by existing claims, publishing the idea only assists competitors. If the idea is already covered by patent claims, but the existing patent claims are weak or poorly enforceable, then the additional layer of protection provided by another patent may be needed to buttress the protection provided by the patent portfolio as a whole. If the idea is embodied in a product with long-term marketability, say a new drug product, then the expense of obtaining patent coverage is likely to be justified by the extended patent protection. For a product that brings in over $1 billion per year, even one additional month of patent term can be worth tens of millions of dollars in revenue.

Other examples of potentially effective publications include:

- **Uses of a core technology that are not strong candidates for patent protection.** Even though they are not strong candidates, a competitor may convince the patent office to issue a patent. An issued patent, even if it is invalid, is nevertheless entitled to a presumption of validity. Expensive litigation may be required to overcome this presumption. Publishing the idea may prevent this outcome.

- **Inventions in filed applications.** Patent applications are published 18 months after the initial filing. This practice results in an 18-month window during which a patent application can be filed in a foreign country. Early publication of a company's patent application (i.e., before the 18-month publication) can eliminate some or all of the 18-month window. Keep in mind, however, that early publication can also be used against the company's own subsequently filed patent applications.

- **Inventions in catalogs or other advertising material.** Catalogs, Web sites, and other customer information all qualify as prior art. However, often patent offices do not search these areas. Publication of such materials in a searchable database can ensure that the world's patent offices have access to this otherwise unsearchable information. For example, publication of catalog and Web site information in a form that is readily searchable by patent examiners can increase the probability that they will find these publications and use them against your competitor's patents.

What Are Defensive Publications?

The balance of the patent deal discussed in detail earlier in this chapter sets the context for the use of defensive publications. The impact of a successful defensive publication is the intentional and targeted destruction of this balance for competitors' patent applications. Defensive publications achieve this purpose by placing an invention in possession of the public. If the defensive publication predates the filing of the competitor's patent application, the patent deal for that application is out of balance—the competitor has nothing to offer the public, since the invention has already been disclosed and is thus already possessed by the public. Technically speaking, the novelty and nonobviousness (or inventive step) requirements help to ensure that patent rights are granted only where the invention is new—that is, when the public actually will obtain something new from the disclosure. Defensive publications render competitor's patent applications obvious and lacking in novelty.

Writing a Defensive Publication

The probability of executing a successful defensive publication strategy is vastly improved if the strategy is a component of a comprehensive iProperty strategy. As noted, defensive publications relating to important company technology are best employed only where the company already has effective patent protection. For this reason, it is necessary to analyze the claims of existing patents prior to publishing to be sure that they encompass the alternatives being described in the proposed defensive publication.

In the absence of such protection, the defensive publication may simply assist a competitor to engineer around your own patent.

To knock out a patent application, a publication cited against that patent application must *enable* the invention claimed in the patent application. In the United States, this means that the publication must "disclose every element of the challenged claim and enable one skilled in the art to make the anticipating subject matter."[15] An assessment of the probable value of a defensive publication should take into account the fact that the publication typically will not prevent others from patenting aspects of the invention that are not enabled by the publication. In complex fields, such as biotechnology, where the efficacy of conceptual inventions is viewed as unpredictable, this application of the enablement requirement means that the defensive publication should provide a detailed, working protocol and generally should describe empirical work demonstrating the validity of the inventive concept.

For example, consider the publication of a new gene sequence. Publication of the sequence enables an ordinary molecular biologist to make a gene having the sequence. However, publication of the sequence may not enable an ordinary molecular biologist to use the gene in a specific gene therapy application. The publication would destroy the right of others to patent the isolated or synthetically produced nucleic acid encoding the gene but may not destroy the patent rights of one who later succeeds in using the nucleic acid in an unpredictable gene therapy application.

To strengthen the impact of the publication, consider including alternatives to the basic idea being published. Including alternatives will protect against competitors who wish to engineer around or improve the published idea to generate patentable alternatives. Patent counsel can assist by providing language commonly used in patents to broaden the scope of an invention. Broadening the defensive publication in this manner will reduce the risk that others will build off the published idea to develop additional patentable ideas; however, surprising improvements or alternatives still may be patentable, even in light of the defensive publication.

Where to Publish

Options for publishing defensive publications range from traditional peer-reviewed journals to dot-com sites dedicated to online publishing. Publication in peer-reviewed journals is desirable, because such publications are important to the advancement of a scientific career, and the critical review such publications afford is important for the advancement of science.

Moreover, the traditional requirement of repeatability in peer-reviewed publications parallels the enablement requirement, helping to ensure that the latter is satisfied. The difficulty with traditional journal publications is that, assuming that they actually agree to publish your submitted article, they can take months to publish, and speed is critical to a defensive publication strategy. If another company files a patent application before the defensive publication becomes public, then the strategy is defeated.

A tempting forum for defensive publishing is the company Web site. However, most standard Web site publishing does not include a method for verifying the date of publication or the authenticity of the publication. Additionally, the content of Web sites is constantly changing, and Web-based searching is still not as accurate as traditional information databases. The world's patent examiners may not identify the publication. If this happens, the competitor's patent application could be examined and granted without knowledge of the defensive publication, and the publication would therefore not have its intended effect (i.e., use by a patent examiner as the basis for rejecting a competitor's patent application).

It should be noted that ideas described in patents but not claimed are also considered published subject matter and are dedicated to the public. One publication option is to describe the ideas to be published in a patent application without submitting claims that protect the ideas. This option has the advantage that if, during the pendency of the application, the applicant decides to elect to patent the ideas rather than publish them, the applicant may have the option to submit claims covering the ideas. In other words, publishing ideas in a patent application can be a way to defer the finality of a decision between patenting and publishing.

Another option for defensive publishing is IP.com. This savvy Internet-based company, founded in 2000, has created a prior art database that provides a quick and effective way to put defensive publications in the hands of the public. The company has a wide variety of clients, including IBM, General Electric, Motorola, Abbott Laboratories, and Eastman Kodak. IP.com electronically date stamps and protects the integrity of each defensive publication to ensure that its publications have legal significance for the world's patent systems. Documents published by IP.com become part of a text-searchable database, accessible to patent examiners in the world's patent offices. The disclosures also are published monthly in the *IP.com Journal* to ensure compliance with accepted legal standards. The journal is housed in 35 libraries and patent offices around the world.

Tom Colson, chief executive officer of IP.com, observes that a recent Supreme Court case, *KSR v. Teleflex*, heightened the nonobviousness requirement for U.S. patents and, in doing so, made patents and patent applications more vulnerable to defensive publications. In that case, Justice Kennedy, writing for a unanimous court, emphasized that "the results of ordinary innovation are not the subject of exclusive rights under the patent laws. Were it otherwise patents might stifle, rather than promote, the progress of useful arts." In taking this position, the Court pushed back on the U.S. Patent Office's recent tendency to grant easy patents, holding that the patent at issue was invalid due to the existence of published patents describing similar devices. Colson points out that, as a result of this ruling, "patents will be harder to get and easier to invalidate." This change suggests that in many cases, defensive publications will be an even more desirable strategy than has been the case in the past. "Simply put," Colson says, "competitive patents are more dangerous than your own patents are valuable."[16]

Is your company taking advantage of the defensive publication strategy where appropriate?

Many organizations work hard to identify inventions that should be filed as patent applications. However, few organizations make a concerted effort to identify information that should be placed in the public domain as a defensive publication. Defensive publication is less expensive than patent protection, and proper strategic use of defensive publications can help companies and universities to protect their iProperty space from the patenting efforts of others. Further, integration of a defensive publication strategy into an iProperty strategy can preserve resources to be invested in patent applications that are likely to provide the greatest return on investment.

SHOOT FIRST, AIM LATER

Like every stage in the development of an iProperty portfolio, the selection of options for protecting novel ideas must be accomplished in the context of an insightful iProperty strategy by a fully functional iProperty team. All the various pieces of the puzzle that combine to assemble the iProperty portfolio must be designed in precise relation to each other, requiring the strategic decision maker to have a holistic understanding of the business strategy, the iProperty strategy, the competitive landscape, and the company's existing iProperty portfolio. For example, an ill-conceived publication strategy can devastate the company's own patent strategy and vice versa. The two must work together in order to be effective. However, it is usually a mistake to be so precise and deliberative that speed is sacrificed. In many cases, speed is more important than precision, and a "shoot first, aim later" approach is preferred. A beautifully assembled portfolio can be worthless if a speedy competitor beats you to the patent office.

NOTES

1. Bill Landes and Richard Posner, *The Economic Structure of Intellectual Property Law* (Boston: Harvard University Press, 2003), 356.

2. Thomas Friedman, *The World Is Flat: A Brief History of the Twenty-first Century* (New York: Farrar, Straus and Giroux, 2006), 217.

3. Paul Beamish, "The High Cost of Chinese Labor," *Harvard Business Review* (June 2006).

4. Landes and Posner, *Economic Structure of Intellectual Property Law,* 357.

5. See Lester Thurow, *Fortune Favors the Bold: What We Must do to Build a New and Lasting Global Prosperity* (New York: HarperCollins, 2003), 169–176.

6. See Henry Beck and Xichun Pan, "Licensing and Technology Transfer to China: A Roadmap," *Licensing Best Practices: Strategic, Territorial and Technology Issues* (Hoboken, NJ: John Wiley & Sons, Inc., 2006).

7. Landes and Posner, "Economic Structure of Intellectual Property Law," 358.

8. Karl Jorda, "Patents Come and Go—Trade Secrets Are Forever," *From the Editor: An Excerpt from Pierce Law Center's Germeshausen Center Newsletter* (Summer/Fall 2006), 3.

9. Ibid, 3–4.

10. 35 USC §112.

11. Karl Jorda, "Intellectual Property Protection Policies & Strategies: Synergistic Integration of Patents & Trade Secrets," unpublished paper, 15.

12. Bharat Anand and Alexander Galetovic, "How Market Smarts Can Protect Property Rights," *Harvard Business Review* (December 2004), 72–79.

13. "Employee Dives into Water Again," *Orange County Register*, July 31, 2006, www.ocregister.com/ocregister/money/homepage/article_1227510.php.

14. Karl Jorda, supra note 8, 5.

15. *PPG Industries, Inc. v. Guardian Industries, Corp.,* 37 USPQ 2d 1618 (Fed. Cir. 1996).

16. E-mail interview with Tom Colson, CEO of IP.com, June 12, 2006.

Index